JIM AUBREY

is the executive spokesperson for Australians for a Free East Timor (Vic) and the director of a human rights consultancy body, Humanity First. He has directed campaigns and actions against the Timor Gap Oil Exploration Treaty, the Australia–Indonesia Security Agreement, and, with East Timor as his platform, he stood in the 1996 Federal election for the Australian Democrats against the then Australian Foreign Affairs Minister. That year Mr Aubrey also lobbied the nations of the UN General Assembly against Australia's application for the vacant non-permanent Security Council seat, citing Australia's complicity in the genocide in East Timor as reason for concern over Australia's bipartisan credentials and the need of the successful member to express an unequivocal belief in the UN tenet of self-determination. Australia lost the vote to Portugal. Mr Aubrey has just returned from a tour of several of the world's capitals with a photo exposition on the genocide in East Timor. While in the USA he received an invitation to address the Congressional Human Rights Caucus in Washington DC in October 1998.

FREE

AUSTRALIA'S CULPABILITY IN EAST TIMOR'S GENOCIDE

EAST TIMOR

EDITED BY JIM AUBREY

V

VINTAGE

Published by
Random House Australia Pty Ltd
20 Alfred Street, Milsons Point, NSW 2061
http://www.randomhouse.com.au

Sydney New York Toronto
London Auckland Johannesburg
and agencies throughout the world

First published in 1998

National Library of Australia
Cataloguing-in-Publication Data

    Free East Timor

    ISBN 0 09 183917 3.

    1. Human rights – Indonesia – Timor Timur. 2. Civil rights
    – Indonesia – Timor Timur. 3. Timor Timur (Indonesia) –
    Annexation to Indonesia. I. Aubrey, Jim.

323.095986

Cover photograph: David Hancock, 7 December 1995 Darwin, at a
demonstration outside the Indonesian embassy. An East Timorese
smashes an effigy of Suharto.
Backcover photograph: David Hancock, 7 December
1995 Darwin. Indonesian military flags burning
outside the Indonesian embassy.

Design by Gayna Murphy
Typeset by Asset Typesetting Pty Ltd, Sydney
Printed by Griffin Press Pty Ltd, Adelaide

ACKNOWLEDGEMENTS

Dedicated to the memory of all those who have perished in the genocide in East Timor and to those who have fought and struggled against all odds for freedom. Especially dedicated to the suffering children and to those who even today continue to be tortured, raped and murdered. In memory of Resistance leader Konis Santana who died as this book was being finished.

Special gratitude to Alison White, Marj White, Harry Levy, Natasha Stott Despoja, and Sean Doyle for their help and generosity in getting the book finished; Ann Treseder (San Francisco) for coming to the rescue; Gareth Smith and Maxine Caron (Canberra), Trish Reid, Chris Tyler and Maureen Tolfree (London) for their kindness and support.

Many thanks to Pedro Batista, Amandio Gomes and his niece Roselia, David Bowling, Sid Spindler, Ben Stranieri, Robyn Neate, Peter Shumpeter, Lyn Allison, Mathew Townsend, Miranda Sissons, Joyce Evans, Emmanuel Santos, Andy McNaughtan, Juan Federer, Robbie Casey, Vivian Porzsolt, Jefferson Lee. Members of the 2/2nd and the 2/4th Independent Companies. The Jewish Holocaust Museum, Melbourne, Australia. Descendants of the Shoah, Melbourne, Australia. Antonio Barbedo Magalhães (Portugal). Tom Hyland and the entire East Timor Ireland Solidarity Campaign—Carl, Michael, Sean, Luciano, José, Dino, Barney. *Tapol*—Camel Budiardjo, Paul Barber and Roger Willot (London). Joao Crisostono (New York). American Jews Against Genocide—

Sharon Sibler, Meryl Zegarek, Eileen Weiss, Jack David. Dan Berrigan, Owen Daley and my other Jesuit friends in Upper Manhattan. Mark Van Hollebeke, GSA—Fordham University and Jim, Vanessa, Danielle, Anne, Andrew. Arieh Lebowitz—American Jewish Labor Committee. Israel Charny—Institute of the Holocaust and Genocide, Jerusalem. Edy Kaufman, Pamela Lubell—the Truman Institute at the Hebrew University, Jerusalem. Gideon Remes, Miri Scharf, Tziona Orr, Aliza Sara June, Michelle (Jerusalem). Human Rights Alliance, Washington DC—Kathryn Porter, Bakhtiar Amin. His Holiness the Dalai Lama and Bishop Desmond Tutu for their encouragement in the project Stop Operation Annihilation.

To the foundations and individuals whose generosity has kept our activities ongoing.

Ken Fry for his kind cooperation with my research. John Pilger and Rob Wesley Smith for their encouragement. All the authors in this book who graciously waived their normal fees and for their inspiration. Photographer David Hancock for the same.

Politicians from the Australian Democrats, the Australian Greens and Parliamentarians for East Timor for showing that honour and integrity are not a lost cause in politics.

Many thanks to Jane Palfreyman at Random House for her encouragement.

For my family in Australia and Israel, especially my children.

For the truth; for the sovereignty of human rights.

Thank you.

CONTENTS

FOREWORD
1

More than two decades have passed since the Balibo incident—the killing of Australian journalists at the hands of the Indonesian military—which marked the first major military operation against East Timor by Indonesia's armed forces. In spite of the consequences of the invasion of East Timor by Indonesia, its brutal aftermath, and the repeated calls of the international community, Indonesia's defiance has gone virtually unchallenged by the United Nations system and the UN is still yet to take firm action on the issue. Indonesia's illegal annexation of East Timor has also been unchallenged by those very forces who, in 1991 (and who appear likely to again), rallied with massive military power to force Saddam Hussein to abandon his illegal annexation of Kuwait. Despite international concern since the Santa Cruz massacre of November 1991, Indonesian military personnel have faced no such pressure to make the kind of concessions that might help redress the terrible wrongs suffered by the Timorese people.

In Australia we have little to feel proud of in successive Governments' policies on East Timor. We have seen deliberate attempts to bury the East Timor question, most cynically when the Hawke Government signed the Timor Gap Treaty, and the Keating Government signed the Indonesian security treaty thereafter. The Coalition Government sees no need to reverse Australia's *de jure* recognition of East Timor's annexation.

Successive Australian Governments have abstained from voting on UN resolutions on East Timor, even those granting the East Timorese the right to self-determination and independence. The *de jure* recognition given to Indonesia by Australia, and Australia being the only Western nation to give such legal endorsement, has been of value to the Suharto regime internationally. At annual sessions of the UN Commission on Human Rights, Australia has either supported Indonesia when its human rights record has been under scrutiny, or challenged resolutions in order to minimise offence to the Suharto regime.

On the other hand, individual parliamentarians care very deeply about the East Timor question. They do make some effort to pressure both the Indonesian and Australian Governments to make concessions, and to recognise the public disquiet in Australia at the way the issue has been handled over the last two decades.

The awarding of the Nobel Peace Prize to José Ramos Horta and Bishop Carlos Filipe Ximines Belo gave the international community some hope of a renewed effort to solving the East Timor problem. At the very least, it has become an international *cause célèbre*.

The problem of East Timor will not go away, and we must not condone the inaction of our Government to address the significant human rights abuses in East Timor by remaining silent. Listen carefully to some of the voices in this book. Voices with an intimate knowledge of East Timor. East Timorese leader Xanana Gusmao says, referring to Australia, 'it is inconceivable and unacceptable that a democratic country with a Western way of life, a country which claims to be the defender of human rights, should profit from the blood of other people'.

Journalist Roger East, commenting on the Indonesian invasion and Australia's reaction, just prior to his death, 'For Australia to pretend the situation is otherwise must reflect either on their intelligence or their integrity.'

The 2/2nd commando Paddy Kenneally states that 'our governments have abandoned and betrayed the people of East Timor ... have waded through a sea of Timorese blood, and climbed over a mountain of Timor's dead, to sign the Timor Gap Treaty for economic gain with Timor's invaders'.

And the words of human rights activist Jim Aubrey, '… with just cause our children and our children's children will condemn us for our indifference, our apathy, and our Government's appalling record of complicity in the genocide in East Timor.'

Our Government wants a greater role for Australia in our immediate region. We hope this commitment will have some positive effect for the Timorese people. Timor's remoteness from most democratic governments with influence in Jakarta means that little positive action can be taken unless Australia plays a key role. As James Dunn has once so eloquently written, the real test of a government's commitment to the universality of human rights is a measure of the state of our civilisation. It is incumbent on Australia to resolve to work within the international community to remedy a gross violation of those standards against a small and vulnerable people.

The tireless efforts of the many committed people working for East Timor should be acknowledged. Their task will be harder the longer it takes for our Governments—whatever their persuasion—to reverse their policy. We need to continue to support their efforts, and to pressure for East Timor's self-determination and independence.

Natasha Stott Despoja
Australian Democrats, Canberra

FOREWORD
2

Fifty-five years ago I was in East Timor. I was part of No. 4 Independent Company and we were behind Japanese lines conducting guerrilla warfare in the mountains, eight to ten thousand feet above sea level. Both No. 2 and No. 4 Companies were keeping 22,000 Japanese busy. By the same token they, in turn, were keeping us busy. We operated in small groups of ten to twelve men. We had relieved No. 2 Company in September 1942. Each Company of 250 men kept two divisions of Japanese on the alert for twelve months, but I do not wish to tell you what we did. Rather, I wish to tell you what the indigenous Timorese did for us.

How did 250 men in each Company survive? We had no Navy, no Air Force, nor vast legions of Army supply units to support us. Our only support was the Timorese. They sent their young sons, aged ten to sixteen years, to guide us, to succour us, to feed us, and to show us all the Timorese trails. They carried our gear. We lived in their villages. They came on ambushes with us. They were with us when superior Japanese forces attacked us; these young boys saved us by taking us on secret trails and tracks. We were always in danger of annihilation. The Japanese put a price on our heads: 8 pounds dead or alive.

Never once did the Timorese betray us. They were unbelievably loyal to us. That loyalty is why we survived and why I am able to stand here more than five decades later, to tell you of the debt my comrades and I owe the Timorese people. It is a debt that we owe unto the third and fourth generations, and all the generations to come. A blood bond was established with these Timorese people. Although we withdrew in 1943, Australia continued to send in special missions, and maintained this link with the Timorese.

In 1944 leaflets from the Australian forces and the Government were dropped by the RAAF over Portuguese Timor. The leaflets promised the Timorese liberation from the Japanese forces, stating that Australia would never forget the people of Timor. My surviving comrades and I continue to support the Timorese people in their struggle for independence.

Why has the Australian Government forgotten the Timorese? Here I am, at the age of 77, to plead with you to support the Timorese people. In 1942–43, at least 20,000 Timorese were killed by the Japanese, and by the war's end that figure had reached up to 60,000. That was the price the Timorese paid for helping us! More than 200,000—that is, over one-third of the Timorese population— have been massacred by the Indonesians since 1975. This is genocide!

It is not a case of Australia going to war with Indonesia. That would be stupid. It is not a case, as it was when I was a young man, of what the Timorese can do for Australia. It is a case of what Australia should do for the people of East Timor. The people of East Timor have a right to self-determination, a right to a free and independent homeland. My comrades and I will never forget, even if our leaders have, how they once sacrificed themselves to maintain our freedom. Like the children of Israel described in the Bible, Indonesia must let the Timorese people go. May I and my fellow comrades live to see the day of their freedom. Viva Timor!

Harry Levy
2/4th Independent Company

INTRODUCTION

As I write this introduction, the words I heard two weeks ago on the TV news are still echoing in my ear. 'Some things are worth fighting for,' stated the United States Secretary for Defence, William Cohen. He was referring to the current Gulf crisis and the mobilisation of American-led military forces for a second showdown with Saddam Hussein. Hussein's mistake: he has not upheld United Nations Security Council resolutions regarding free access of UN inspection teams searching for bio-chemical and nuclear weapons sites.

President Suharto has ignored at least a dozen UN resolutions calling for his withdrawal from East Timor. One-third of the population of East Timor has perished, and there has been no cavalry to the rescue for what has been one of the longest ongoing acts of genocide since the Second World War. The world is guilty of being a bystander to this genocide. In an act that really epitomises what this tragedy is all about, while the suffering, torture, rape, sterilisation and killing continue, the International Monetary Fund is offering a 40 billion dollar bail-out package to the corrupt Suharto regime over the currency crisis that has decimated Indonesia and parts of Asia these last six months.

In *The Myth of Rescue*, one of the most controversial books published last year, William Rubenstein came to the view that the Allies had done all they could to rescue European Jewry from the Holocaust during the Second World War and, in fact, could not have done any more than they did. I have no doubt that in years to come, someone will come to a similar view concerning the struggle for freedom in East Timor, and state that the Australian Government did all they could to help East Timor and could not have done any more.

This book, *Free East Timor*, is in anticipation of this future transgression. It is a testimony for the historical record, to document some of those who did everything they could to help East Timor—average, everyday people ashamed of their Government's indecent obsession with Indonesia and its complicity in Indonesia's genocide in East Timor.

Another book last year, *Hitler's Willing Executioners*, by Daniel Goldhagen, portrays the perpetrators of the Holocaust as normal people who fulfilled their roles without mitigating circumstances, such as diminished responsibility. They willingly performed the atrocities regardless of opportunities to disengage from these acts. In contrast to the stock phrase 'I was just obeying orders', in the case of East Timor, it is the leaders of the so-called Western democratic, 'freedom-loving' nations that have adopted postures of accommodation, of apology and of indifference to the genocide of a 'small mountain people'. With full knowledge of the genocide in East Timor they have been 'Suharto's willing accomplices' in the 'death of a nation'.

Then there is the other stock phrase, 'I am just one person, what can I do?' Raoul Wallenberg, a single person, saved 100,000 Jews from the Nazi gas chambers. Oscar Schindler made mercy rather than exploitation his war-time mission. When the Holocaust atrocity photos became public at the end of the war, the world united in condemnation of the Nazis' 'final solution'. Why were people who condemned the genocide of European Jewry, who said 'never again', to become accomplices in the genocide of innocent men, women and children only thirty years later? To be chums with a regime that stands alongside Hitler's Nazi Germany, Stalin's Soviet Union, Pol Pot's Cambodia, the SLORC's Burma and China's Tibet as part of a select group guilty of the worst ever crimes against humanity.

I have only just returned the last fortnight from taking a photo exhibition on genocide to several locations around the world—contemporary photos of the Nazi extermination camps and photos of the genocide in East Timor up to the present day. The current torture photos of young women, including schoolgirls, are a graphic and shocking affront to our senses, to our idea of humanity and to our integrity.

Everywhere I have been in the world, average, everyday people are appalled by the situation in East Timor. I found that a good way to test the waters on arriving somewhere was to question taxi drivers for their opinion. Whether it was London or New York, Washington or Dublin, not one of these drivers agreed with their Government's record on East Timor. Not one favoured sacrificing the East Timorese for their own standard of living. Our leaders, on the other hand, continue to preach pragmatism and national interest.

Anyone who has viewed the current torture photos will surely agree that a 'national interest' which has aided and abetted such atrocities is unacceptable. A national interest that becomes part of the apologetics for the atrocities is itself a corruption of the human spirit, and should be resisted tooth and nail. There are times when it is difficult for me to distinguish just who to condemn the most—the perpetrators or the apologists.

Among the important works on East Timor are those by Jill Jolliffe, Bill Nicol, Carmel Budiardjo and Liem Soei Liong, Jim Dunn, George Munster and Richard Walsh, Brian Toohey and Marian Wilkinson, John Taylor, Peter Cary, Noam Chomsky, John Pilger, Geoff Gunn and Jeff Lee, among others now being published, like Shirley Shackleton's fictionalised account of the whole tragedy which, I believe, having read some of her manuscript, will rank at the top end in our literary heritage. Carmel again, with *Tapol*, and Pat Walsh's *Inside Indonesia*, two excellent monthly publications on Indonesia and East Timor. Then there are filmmakers Gil Scrine, James Kesteven, Mandy King and Denis Freney, John Pilger and David Munro, Max Stahl, Dom Rotheroe and photographer Steve Cox. I can never forget the images of their courageous work. They have honoured our 'blood debt', as have several journalists who have kept this tragedy alive in the public arena.

Deserving of very special attention is the work by Michele Turner, *Telling East Timor*, perhaps the most courageous and inspirational subject matter undertaken by any of us: the documentation of the testimonies of participants and survivors from the Second World War to the post-invasion period.

So, *Free East Timor* should not be considered in any definitive form, but merely as part of the testimony of a stand taken by a small group of people in defence of values of freedom and freedom from abuse, values that we believe are as Mr Cohen said 'worth fighting for'. It is indeed a privilege to call these people both friends and colleagues, and they, more than our Government's treachery and indifference, reflect who we are as a people and what humanity is all about.

Jim Aubrey
Australians for a Free East Timor
Melbourne, February 1998
Free_East_Timor@bigfoot.com

*The Hobart East Timor Committee boasts some excellent lobbying work
done at the United Nations and has included among its membership the
magnificent activist Michele Turner, who passed away during 1996.
Her book* Telling East Timor, *will remain one of the most important
testimonies of the tragedy of East Timor. This chapter highlights the
Allies' contest with Japan during the Second World War on the island of
Timor and the fatal impact this had upon the East Timorese.*

1

WORLD WAR II AND EAST TIMOR

THE HOBART EAST TIMOR COMMITTEE

The understanding that the Governments of Japan and Australia
have a continuing unpaid debt to the people of East Timor has
gradually gained acceptance. Three areas of culpability can be
delineated: (a) The violation of Portuguese neutrality, by Australia
in December 1941 and by Japan in February 1942; (b) the failure by
both parties to take adequate measures to protect civilians including
the failure to avoid population centres when planning military
actions; (c) and the failure by both Governments to pay postwar
compensation for the killing of neutral civilians, as well as for
physical and mental trauma, and the damage done to roads, bridges,
airfields, public and private buildings, livestock, crops and
plantations.[1]

But this paper has been produced to ask some of the questions which appear never to have been asked and to question some of the assumptions which have long been accepted as correct. In particular, we would like to raise the possibility that three other nations may have much larger responsibilities towards East Timor, dating from World War II, than has previously been acknowledged.

UNITED STATES OF AMERICA

Radio operator Patricio da Luz gave an eyewitness account of American bombing of East Timor: 'There were Australian and American bombers and they all make mistakes but the Americans make more. The Australian pilots were more careful. The Americans would come and bomb palm trees! In the moonlight they see the palm trees glowing like galvanised iron roofs and bomb them. When they bomb a place they do it with a lot of force, as many bombs as they can and flatten everything and always more planes than necessary.'[2]

Officially, the United States Air Force carried out three bombing missions over Portuguese East Timor in 1942, eighteen in 1943, and nine in 1944. The number of aircraft per mission varied from one to twelve with each able to carry up to a 4000-pound bomb load. General George Kenney was in command, but received 'strategic direction' from General Arnold in Washington.[3]

But the greatest damage done by the Allies to East Timor between 1943 and 1945 was as a result of the 'Z Special' operations. In various parts of the Pacific, such as on some of the islands of New Caledonia and the Solomons, Japanese troops cut off from resupply began vegetable gardens and went fishing, becoming what have been called 'self-supporting prisoners of war'.[4] This was not possible in East Timor, because of the continuing clandestine insertions of the 'Z Specials' and, to a lesser extent, because of the decision to bomb all shipping to the north of Timor, making it difficult for the Japanese either to be resupplied or to be moved from East Timor. Any attempts by Timorese villagers to create some kind of compromise with the occupying Japanese were rendered unsuccessful by these operations. The arrival or rumoured arrival of secret Australian missions constantly undermined Timorese attempts to develop some form of modus operandi and reduce pressures on limited food stocks.

The 'Z Specials' have always been described as an intelligence-gathering operation, under the auspices of the Allied Intelligence Bureau, but we think this description should be questioned, for three reasons. First, by 1943, regular reconnaissance flights over Timor were monitoring all shipping movements, use of airfields, et cetera. Any intelligence gathered 'on the ground' would be of very limited value. Second, if intelligence on Japanese numbers/ movements was of vital importance, why were no similar operations mounted into West Timor or the surrounding islands? Third, the second intelligence party landed lost its ciphers, which were then used by the Japanese for nearly two years, thus compromising other parties inserted. The repeated failure of radio operators in Australia to realise anything was wrong suggests these parties, and any intelligence they sent, received very low priority in Australia.[5]

We would suggest that instead their role was to provide, and to encourage the East Timorese villagers to provide, low-grade harassment of the Japanese, thus helping to keep large numbers of Japanese troops tied down in Timor. It was this policy which led directly to the widespread starvation experienced in East Timor between 1943 and 1945. However, even this does not explain why more 'Z Special' parties were sent into Portuguese Timor than into any other territory of comparable size.

The 'Z Specials' have always been seen as an Australian operation. In fact this is not so. In March 1942, the Governments of the UK, USA, Australia, New Zealand and the Netherlands set up the 'South-West Pacific Area' (SWPA) which covered Timor, and nominated General MacArthur as Supreme Commander. John Hetherington, in his biography of General Blamey, says: 'He lashed out in December 1942 when he learned that the Advisory War Council had gone far beyond its province by asking the Australian Chiefs of Staff to prepare plans to capture Timor. He pointed out that nobody but MacArthur was empowered to authorise such an operation,' and MacArthur made sure that no action was taken in SWPA without his knowledge or approval. His headquarters set up the Allied Intelligence Bureau (AIB), under Major-General Willoughby, on 6 July 1942. The AIB included Special Reconnaissance Department (SRD), which had responsibility for the 'Z Specials', and the Far East Liaison Office (FELO), which prepared propaganda leaflets to be dropped over Portuguese Timor.[6] Final authorisation for the 'Z Special' operations and target areas came from MacArthur. But MacArthur always intended to move directly to the Philippines, cutting off Japanese supply lines to Timor and the Netherlands East Indies and leaving Japanese troops to 'wither on the vine'; he saw Timor as largely irrelevant. That he authorised 'Z Specials' into East Timor simply to give keen young Australians 'something to do' has never been canvassed.

To understand their impact, it is important to put the situation in perspective. The number of Japanese troops in East Timor reached approximately 15,000 in December 1942 and remained at that level for more than two years because of the Japanese belief that the Allies intended to retake East Timor after the initial withdrawal in early 1943.[7] The 'Z Specials' constantly reinforced this suspicion. The 1942 Allied campaign was fought predominantly in the three western provinces. East Timor was divided into six provinces in the 1940s—Fronteira, Dili and Suro. The 'Z Specials' were inserted mainly into the three eastern provinces of Sao Domingos, Manatuto and Lautem. Because the Japanese regarded the people of the western provinces as being 'pro-Australian', they maintained both their own troops and a number of West Timorese in those provinces, whilst sending large 'search and destroy' missions into the eastern provinces, which had, until the arrival of the 'Z Specials', been relatively untouched by the war, except for the bombing of towns along the north coast.

This meant that every province in East Timor came under pressure to provide food for the Japanese troops whilst suffering severe disruption during planting and harvest, as well as the loss of livestock, either as food for occupying troops or to deny the 'other side' such food. Livestock were also lost in bombing raids and when the Japanese carried out 'scorched earth' policies. Livestock were needed for milking, meat, ploughing and transport. Each harvest was significantly smaller than the previous one. By 1944, people were reduced to eating their vital seed stocks in the desperate attempt to stave off starvation.[8]

The pressure of large numbers of troops needing to be fed in a small country which received no outside food supplies for several years, along with disruptive military operations, is best understood by remembering that East Timor would fit approximately: 6 times into Portugal, 15 times into the UK, 25 times into Japan, 515 times into Australia and 650 times into the USA.

The United States cannot walk away from its obligations to East Timor.

BRITAIN

By late 1941, enthusiasm for sending Australian troops to Europe and North Africa was diminishing, partly because of the debacles in Greece and Crete, which many Australians blamed on the British High Command, and growing fears of Japanese intentions. Churchill wanted to keep Australian troops under British control; the Labor Government which took power in October 1941 wanted them brought home. Yet Churchill and his generals acquiesced, apparently without a murmur, to the sending of Australia's elite commandos, the 2/2nd Independent Company and later the 2/4th, into neutral Portuguese Timor, rather than to Europe or key areas in Southeast Asia such as Malaya. The Independent Companies grew out of a British War Office initiative. A secret British military mission was sent to Australia for this purpose, and the men received British commando-style training, in some cases using British experts. After expending much organisation and hard work to develop the initiative, the British apparently made no attempt to have these elite troops used in the protection of any British territories. It has become almost an article of faith to present this action as an Australian initiative about which Britain was less than happy.

But a survey of the cables sent by UK Secretary of State for Dominion Affairs, Lord Cranbourne,[9] suggests not only a strong commitment to getting Australian troops into Portuguese Timor but also a willingness to put extreme pressure on Portugal, ignoring Portugal's position that any breach of neutrality in Timor could lead to Japanese reprisals against Macau.[10] Britain, based in nearby Hong Kong, was well aware that the predominantly Chinese population of Macau had no conceivable protection except adherence to a policy of strict neutrality. In the wake of the Nanking and Chungking massacres in nearby China, the fears for Macau were very real.

Three reasons are usually given for supposed British reluctance to support the Timor campaign. First, Britain wanted Portugal to remain neutral, because if Australia breached Portuguese neutrality in Timor, this might encourage Salazar, the Portuguese Dictator, to give support to the Axis powers. Second, Britain hoped to gain facilities in the Azores, the Portuguese islands in the mid-Atlantic, and if Australia breached Portuguese neutrality in Timor, these negotiations could become considerably more difficult. Third, Britain wanted to keep its 'ancient alliance' (the Anglo-Portuguese Treaty of 1373) in reserve, in case it should need to invoke it during a future emergency. Australian actions might be construed as disrespect for the alliance and, therefore, as weakening Britain's bargaining position.

These reasons do not stand up to close scrutiny. We may even have been looking at them back to front. It may be that Britain wanted Australia to take the tough line so it could step in with what seemed a compromise position which would nevertheless weaken Portuguese neutrality; David Day says the troops were sent to Timor 'at Britain's instigation' but that 'London went cold on the project'.[11]

Britain always knew it was unlikely that Portugal would change its stance on neutrality while Spain remained out of the war, for Portugal was under tremendous pressure from Spain to remain neutral. Paul Preston says that in 1939, 'Through his brother in Lisbon, Franco put pressure on Portugal to ignore its commitments to Britain and to maintain neutrality,' and in 1940, 'In Britain and Portugal, it was assumed that non-belligerence meant, as it had for Mussolini, a prelude to a declaration of war. Franco consistently tried to use the Portuguese to deceive the British. For months he had been assuring the Portuguese Ambassador, Pereira, of his commitment to neutrality and of his lack of acquisitive plans. He did so again on 10 June, the same day that he wrote to Mussolini to offer non-belligerence. On the day that non-belligerence was announced, he sent his brother Nicolas to assure the Portuguese Foreign Ministry that it constituted no divergence from Spain's existing neutral line. The Caudillo saw Lisbon as a useful conduit to the Foreign Office, to be exploited, while the Axis was winning, to mask his own position. In 1943, when the outcome of the war seemed more doubtful, he would use Lisbon to endorse his neutral credentials in the eyes of the Allies. In the summer of 1940, however, he harboured predatory thoughts about Portugal.'[12]

This came about partly through the growth, as a popular movement in Spain, of Pan-Iberianism, which promoted the 'absorption' of Portugal into Spain, but also partly through Franco's more secret plans. More than Portugal itself, he wanted Portugal's empire; he never forgave the Spanish Government for 'losing' Spanish Morocco. It would be remarkable if Salazar, a shrewd observer, was unaware of feelings in Spain. A commitment to Britain, possibly provoking an Axis response, would have played right into Franco's hands. A move into Portugal could be cloaked as 'help for our little Iberian brother'.

It has been suggested that Portugal gave Britain air and naval facilities in 1943 because it had been selling wolfram to Germany and wanted to be seen as 'even-handed'. This is a misunderstanding. As a neutral nation, it was free to sell its products on the open market (though it began selling wolfram to Germany only in 1942). The Azores' facilities, however, involved questions of sovereignty and undermined Portuguese neutrality. We would like to suggest that Churchill supported the violation of Portugal's neutrality in Asia in the hope that it would make the violation of Portuguese neutrality in Europe much easier. Portugal agreed to allow the base when Britain invoked the 'ancient alliance', but specified that only Britain should benefit. When Britain opened the facility to the Americans, Salazar protested strongly. In response, Churchill telegraphed Eden: 'There is no need for us to be apologetic in dealing with any of these neutrals who hope to get out of Armageddon with no trouble and a good profit.'[13] His respect for neutrality was minimal.

Britain, in its negotiations with Portugal over Timor, claimed that Australian troops sent to the island to 'protect' its people were doing so because of British respect for the 'ancient alliance'. Portugal responded by saying that the only respect it wanted was respect for its neutrality in Timor. Britain clearly interpreted the 'ancient alliance' in terms of its own needs; but it could also, by using Australian troops, be said to have covered its back in the event of any later claims for damages done by those troops through Royal Air Force squadrons based in northern Australia which carried out at least one bombing mission into East Timor, in June 1945.

We would go further and suggest that, as far as Britain was concerned, the 'ancient alliance' was an irrelevance. In 1914, the

British Government and the German Ambassador to Britain, Prince Lichnowsky, drew up a secret agreement by which the two nations would carve up Portugal's African empire between them.[14] The First World War prevented the implementation of this plan and, 'Although the Allies won the war, and Portugal's colonies were safeguarded, the 0.75 per cent of the war indemnity paid by Germany to Portugal was scant compensation for the heavy costs incurred, both in the field and at home; the casualties of the African campaigns and the western front; the alienation of a portion of the army officer corps; crippling war debts to Britain; intense inflation; and a scarcity of food and fuel.'[15] However, neither Britain nor Germany gave up their individual ambitions in regard to Portugal's empire, and 'leading far-right-wing members of the Chamberlain Government had, in that time of frantic attempts to contain the burgeoning Nazi behemoth, proposed appeasing Germany by giving it economic and settlement rights carved out of Portuguese Angola'.[16] By June 1943, Britain and Australia were discussing a postwar future for East Timor which did not include Portugal.[17]

More civilians died in tiny East Timor in World War II than died in Britain.[18] Yet Britain's 'back room' role has always allowed it to walk away from any responsibility for events in East Timor.

HOLLAND/NETHERLANDS EAST INDIES

The entry of Dutch troops into neutral Portuguese Timor is rarely mentioned, let alone criticised, possibly because it has been seen as an admirable initiative by individual Dutch officers to fight on rather than surrender. This is incorrect. Dutch troops entered East Timor on 17 December 1941, after threatening the Portuguese Governor in Dili with bloodshed if they were not allowed to land, and well before Japan invaded the Netherlands East Indies. The Dutch military command was still intact, so it must be assumed that they violated Portuguese neutrality on orders from their

Government or from their Commander-in-Chief, General Hein ter Poorten, in Jakarta. Why did Dutch troops violate East Timor's territory when good relations between two powers sharing the island would seem desirable and when military needs would suggest these men were better placed elsewhere? Furthermore, Portugal respected Dutch neutrality in the First World War, so why was this respect not returned in the Second World War? The Dutch were aware of Portugal's wishes, as they ran a weekly flight between Kupang and Dili and maintained a Dutch Consul in Dili.

The usual explanation, that the Dutch wanted to prevent the Japanese from using Portuguese territory for a 'back door invasion' of Dutch Timor, does not hold up to scrutiny: 'The Dutch, in the 20th century, were not a military inspired nation. No attempt had been made by them to strengthen their small force on Timor either before or after our arrival, yet there had been much talk about this,' and: '(Brigadier) Lind was by now extremely critical of the Dutch failure to complete preparations agreed to much earlier in the year' are two Australian comments on the fact that the 'front door' was standing wide open.[19] The prize for the Japanese in the Netherlands East Indies was the oilfields of Kalimantan and Sumatra. Japan's desire for oil was a major war aim, yet instead of making the defence of these fields a priority, forces were spread out across the Netherlands East Indies in sufficient numbers to provoke a Japanese response, but in insufficient numbers to either hold the individual islands or draw Japanese troops away from the assaults on the oilfields. Dutch claims of empire always appeared to be in conflict with war strategies. At the same time as the Netherlands East Indies Government was concerned that an Australian force on Dutch Timor[20] could provoke a Japanese invasion, their Commander-in-Chief was asking General Wavell to send troops. (Decisions about deployment of Australia's elite commandos, the 2/2nd, into neutral Portuguese Timor and a regular army battalion, the 2/40th Australian Infantry Forces (AIF), into Allied Dutch Timor, were apparently made as early as mid-1941. Clearly there are many unanswered questions about Dutch, British and Australian decision-making in regard to Timor in this crucial period.)

The Dutch made no attempt to garrison the border between East and West Timor, nor to fortify any anchorage except Kupang. Timor, as a whole, has the longest dry season of any area in Southeast Asia; food constraints were always going to undermine any strategic value the island might have. In 1941, it was still believed that Singapore was 'impregnable' and that the Japanese would easily be stopped in Malaya.

East Timor could have only very limited value to the Japanese. It could be used to bomb northern Australia but, equally, northern Australia could be used to bomb Timor, which was far more vulnerable than any part of Australia. All the harbours of East Timor were open and vulnerable to air attack; it had little flat land for the easy building of large air bases; the pattern of habitation, as a dense grid of tiny hamlets, unlike northern Australia, where towns are surrounded by huge areas with a sparse population, meant no airfield would be more than two kilometres from civilian settlement; almost all the women and children, except for army nurses, were evacuated from the towns of northern Australia, whereas the Portuguese had nowhere to evacuate the more than 300,000 women and children in their territory; and Australia did not depend on food grown in northern Australia for its survival. The decision by Britain, Australia, and the Netherlands East Indies to 'garrison' Portuguese Timor, against its wishes, made it strategically important to Japan.

The assumption that Portuguese neutrality was the 'Achilles' heel' of Dutch defences is incorrect. That the Dutch surrendered to Japan on 8 March 1942, only weeks after the Japanese invasion, has to do with military unpreparedness, confusion over objectives, the nature of its military decision-making, and the influence of the Sukarno-led independence movement in Java. It had nothing to do with Portugal. So why did the Netherlands East Indies send several hundred crack infantry troops into neutral East Timor?

It has been suggested that the Dutch could not guarantee the loyalty of their subjects and Portugal could, but this was definitely not the pre-war view. A secret report prepared in mid-1941 for the Australian Government praises the Dutch administration in West Timor and is very critical of the Portuguese in East Timor. For example: 'In the educational field, the Dutch authorities are much more active than the Portuguese ... The natives of Dutch Timor are subjected to very much lighter taxation, both actual and relative, than those of Portuguese Timor ... Generally speaking, the natives appear on the average better nourished, more alert and more active in the Dutch colony than in the Portuguese. Certainly they have a much better time.'[21] Portuguese racial tolerance and their willingness to meet socially with the small Japanese community in Dili (which numbered thirteen people including a woman and two children) were interpreted as being pro-Japanese. The British, Dutch and Americans were astonished when supposedly humble 'Chinese' barbers, cigarette sellers, gardeners et cetera were suddenly revealed as high-ranking Japanese officers, but the Portuguese knew the military rank of all the Japanese in their territory.

But no-one could predict how the Timorese tribes would react to the arrival of foreign soldiers in their villages, or to the pressures of a little-understood war being fought across their land. The Dutch certainly did not enter Portuguese territory because of a belief that 'Portugal's natives' would be more loyal.

Equally, the behaviour of villagers in Dutch Timor has been attributed to the effectiveness of Japanese propaganda. This does not explain why they were willing to abandon their tribal lands and villages, at the behest of foreigners with whom they could carry on only the most minimal of conversations, and cross the border into East Timor to carry out attacks there. The real reason would appear to be that they knew their Dutch colonial masters were in Portuguese Timor and the Japanese offered them encouragement, and freedom from later Dutch reprisals. The Dutch surrender three weeks after the arrival of the Japanese in West Timor gave weight to Japanese proclamations at a time when the Dutch administration was falling apart; to go after them and vent their simmering resentment for the forcible relocations carried out in Dutch Timor in the 1920s.[22] The Dutch decision to violate Portuguese neutrality took the results of Dutch pre-war administrative policies into Portuguese territory and caused great suffering in the areas adjacent to the border.

Dutch exiles in northern Australia formed No. 18 Squadron, which was regularly in action over East Timor from January 1943 onwards. 'Mitchells of No. 18 Squadron continued nightly attacks on Koepang, *Lautem*, *Fuiloro* ...' (August 1943); 'Mitchells of No. 18 Squadron visited Koepang, *Lautem*, Penfui and *Dili* ...' (April 1944); 'In the first week of May Nos. 1, 18 and 31 Squadrons bombed Penfui, *Cape Chater*, *Manatuto*, Koepang and other targets on Timor'; 'No. 18 ... heavily attacked *Cape Chater* airfield on 19th June dropping bombs on the runway and dispersal area. It also sank a small vessel and two prahus off Timor'; 'As a counter-propaganda measure Nos. 2 and 18 Squadrons carried out a series of widespread raids on villages in Timor on 1st January (1945), a day on which the Japanese usually held festivities in Timor towns. Seven targets were successfully bombed and strafed.'[23]

But was there a secret agenda beneath Dutch willingness to violate Portuguese neutrality and attack the territory thereafter? On 4 October 1904, Holland and Portugal signed a treaty to delineate their border in Timor, but Holland was not satisfied and on 25 June 1914, the World Court in The Hague (the Permanent Court of Arbitration) ruled in favour of the border that Holland had sought. By actively compromising Portuguese neutrality, by the possible spilling of Dutch blood on Portuguese soil, even by burying Dutch 'patriots' in Portuguese territory, Holland's legal, moral and emotional claim to East Timor would be strengthened. If the Portuguese administration broke down (which was expected—it was seen as ramshackle and poverty-stricken, while the Portuguese, regarded as 'dagoes', were not believed to be courageous or tenacious), the Dutch were then admirably placed to step in with their administrative experience in West Timor. With the Dutch Government-in-Exile having the ear of the British Government, and the Netherlands East Indies Government-in-Exile the ear of the Australian Government, the Dutch were well placed to press their claim in any postwar distribution of colonial territory.[24]

Whether or not Dutch/Netherlands East Indies actions in East Timor were motivated by a desire to absorb this small colony into the Netherlands East Indies, Holland does have a responsibility towards the people of East Timor which it has never acknowledged.

It could be argued that the Sukarno-led liberation movement in Java prevented any Allied ambitions to take over Portuguese Timor. But we would like to suggest that insufficient attention has been paid to the part played by the Governor in East Timor, Captain Manuel Ferreira de Carvalho, and other administration officials.

Under the Hague Conventions, to maintain the *legal* status of neutrality, a nation had to deport or intern invading forces. Portugal's position was strengthened both by the League of Nations Covenant and by the Kellogg-Briand Pact, whose signatories pledged to negotiate rather than go to war with fellow signatories. Japan, Britain, Holland, the USA, Australia and Portugal were all signatories to the Pact and all except the USA were signatories to the Covenant; Japan withdrew from the League in the 1930s but did not repudiate the Covenant itself. It might be argued that Portugal's claim to neutrality was compromised by its failure to intern invading Dutch, Australian and Japanese forces (though it is hard to see how it might have done so), but this compromise is offset by the later agreements. The territory's impeccably neutral status, upheld by the Governor on behalf of the administration and his colonial subjects despite immense pressure, provocation and personal hardship, could be said to uphold the moral right to have its neutrality respected.

This is strengthened by two other points. Australia, for example, declared war on Thailand on 2 March 1942, on the grounds that it had been occupied by Japan. Yet Japan did not use the excuse that East Timor was occupied by Australia and the Netherlands East Indies (both of whom had declared war on Japan on 9 December 1941) to declare war on Portuguese Timor; nor did any of the Allies declare war on Portuguese Timor on the grounds that it had been occupied by Japan. Furthermore, Portugal was excluded from all postwar deliberations on reparations and compensation, nor was any postwar aid offered to Portuguese Timor, ostensibly because of its neutral status.

We believe that Japan, Holland, Britain, Australia and the USA all have unacknowledged and unpaid debts towards the people of East Timor.

Endnotes

1 Japan caused the highest number of deaths in East Timor while Australia caused the greatest amount of structural damage. Australia has always been more open about the damage it caused—for example, the RAAF's Directorate of Public Relations stated in 1943: 'Dili, Bobonaro, Manatuto and Baucau squirmed and smoked under the rain of bombs and machine-gun fire the Hudsons loosed.' But this division is not rigid. Japan first bombed East Timor in February 1942 and carried out a number of subsequent raids. Lieutenant Colin Doig in his history of the 2/2nd Independent Company wrote: 'there was no satisfaction at all in killing natives, also it was a fruitless task; what were a few hundred or thousand of them out of the hundred thousand native men in the colony?'

2 Michele Turner, *Telling East Timor*, University of New South Wales Press, Sydney, 1992, p. 41.

3 United States Air Force archives.

4 See for example, Peter Charlton, *The Unnecessary War*, Macmillan, Melbourne, 1983.

5 'Lagarto' party 01/07/43 lost its codes; it was not until 'Sunlag' party 29/06/45 that this loss was discovered. Alan Powell in *The Shadow's Edge* (Melbourne University Press, 1983) quotes from

Operations of the Allied Intelligence Bureau, Volume IV: 'When these moves are studied in conjunction with the party's earlier history of being hounded from place to place, with the Japanese learning of its movements by killing and torturing the natives in the areas through which it passed, it is incomprehensible that SRD Headquarters did not deduce that the party had been captured', and he rightly remarks, 'Incomprehensible indeed'.

6 The leaflets for Portuguese Timor were prepared predominantly by Australian personnel and dropped into the territory on an *ad hoc* basis by Australian and American aircraft. They were an uneasy blend of promises: 'Timorese! Your Friends Do Not Forget You', 'For you, Timorese, the day of liberation is drawing nearer. The day is not far off when we shall go back there, counting on your friendship and goodwill to work with us and help us in driving out forever from your country these cruel pygmies'; exhortations: 'Prepare with all your strength to be able to fight on this day on the Allied Nations' side'; war news: 'Bangkok again attacked by British and American bombers. Fires visible 150 kms away'; and threats: 'HEED OUR WARNING. If you do not stay away from the Japanese you may be killed', 'REMEMBER: Keep away from the Japanese or we will be forced to attack you'. (As many Timorese were doing forced labour on roads, bridges and airfields, though this may have salved consciences in FELO, it was of no comfort to the people at whom it was aimed.)

7 The removal of Japanese troops from East Timor in August/September 1942 has mistakenly been seen as a permanent removal. In fact it was only temporary. 'On 5 Dec it was reported that the enemy strength in Portuguese Timor was 7000. On the 15th Dec this number was reinforced by a further 3000 and on the 22/24 Dec a further 5000 were landed at Laivai making the total in Portuguese Timor 15000' (Secret Situation Report to 11 January 1943, Australian War Memorial). It was not until March 1945 that Japan sought to move the bulk of its troops north from Timor and surrounding islands; this was only partially completed, because of Allied bombing and lack of ships.

8 Because the 1940 census figures were lost in the destruction of Dili, no precise figures for population loss can be given. The 1920 census showed a population of 397,875. The 1930 figure was 472,221, a rise of 74,346 in ten years, so it can be assumed that the

1940 figure was at least 546,567. It was probably slightly higher. The health survey and census carried out in 1946 showed a population of 403,232. East Timor's population had dropped by at least 143,335 and probably more. (A despatch from the Australian Consul in Dili, dated 19 May 1946, says: 'I have been given by Government Officials the approximate figure of 100,000 deaths of Portuguese Timor natives from starvation and other causes during the Japanese occupation. I consider this a high estimate from a population of some 450,000', but, strangely, he never provides the result of the 1946 census.) This does not allow for people left with chronic ill health, nor for the generation of children exposed to severe malnutrition. Figures for other small territories are also very high. For example, the Native War Damage Compensation Committee reported that: 'one quarter of the population of Bougainville may have perished ... The invasion and war activities ... have had effects upon the natives so calamitous and so far removed from anything with which their experience and way of life have made them familiar, that it is beyond their power to cope with them.' What was called a 'defence screen' in the 1940s and 'forward defence' more recently has actually involved a racist and callous attitude towards our small island neighbours which has accepted without question the belief that it is better to fight our wars on their territories than on our own. We need to develop sufficient moral integrity and maturity to consign this attitude to the scrapheap of history.

9 The article 'Timor 1941: Unwelcome Visitors' by Sydney lawyer, Rodney Lewis, gives a good overview of the cable traffic.

10 See for example, L. Woodward, *British Foreign Policy in the Second World War*, in the series *History of the Second World War*, 1962.

11 See David Day, *The Great Betrayal*, Angus & Robertson, Sydney, 1988.

12 Paul Preston, *Franco*, Harper/Collins, London, 1993.

13 Churchill to Eden, 12 January 1944. It is debatable whether living in Salazar's police state could be described as 'no trouble'. Salazar, whatever one may say about his politics, was incorruptible in a personal sense—as both Allied and Axis powers discovered—and he would probably have found Churchill's lifestyle, even in the war, ostentatious and wasteful.

14 See *World War 1*, Volume 4, Marshall Cavendish, New York, 1984.

15 *Encyclopaedia Britannica*. Attitudes had not changed much over the previous century. H. V. Livermore in *A New History of Portugal* points out that 'The Napoleonic wars ... had devastated the Iberian Peninsula and dislocated its traditional commerce', yet Portugal received only 0.286 per cent of French reparations. Cambridge University Press, Second Edition, 1976.

16 Jerrold M. Packard, *Neither Friend Nor Foe*, Macmillan, New York, 1992.

17 Australia's Minister for External Affairs, Dr Evatt, discussed with his British counterpart, in June 1943, possible British help to Australia in gaining East Timor as a colony. This matter appears to have been raised again in 1944, when Britain thought the war in Europe would be over by the end of the year and a British expeditionary force might then be available for use in Southeast Asia. The Americans were also interested; Paul Hasluck writes: 'at the Pacific Council on 31st March 1943 the President said that he had discussed with Mr Eden the island territories in the Pacific, including the question of the Japanese mandated islands and Timor.'

18 Civilian deaths in Britain have been put at 60,595. Thus the combined total for civilian deaths in Britain, Australia and the USA is less than the death toll in East Timor.

19 Quotes are from *Samurais and Circumcisions*, by Leslie Poidevin, Adelaide, 1985 (published by the author), and *Doomed Battalion*, by Peter Henning, Allen and Unwin, Sydney, 1995.

20 Australian Archives. 14 June 1941. CRS A2671 109/1941.

21 A secret report—the Archer Report prepared in 1941.

22 See for example, Andrew Gray, IWGIA Document 50, edited by Torben Retboll. 'They forced mountain dwellers in West Timor to move into more accessible places for purely administrative convenience' and 'These *kampung* settlements were set up in the 1920s, initially near military supply roads and later along trunk roads. They were artificially large villages'. By contrast, the Portuguese in the 1930s began a programme to survey all tribal lands and acknowledge traditional land ownership in East Timor.

23 Quotes from *Air War Against Japan 1943–1945*, by George

Odgers, Australian War Memorial, Canberra, 1957. Places in East Timor have been put into italics.

24 See eg. Rupert Lockwood, *Black Armada*, Australasian Book Society, Sydney, 1975. The Netherlands East Indies Government-in-Exile retained the close support of the Australian Government throughout the war and into the postwar period. 'In this South Seas diaspora the bread of banishment was seldom bitter to Dutch taste. Australia provided the Wacol establishment with military camps, housing, armaments, officers to train its armed forces, hospitals, shipyard berths, airfields, workshops, clothing, food and drink, some of the latter in the comfort of beer gardens.' Nevertheless, the arrival of political prisoners from the infamous Bovun Digul camp in West New Guinea helped alienate the sympathy of ordinary Australians, and led directly to the boycott of the stevedoring of Dutch ships in Australian ports in the immediate postwar period. Compare the Dutch treatment with the miserly and carping treatment given to the small number of Portuguese exiles, including former administrators Sousa Santos and Lemos Pires, who had risked their lives and their careers to provide help to Australian and Dutch troops.

Roger East is one of our great unsung heroes. While Australia's political leaders were cosying up to those Indonesians responsible for murdering the five Australian and Australian-based television newsmen in October 1975, Roger East took it upon himself to go into East Timor in order to find out what had happened to his colleagues. On arrival in Dili he set up the East Timor News Agency. Refusing to leave with the invasion imminent— 'I can't leave these people, everyone else has, but I can't leave them'—he paid for his unique and courageous concern for those journalists and for the East Timorese with the greatest sacrifice: his life.

According to a radio message sent out by Fretilin's Minister for Information and National Security, Alarico Fernandes, and received in Australia on 4 January 1976, Roger East had been murdered on the day of the invasion, along with hundreds of East Timorese, on the wharf in Dili harbour. His last article was printed in the Australian Left Review *in June 1976, and is reproduced in full here with their kind permission.*

2

EAST TIMOR'S BORDER WAR
AN EYEWITNESS REPORT FROM ROGER EAST

Australia's nearest neighbour, East Timor, has cast the die. In three convulsive months this tiny Portuguese colony has springboarded from passive politics into an armed camp crusading for independence. The standard-bearers are Fretilin, a loosely knit grouping of many political shades cemented together only by the beckoning beacon of freedom. It is unchallenged now, and unchallengeable. Their opponents, UDT and Apodeti, were thrashed on the battlefield of their own choice and are now despised by the

Timorese for accepting the patronage of Indonesia to recoup their losses. For Australia to pretend the situation is otherwise must reflect either on their intelligence or their integrity. Canberra's studied neutrality has elevated the possibility of Indonesia embarking on all-out war against the East Timorese.

BOGONARO (on the border): The monsoon rains are now whooshing down on these mountain passes to create a new scenario for this border war. Within days, these snaking rivulets will be fast-flowing streams. Beneath me, at this hour, on the now sodden valley, the Indonesian-led troops are now marooned in Maliana.

They know they are going nowhere in the next five months, except to a wider war or the comforts of home. The Fretilin soldiers viewing the foe are exuberant. In this dense low-lying cloud cover and driving rain, they are being provided with a custom-made camouflage for their hit-and-run forays.

The initiative has passed to Fretilin. The firepower which, to date, has blunted their offensives, will be dramatically reduced by the weather.

Thousands of mortars and shells have rained on them in the past eight weeks, most to explode harmlessly against the mountain face or valley bed. Fewer than twenty have died as a result. In their rock crannies, it is a weapon they treat with contempt. On the valley floor in the open countryside it wins a grudging respect.

The Indonesian firepower has been massive on occasions. Yet they are largely beleaguered in their bases at Maliana, Balibo and Batugade on the coast. Their numbers have been estimated by Fretilin commandos at around 5000, but they admit their counting could be faulty. These Indonesian forces, which include the survivors of the East Timorese political parties, UDT and Apodeti, are now anchored along the border in a corridor about 40 kilometres long and which juts no deeper than eight kilometres into East Timor.

Earlier reports, emanating from Djakarta of fighting near Baucau, Aileu and Dili, were either patently untrue, or the singular exploits of a phantom army.

On October 16, Indonesia's censored war began with a ship and shore bombardment of Maliana. At dawn that day, Fretilin forces were in disarray following their first real encounter with shell and mortar.

Thirty kilometres away, Balibo was falling in the same offensive. That was the morning the five Australian newsmen died. Ten kilometres towards the coast, Batugade was already occupied. Maliana was captured within hours and the Indonesian-led force swept on to over-run Sabarai and the mountain strongpoint of Tapo, roughly ten kilometres from the frontier. This was their deepest penetration into East Timor.

(In the second week of September, a 100-strong force over-ran Atsabe, about 50 kilometres from Maliana, and killed 30 villagers before being repulsed. It is now believed they were largely Apodeti recruits.)

Fretilin was to re-muster and counter-attack in the mountains and the offensive became a rout. By the evening of October 17, the Indonesians were back in Maliana.

One of Tapo's two military commanders, Lamos Furril, told what happened. 'They swarmed across the valley and up the mountain-side. It was the first time we had seen the Indonesians. We were being shelled and mortared and we kept falling back. We backed off all that day and through the night.

'We had crossed a mountain range, a valley, and were climbing another mountain. Next morning we were surprised to see the Indonesians sitting down, lying down and leaning against trees. They were completely exhausted.

'We attacked and they offered little resistance. They were running and falling back the way they came. It was easy killing them.'

And so ended the first and only real attempt by this across-the-border force to penetrate East Timor's hinterland.

In Maliana the guns are rarely quiet. The harassed defenders are daily switching their fire to five different mountain targets in an arc of almost 270 degrees. Their 90-degree sanctuary is a road corridor to the border and a craggy hill two kilometres distant. All else is No-Man's Land or Fretilin's.

Along the corridor, three helicopters scurry during lulls in the fighting. Two are white and display the red cross. The third is equipped with machine-guns. The two Second World War bombers which stooge around each morning are largely toothless at this hour. From the safety of about 3000 metres they machine-gun at random. To date, no bombs have been dropped and their daily targets are the former Portuguese cavalry outpost at Bogonaro or Atabae to the north. One is silvery white, while the other is brown, and both are unmarked.

Casualties are few, and will get fewer when soldiers and civilians learn to give up gawking and go for cover. Three times in the past four days I have been in the line of fire which reflected neither competence nor a high degree of courage on the part of the cloud-clinging warriors.

Excited soldiers occasionally ignore orders and release a fusillade from their Mausers. Stone-throwing would be equally effective.

Whither Indonesia?

It is obvious from here that it must commit its forces to a full-scale intervention or accept the verdict that its proteges, UDT and Apodeti, are a part of history. It was here in these regions that UDT had its greatest strength, and this rested largely on a platform of independence, and its respectability in the eyes of both the Catholic Church and the Portuguese administration.

The Church leadership is now fragmented and the Portuguese have gone. UDT is now being judged as either war criminals or quislings and they face short-lived lives if they return.

The anger is genuine and the bitterness deep.

UDT's leadership is now split three ways. Some are languishing in Timorese jails and others in the more comfortable surrounds of Australian cities. The remaining standard-bearers are in Indonesia, hosted and promised a triumphant return, albeit in the wake of mortar bombs.

Their platform of independence which, only a year ago, saw them in a political alliance with Fretilin, is now abandoned. They are opting for Indonesia after 450 years of Portuguese domination.

Apodeti is a bad bar-room joke. Its political rallies could be staged in the proverbial ten by four room which includes a table. Founder and President is Arnaldo Araujo, 62, a respected horse thief, who is currently being detained at Fretilin's pleasure in Aileu. The prison routine revives for him memories of former times. The Portuguese administration jailed him for nine years for war crimes committed against the Timorese during the Japanese occupation.

This leaves only Fretilin, which would embrace an offer of a UN-supervised plebiscite in the knowledge that it would win by the handsomest of margins. This 'front' would appear to have struck the right note at a historical moment. It gathers in intellects, passions and aspirations of varying degrees and intensity.

The mortar that binds them is the singular and irrevocable process towards independence. East Timor will settle for nothing less. This commitment to independence is symbolised in the clenched fist, and the unspoken 'strength and unity' which this implies. It is the greeting at all hours and in any situation.

The fist belongs to children, their parents, the elderly, the soldier, the peasant, the peddler. Young women, clutching traditional household appliances, emphasise their emotional intensity by the whiteness of their knuckles.

Moral reasons are necessary to wage an immoral war. And Djakarta has elected to win support from its nervous neighbours by attaching the 'red' label to Fretilin. Visions of Chinese sampans, Hanoi dhows and Russian cruisers riding at anchor in Dili harbour are sufficient for ASEAN states, countering communist insurgencies, to see the threat and applaud its removal.

Fretilin is indisputably anticolonial, which may be accounted for by the 30 dollar per capita income it enjoys after 450 years of Portuguese rule.

Its initial planning is a blending of socialistic and cooperative policies, which would again appear natural for a colony bereft of secondary industry and winning from the soil a subsistence existence.

The membership by an Australian measure would include thinkers from the centre to the extreme left, the latter a fringe grouping in the 500-strong Central Committee, Fretilin's policy council.

Secretary of the Department of Foreign Affairs, Jose Ramos Horta, admits that the committee's views vary on many issues, the sole exception being independence.

'I expect to see a multi-party set-up in East Timor after we cross this hurdle,' he observed. 'We are a tolerant people who have waited a long time for the democratic process. We'll share it when it comes.'

The crucifixes on the chests of Fretilin's soldiers are the trademarks of their education. Many are outspokenly anti-communist, but how the majority thinks must await events.

Refugees who fled East Timor, many under duress, have told on their return of forced labour conditions in Indonesia, primarily on building roads to the frontier.

Djakarta's generals may now be weighing their options. Certainly, the construction of tourist autobahns into East Timor is not among them. It would appear that the generals are prevailing and that an open conflict may be in the offing. If it comes, the curtain will be lowered on the censored war and raised on an aggressive one. Such an event will embarrass East Timor's neighbours, including Australia, in the short term and shame them in the long run.

Indonesia's 130 million certainly have the numbers and the military hardware to subdue 650,000 Timorese, but only along the coast and in the few centres of population. On present border form, its army on the hinterland will haemorrhage to death.

Ken Fry was a Member of Parliament in the Gough Whitlam Government (Member for Fraser, ACT, 1974–1984). He was a member of two 1975 bipartisan delegations that went to East Timor before the invasion. In 1976, Mr Fry was invited to address the United Nations General Assembly on the subject of East Timor, based upon his personal experience. Reproduced here for the first time: a parliamentary report made by Mr Fry on his second visit to East Timor in September 1975 (Part A); pre-invasion telegrams sent by East Timorese leaders including José Ramos Horta (Part B); the address to the General Assembly (Part C); a background briefing by Mr Fry of the political complications and nuances at the UN at the time of his 1976 visit (Part D); a series of letters believed to be sent from someone within the Department of Foreign Affairs (Part E). All make fascinating reading, and provide us with a first-hand view to the grave situation on the ground inside East Timor just before the invasion, as well as to the present-day machinations of 'working' the UN and the political faithlessness generally prevalent in Canberra. Mr Fry has continued his support for the rights of the East Timorese to self-determination and to freedom from human rights violations. His last public display of solidarity was on 24 April, the day before ANZAC Day 1997, when he joined several people on the stairs of the Australian War Memorial in Canberra to commemorate East Timorese who had died helping Australian commandos during the Second World War. (The background briefing has been edited for the purpose of not reproducing the author's summarised context of his General Assembly speech. This obviously can be better appreciated in the original text—Editor.)

3

LEST WE FORGET EAST TIMOR

KEN FRY

Part A

REPORT ON VISIT TO PORTUGUESE EAST TIMOR BY SENATOR GIETZELT AND K. L. FRY 16–18 SEPTEMBER 1975

This is a brief report of our visit in chronological order. On arrival at Dili on the morning of Tuesday, 16 September 1975, we immediately met the Central Committee of the Fretilin party at the Army Headquarters in Dili. The President, Xavier do Amaral, gave us a brief outline of the events leading up to the UDT coup which took place on 11 August. He stressed that Fretilin knew of the proposed coup some two weeks in advance and had made several requests to the Governor, Col. Lemos Pires, to take some action to forestall it. He also stated that many Fretilin members had been arrested without charge by the Chief of Police, Lt Col. Maggiolo Gouveia, who later commanded the UDT military operations. Fretilin leaders had withdrawn from Dili and had gone to a pre-arranged headquarters in the mountains only fifteen minutes before the UDT coup commenced. They claimed that many Fretilin followers were killed in the fighting in the coup, and many had been murdered in cold blood after being taken prisoner. The President claimed that any Fretilin supporters who were considered to be communist, or sympathetic to the communists, were murdered without question. This included a number of students. He was critical of the Governor for not exercising any control over the UDT forces, despite the fact that he was well informed on what was being planned. Pires is generally considered to have collaborated with the UDT. He was also critical of the Governor's action in leaving Portuguese East Timor and going to the island of Atauro, and particularly his action in forcibly taking with him the only surgeon at the Dili Hospital where hundreds of wounded were awaiting treatment and operations. He also took with him two Portuguese helicopter pilots.

The President stated that the food supplies were being well controlled by the Fretilin forces, but that they were running short and expected to be out of supplies of staple foods such as rice and flour in four to six weeks. They could not expect relief until the rice harvest in November. People who have come down from the villages to Dili were being sent back to tend their crops, and conditions at this stage were favourable for a satisfactory rice harvest.

The main areas of food shortage were in the north-west highlands, centred around Maubisse. In this area, children were also suffering from cold and he requested clothing supplies from Australia if available.

We inspected a large wall map showing the military situation in detail. At that stage, according to the map, Fretilin had full control of the whole area of Portuguese East Timor with the exception of a small pocket of resistance around Batugade. Here they claimed 40 to 50 UDT supporters were holding a number of Fretilin women and children as hostages in the village, which prevented the surrounding Fretilin forces from firing on them. It was the Fretilin intention to keep the village under pressure in the expectation that the UDT forces would ultimately withdraw to Indonesian Timor as most of the other forces along the border had done.

The map showed where UDT forces along the coast north of Dili at Liquica and Maubara had been evacuated to Indonesian Timor by barge. There had been an action by UDT troops at Bobonato which had been repulsed by Fretilin forces who claimed to have killed one soldier wearing Indonesian uniform (red berets) and taken two prisoners. Fretilin were awaiting the return of the dead soldier and the prisoners to Dili but they had not arrived before our departure. Fretilin claimed that they were holding about 500 political prisoners in all.

Fretilin claimed that UDT supporters who were the top administrators and manage the Government Bank took all the currency with them when they withdrew from Dili. They also claimed that Chinese merchants took all their currency with them. Later the UDT supporters told us that the bank vault had not been opened and that money was still in the bank. Whatever happened to the money, it is obvious that there is very little currency in Dili and certainly no-one is being paid, and virtually everyone is being fed by the Fretilin forces.

It is claimed that UDT took 20 tractors from the Maliana area. It was claimed as well that there had also been heavy casualties among the Fretilin forces in this area—500 to 5000. It was not possible to confirm any of these figures but they tend to be refuted by the reports of the doctors of the Dili Hospital that there were only small numbers of wounded evacuated to the hospital from that area.

Following discussions with the Central Committee, we then inspected the jail near the Army Headquarters in Dili where about 80 prisoners were held. They were mainly UDT political prisoners but also included some Fretilin supporters who had been jailed for breaches of discipline and some civil offences. The jail was crowded but the prisoners generally looked to be in good condition and were being fed the same food rations as everyone else in Dili. A small number of them had obviously been bashed when they were taken prisoner, several bearing body bruises and lacerations and some had head injuries. These people were generally described by Fretilin as being very 'bad' people who had been responsible for murdering many Fretilin supporters. They included the Chief of Police, Lt Col. Maggiolo Gouveia.

We then visited the Dili Hospital and spoke with some of the UDT patients there, including the Vice-President, Mousino, a former Mayor of Dili, who was taken prisoner at Baucau. He told us that when he had visited Australia, with the President of the UDT, he had had discussions with Mr Feaks of Foreign Affairs and Mr Morrison in Canberra, and had spoken to ex-Timor commandos and the RSL in Sydney. He stated that he had been encouraged to break the coalition with Fretilin on his return, by people in Australia.

In order to compare the claims of control of the island made by Fretilin forces, we chartered a private aircraft which was owned by an Australian, Mr Frank Favarro, who is a UDT supporter, to inspect a number of widely separated points on the island.

BAUCAU

Our first call was at Baucau, east of Dili, which was a former UDT stronghold. When we arrived at Baucau airport, a platoon of well-dressed Fretilin troops paraded to meet us accompanied by 200 to 300 of the Baucau people who indicated that they were enthusiastic supporters of the Fretilin movement. We went to Baucau where several hundred people had gathered. They too cheered the Fretilin leader, Alarico Fernandez (Secretary-General of the Central Committee), who distributed leaflets containing a message from the Fretilin leadership. We inspected the jail where 58 UDT and one Apodeti prisoners were being held. Their quarters were clean and less crowded than in Dili. They were being well fed and with one or two exceptions bore no signs of having been bashed. Some of the UDT supporters claimed that they had been threatened and coerced by Mousino to fight against Fretilin.

They claimed that Fretilin had always been presented to them as communists who would murder them if they got control. The Fretilin leaders claimed that some of the UDT political prisoners were being held for their own protection. They had murdered Fretilin supporters whose friends and relatives may seek revenge. The Fretilin leaders claimed at many stages that their philosophy was that independence was more important than revenge and that they constantly impressed this on Fretilin supporters. They claim that as soon as the situation quietened down they would set up a commission to try the prisoners and expected to release as many as possible and that they would not be seeking the death penalty for UDT leaders. They were hopeful that Portuguese authority would return to help them set up such a commission.

We called at a Catholic school in Baucau where about 20 Catholic priests and lay teachers taught about 1000 pupils. The disturbances had taken place during the school holidays and it was anticipated that the school would resume normal life when the holidays had ended.

We visited a hospital where we found only five patients and fifteen empty beds. We were given a meal at Hotel Baucau, which included fresh goat and buffalo meat, as well as locally grown potatoes and tomatoes. There appeared to be no damage to buildings in Baucau. It was claimed that 30 Apodeti supporters had met at Baucau on 15 September and had made a decision to support the Fretilin administration. We also heard that this had happened in other areas.

VIQUEQUE

We then flew to Viqueque where again we were met by detachments of Fretilin soldiers both at the airport and at the former Army Headquarters. Here about 30 UDT prisoners were being held, three of whom appear to have been bashed when arrested. Twenty other UDT supporters who had not been involved in the fighting were being held under house arrest. The UDT prisoners were alleged to have been involved in Fretilin killings in

Same and had to come to Viqueque for ammunition supplies. There was no actual fighting in Viqueque. At the Administration Headquarters, a large crowd of about 300 Timorese people had gathered and were addressed by Fernandez. He was given a very enthusiastic reception. Viqueque appears to be a very fertile area with coconut plantations, paw-paws, tobacco and maize being grown. There was also a cane furniture factory which was sponsored by the Portuguese Government, but which was not now in production.

SUAI

We then flew on to Suai on the south-west coast, only about 30 kilometres from the border with Indonesian Timor. Here we were met by Catholic nuns from a small local hospital, where we were asked to make our aircraft available to take a young woman who had been haemorrhaging for eight days, to the Dili Hospital. This operation was carried out successfully but delayed our return to Dili where we had to make a hazardous landing with the aid of car-lights on the unlit airstrip.

In Suai, we found conditions quiet and orderly, with Fretilin troops in full control. All the Chinese shops in the village were opened and none of the Chinese merchants had left the village. They were addressed by the Fretilin leader, who assured them that Fretilin was confident of retaining control and did not want to interfere with their activities.

Suai appears to be a fertile, agricultural area and on our drive out to the airstrip we saw several groups of Timorese people returning to the township heavily laden with produce from the fields. There had been no fighting in Suai but we saw three houses which had been burnt down and we were told that these were destroyed by Fretilin forces after UDT supporters had withdrawn across the Indonesian border.

Before leaving Dili on Thursday morning, we had further discussions with President Xavier who supplied us with a list of the quantities of foodstuffs which he estimated would be required to see them through until the rice harvest. He stressed that, although they were in virtual control of the island, apart from the need for food and clothing, there was an urgent need for talks with Portuguese representatives with the object of re-establishing a skeleton Portuguese administration in Dili. There was also an urgent need for technical aid. At that stage he had received no response from Portugal to his requests for talks in Baucau on 20 September. He also stressed the grave economic problems facing them in the virtual absence of currency. He was adamant that Col. Pires would not be accepted back as Governor, as he had been discredited in the eyes of both Fretilin and UDT supporters. He made a very strong plea to us for urgent relief of the impending food shortage.

SUMMARY OF THE GENERAL SITUATION

1. We received full cooperation from the Fretilin leadership, both in our discussions and in our movements around the island.

2. There were very strong expressions of friendship with Australia from all Fretilin sources. Any Australians in Timor are generally held in high esteem. There is a general expectation that Australia will assist them, and will not let them down. At the same time, some Australian reporters in Dili have indicated that there is an element of cynicism among the Timorese people that Australia has been too timid in its approach to Timor and may ultimately lose face with them, if it does not help them in the near future.

3. Our tour around the island confirmed the claims by Fretilin that they are virtually in full control of the situation. As well as the areas which we visited ourselves, we had reports from Aid and Red Cross personnel of a similar situation in the areas which they had

visited. Wherever we went, the Fretilin troops appeared to be well disciplined; they were treating their prisoners well and appeared to have the overwhelming support of the local population. There was evidence too that some people who had originally supported UDT had changed sides when Fretilin took control. It was evident to us that statements being released in Djakarta by Antara whilst we were in Timor had very little factual basis and should be regarded as propaganda.

4. We were satisfied that there is an urgent need for food, particularly in the Highlands, north-west of Dili. From our previous visit, we were aware that the population in this area suffered near famine conditions from time to time and this is being accentuated by the current disturbances. We were satisfied that there was no actual fighting taking place while we were in Timor, and that the only position which was not in control of Fretilin was Batugade.

We are also satisfied that there is no genuine basis for the charge by the UDT forces that Fretilin is a communist controlled or dominated organisation. The only evidence we have had of communist influence is from a small number of students who are said to have communist associations in Lisbon. At least some of these were murdered by UDT forces during the coup. We are satisfied from discussions with Fretilin leaders that there has been very little outside influence on their general philosophy or their strategic or tactical approach to their plans for independence for Portuguese East Timor. It is obviously a self-generating concept of revolution for independence based on a surprisingly well-developed political consciousness of the desire for independence by the Timorese people at large. Their leadership impressed us as being moderate, highly responsible, dedicated and intelligent in their approach. To attribute their success so far to outside influence would, in our opinion, be a grave error of judgement and a misperception of the over-riding grass roots desire for independence from Colonial overlords by the indigenous people and their leaders.

Part B

THE PRE-INVASION TELEGRAMS

These telegrams were sent after the so-called 'civil war' between Fretilin and the Indonesian-backed forces of the other Timorese political parties, UDT and Apodeti. This conflict, instigated by Jakarta through a policy of subversion and destabilisation, lasted several weeks during August and September 1975. The 'people's party' Fretilin was unequivocally victorious and quickly consolidated agrarian and education reform, bringing both hope and relief to the impoverished Timorese people. This hope was to be short lived, as Indonesia, not being successful through its orchestration of civil conflict, now aimed to conquer the territory of East Timor. This objective involved the incursion on East Timor's territory by Indonesian soldiers, planes and ships, much of which is described in the telegrams sent by Rogerio Lobato, the military commander of Fretilin, and José Ramos Horta, then Fretilin's Secretary for Foreign Affairs, to Ken Fry MP. (Simple grammatical and spelling errors have been corrected—Editor.)

TELEGRAM
Dili to Canberra
Received 8 October 1975

Ken Fry
Room 204 ASL Building
Ainslie Ave
Canberra City ACT

After being crushed by Fretilin forces in several clashes in the East Timor villages along the border Indonesia has reacted today with a massive military operation stop Indonesian helicopters a navy destroyer and infantry have invaded the village of Batugade this morning stop Such a military aggression against our people and our territory is a violation of UN charter and is viewed by Fretilin as a criminal act that should be countered by all democratic forces in the world stop We are counting on all governments and peoples of all the world to end the criminal military aggression by Indonesia against a small country whose people want to be free and independent stop Although we have indicated very often our willingness to promote friendship peace and cooperation with the neighbouring countries our territory peace and our people are experiencing intimidation and military aggression by Indonesian troops stop The people of East Timor under the leadership of Fretilin will fight to the last man against foreign aggressors stop Such a military invasion of East Timor will bring only long term war and instability in the area stop Another Vietnam is starting by the Indonesian troops stop Independence or death we shall win ... José Ramos Horta

TELEGRAM

Dili to Canberra
Received 10 October 1975

Ken Fry
Room 204 ASL Building
Ainslie Ave
Canberra City ACT

Late yesterday Fretilin forces reoccupied the village of Batugade stop After several hours of massive attack by aircraft jets helicopters infantry and a destroyer the Indonesian forces returned to Indonesian territory and Fretilin forces reoccupied Batugade stop Over the past few days Fretilin forces have captured several weapons American made used by the Indonesian army and three vehicles used by UDT forces that drove them from Atambua in Indonesian

Timor stop We warn all peoples and governments in the world that continuous violation of our territory by Indonesian troops will bring long term instability in this region because the people of East Timor under the leadership of Fretilin will not tolerate further criminal attempts to take over our territory by Indonesian forces stop Indonesian Government will be responsible for war and instability in this region as we have indicated already on a number of occasions our willingness to promote friendship and close cooperation with the people and Government of Indonesia stop We believe that peace and stability can only be a long term reality in this region if the Government of Indonesia respects the will of the people of East Timor for national independence and liberation stop Any attempt to suffocate Fretilin will be countered by our forces and the recent victories of the people of Indochina should be a lesson for everybody as it indicated that there is no force in the world that can halt the march of the peoples towards national independence stop Myself I have endeavoured continuously to placate the Indonesian Generals and to find a way for friendship and co-operation for the benefit of the people of East Timor and of Indonesia stop Fretilin always offered dialogue to settle the conflicts in East Timor but the other factions UDT and Apodeti now non-existent rejected our proposals because they were very confident that Indonesia would back them to crush Fretilin stop Have proposed that a joint peace force should be formed between Fretilin troops and Indonesian troops with equal number on both sides stop This I believe would be the best guarantee for security in the border regions and would develop friendship among the Timorese and Indonesian troops in the mentioned region stop We also would welcome a neutral police force from Sweden to police the border region stop We welcome fact finding missions from every country in the world particularly from Asia Australia and New Zealand to assess the situation in East Timor stop Peace and

order have been restored stop Life is returning to
normality stop The Timorese people are again
working hard in countryside stop Several public
services such as post office communications telegrams and telephones tourism etc have been re-
opened as well as the commerce stop Journalists are
invited to visit East Timor and enjoy free access to
every situation and sources with no restrictions at
all stop The only conditions for peace and stability in
the Indonesian archipelago and in the South east
Asia region are the following stop Indonesian
Government respect the will of the people of East
Timor to be independent and free and accept the fact
that Fretilin has achieved a military and political
victory and is in de facto control of the whole
territory of East Timor including the enclave of
Oecusse stop Indonesian Government should cease
all military attacks against our people and our
territory stop Indonesian Government to end all
military support such as training of troops and
supply of weapons and ammunition to UDT and
Apodeti members in Indonesian territory stop Indonesian territory should not be used as a base for
insurgency against East Timor as it has been done
stop We are aware that the Indonesian Government
would not be very happy if East Timor was used by
the present regime opponents stop Cordially ... José
Ramos Horta Secretary for Foreign Affairs

TELEGRAM

Dili to Canberra
Received 13 October 1975

Ken Fry
Room 204 ASL Building
Ainslie Ave
Canberra City ACT

We have heard of statements by the Indonesian leaders that the present regime of Jakarta has no territorial ambitions and no military plans to take over East Timor stop We also have heard often the Indonesian generals denying that Indonesian regular troops have been involved in military operations in the Portuguese territory of East Timor stop But unfortunately the Portuguese territory of East Timor has been violated several times in the past three weeks only by Indonesian regular troops—some Indonesian army men captured or killed in our territory weapons ammunition documents and other war equipment captured from the Indonesian army are the indication that what the leaders of Jakarta claim is one thing—another thing is what the Indonesian army does stop Fretilin accuses Indonesia for the continuous violation of the Portuguese territory of East Timor continuous military operations against native villages in the border area continuous campaigning of intimidation and terror against our people stop The ex-Apodeti and ex-UDT parties do not occupy an inch of territory in East Timor but their few forces have military training in bases in Indonesian territory particularly in Atambua Kefamanano Mota Ain and Atapupo stop Both enjoy free use of the Government 'Radio Kupang' in Indonesian Timor to carry their vicious campaign of intimidation against our people stop According to some eyewitnesses who have been already exposed to independent observers hundreds of refugees in Indonesian Timor wish to return to East Timor but they have been stopped by Indonesian troops stop Also an Indonesian national Joseph Talik aged twenty from Atambua captured in Zumalai a village in East Timor near the border (states that) hunger and diseases are widespread among the Timorese refugees but despite this fact they are stopped from returning to their homeland stop According to Talik one person dies each day mainly from hunger stop When the refugees left for Indonesia when the war broke they took money and jewellery but the Indonesian police confiscated all their possessions stop The attacks against Batugade on Monday Tuesday and Wednesday were directed by Indonesian regular troops wearing uniform and were identified as Javanese stop About a total of 100 to 120 Indonesian regular troops were engaged in the attack against different villages in the border in the last few days stop Aircraft jets helicopters Australian and French origin a destroyer and a submarine did take part in the operations stop A helicopter was hit by a Fretilin patrol boat and fell in Indonesian territory near Mota Ain stop We call on all democratic forces in the world to oppose the expansionist manoeuvres and actions of terror by the Indonesian militarist Generals against the people of East Timor stop We request immediate withdrawal of Indonesian troops from our territory and cease all military operations in the border stop We invite international observers to assess the situation in East Timor stop Cordially … José Ramos Horta Secretary for Foreign Affairs

TELEGRAM

Dili to Canberra
Received late October 1975

Ken Fry
Room 204 ASL Building
Ainslie Ave
Canberra City ACT

Indonesian involvement in the attacks against the people and territory of East Timor has been confirmed already on a number of occasions by independent observers stop Indonesian territory has been used as a base for military training and attacks against the border villages of East Timor stop Indonesian warships and aircraft have violated our territorial spaces stop The refugee camps in Indonesian territory have become concentration camps stop Hundreds of Timorese wish to return to their homes in East Timor but they have been stopped at gun point by Indonesian forces stop About 300 Timorese have already crossed the border and they claim that many have been shot when attempting to escape from the camps stop According to one eyewitness up to three persons die every day from starvation and lack of medical assistance stop Over the past two weeks Fretilin forces have inflicted the following casualties to the Indonesians—Lebos—130 deaths stop Tapo—16 deaths stop Maliana—56 deaths stop Balibo—80 deaths stop The following weapons were captured—three mortars 81mm one bazooka stop Seventeen machine guns American made stop Twenty seven boxes of ammunition for machine guns and ten boxes of mortar grenades stop One Indonesian soldier was captured when Fretilin forces recaptured Lebos more than a week ago stop Most of the deaths were regular Indonesian soldiers from Java stop Information reaching Dili indicates that most of Indonesian troops stationed along the border with

East Timor were brought from Java as the Indonesian Timorese do not enjoy the confidence of the Government of Jakarta stop At the moment Fretilin forces are well in control of the whole border area except Balibo and Batugade stop Maliana has been retaken by Fretilin forces stop Indonesian forces have been encircled in Balibo by Fretilin forces who have occupied already the surrounding mountains stop According to Indonesian Government Radio Kupang used by UDT and Apodeti the five Australian newsmen were killed because they were communists and they supported Fretilin stop Once again we call on all democratic forces to stop such criminal actions by the Indonesian Generals stop Peace and order have been restored by Fretilin stop Life in East Timor is returning to normality stop Thousands of Timorese are engaged in hard work to increase food production stop Therefore it is alarming the way the world remains silent when the Indonesian generals are carrying out their criminal military operations against our people and our territory stop Cordially yours ... Rogerio Lobato Military Commander Fretilin Liberation Army

TELEGRAM

Dili to Canberra
Received 10 November 1975

Ken Fry
Room 204 ASL Building
Ainslie Ave
Canberra City ACT

We are both disturbed and dismayed by the continuous reports reaching Dili of harassment of the aircraft company and passengers seeking to come here through the actions of the Darwin airport authorities stop This twice a week service is our only physical link with the outside world stop Such policies directed against us imply that unstable conditions continue to prevail in East Timor stop The facts repudiate these conclusions stop Peace and order have been restored more than two months ago with the exception of three tiny villages near the border still in Indonesian hands stop We plead with you to use your good offices to end this unjust and arbitrary harassment which can only affect Timorese population as a whole stop Warmest regards ... José Ramos Horta Secretary Department Foreign Affairs

TELEGRAM   *Dili to Canberra*
                                       Received 17 November 1975

Ken Fry
Room 204 ASL Building
Ainslie Ave
Canberra City ACT

As East Timor lives an historic hour I feel it is incumbent on us to keep you fully briefed on internal developments stop We do so in the knowledge that there have been gross distortions in the Australian media on both situation here and our programmes stop Fretilin Government fully understands that the attitude of Australia must make a major impact on both the substance and outcome of talks on the future of East Timor stop We are solemnly sworn to a policy of neutrality in Southeast Asia and friendly relations with all our neighbours stop Australia's proximity wealth and influence are paramount in these seas and a beacon to East Timor as it emerges from colony status stop Fretilin must be viewed as a nationalist movement in which the unifying web is independence stop We regret that the media continues to label Fretilin as a communist organisation stop We strongly repudiate such labels stop Fretilin is a nationalist movement which respects basic human rights such as freedom of speech worship and association stop Certainly the people of East Timor do not want to pass from one form of totalitarian system to another stop We are anxious for close cooperation with Australia and Indonesia stop We believe that both countries can effectively bring long term peace and stability in this region stop But peace and stability will never be achieved if the Governments of Indonesia and Australia do not make the right and unshakeable will of the Timorese people for national independence stop Fretilin remains in control of most of the territory with the exception of the tiny villages of Balibo and Batugade whose areas represent less than one per cent of the size of East Timor stop Maliana has been recaptured by Fretilin forces stop The mountainous border region is heavily controlled by Fretilin forces and it will be virtually impossible for Indonesian forces to move further into our territory stop Indonesian forces continue to violate our territory with helicopters and warships shelling villages along the coast stop In the attack against Maliana two Indonesian helicopters landed ten times in that region to pick up dead or wounded Javanese soldiers stop Fretilin Government invites fact finding missions from Australia to assess the situation here in first hand stop Warmest regards ... José Ramos Horta Secretary Department Foreign Affairs

TELEGRAM
Dili to Canberra
Received 4 December 1975

Ken Fry
Room 204 ASL Building
Ainslie Ave
Canberra City ACT

Thank you for your kind expressions stop We do need Australian friendship in these difficult times and your message of support lightens the load a little stop Assure you we will fight if aggression is forced upon us stop The issue remains in the balance stop My kind regards to you and East Timor's many friends in your country stop ... Francisco Xavier do Amaral President Democratic Republic East Timor

Part C

ADDRESS BY KEN FRY
AT THE UNITED NATIONS GENERAL ASSEMBLY
14 APRIL 1976

The President: It will be recalled that the Security Council agreed at its 1908th meeting to extend an invitation, under rule 39, to Mr Ken Fry, as requested in document S/12047. As Mr Fry's is the next name inscribed on my list, I now invite him to take a place at the Council table and to address the Council.

Mr Ken Fry: Mr President, members of the Security Council, I thank you for your courtesy in allowing me to address the Security Council on the difficult problems confronting the people of East Timor. I came to New York from Australia at the request of the Democratic Republic of East Timor, but I present my views to this Council as an independent observer who has followed the events in East Timor with a great deal of interest and, I must say, with a great deal of sadness at what has taken place.

In my search for the truth of what was happening in Timor—and I must emphasise how elusive the truth can be from a distance—I and some of my colleagues from the Australian Parliament visited East Timor twice during 1975: the first time in March, during the period of the coalition between the Fretilin party and the UDT party; and then, on the second occasion, in mid-September, when Fretilin was firmly in control, following the abortive UDT show of force in the previous August.

Whilst my views are those of an independent observer, I would assure members of the Council that they generally coincide with the views of those of my Parliamentary colleagues—over 50 of them—who last week signed a petition to the United Nations calling for the early withdrawal of Indonesian forces from East Timor. The majority of those signing the petition are members of the Australian Labor Party, at present in Opposition, but it was also signed by several members of both of the coalition parties of the Government.

I would claim, too, that my views would generally coincide with the views of many private citizens and organisations in Australia that support the cause of the independence of East Timor. These include organisations which have been set up in every state in the Commonwealth for this specific purpose, as well as Church and overseas organisations.

It includes the Australian Council of Churches and the Australian Council of Trade Unions, both of which have expressed support for Timorese independence to the United Nations; and I can assure members that there is a growing body of support for the Timorese independence movement among the public of Australia.

I believe that the Timorese people have been, and in fact continue to be, the victims of a cruel and blatant miscarriage of justice based on a series of misperceptions, bad judgements and misguided, irrational ideological bias. The misperception has been that of Indonesia and other nations of the relative strengths of the political parties which had emerged in East Timor. There was also a misperception of the determination of the people to resist aggression and to fight for their independence.

The bad judgement I refer to was the decision of the UDT party to stage a show of force following what I believe to be ill-advised encouragement from the Indonesian Government whilst the irrational ideological bias, I believe, was that shown by Indonesia in its persistent efforts to create a communist bogey out of the Fretilin party.

It is not possible to get a clear picture of the number of casualties in East Timor, but they are undoubtedly quite extensive as a proportion of the total population, and the conflict in East Timor must be regarded as one of the most sordid, most tragic and most unjustified episodes in the history of modern decolonisation.

When I first visited East Timor, in March 1975, the Portuguese administration was still in firm control, with officers of the Armed Forces Movement carefully nurturing the orderly development of political parties as a stage in the move towards independence. When we arrived we invited all parties to meet with us publicly and separately to discuss their aims and their aspirations. We had responses from three parties only, and I believe that they were then, and are now, the only three parties with any real measure of support in the Timorese community.

At the first meeting we met the Apodeti party, and there were about 50 people present. At the second meeting we met with the UDT officials in a hall in Dili, and we had about 150 people present; and our final meeting was with the Fretilin party, where there were 4000 people estimated to be present. These figures for the meetings in Dili gave us an indication of the extent of support for each group, and this was broadly verified by other gatherings at regional centres which various members of our party visited by helicopter.

At the conclusion of the meetings, the consensus of opinion of our members was that, at a generous estimate, Apodeti would have a maximum support of about 5 percent, UDT would have a support of about 10 or 15 percent, with the overwhelming mass support of at least 80 percent for the Fretilin party. This is as we saw it in East Timor.

We agreed too, that the Apodeti and UDT support, although relatively small, represented powerful minorities—property owners, commercial interests and top administrators—who, naturally, had a vested interest in maintaining a relatively privileged status in the community.

At that stage Fretilin and UDT were working in coalition, as they were both advocates of independence, and they differed only on the question of timing and on the nature of the future relationship with Portugal. It was the breakdown of this coalition which ultimately led to civil war.

In view of Indonesia's well-articulated hostility to Fretilin, and the fact that the breaking of the coalition and the abortive UDT show of force followed soon after a visit of UDT leaders to Jakarta, it was generally assumed that Indonesia was largely responsible for this ill-advised decision to stage the coup. This was later confirmed when we interviewed UDT leaders who were held prisoner in hospital in Dili, during our second visit.

During our first visit to East Timor, we particularly sought evidence to support Indonesia's claim that Fretilin was, in fact, a communist or Marxist party. No such evidence was forthcoming, and the lack of support on the ground for Fretilin from any other country in the subsequent fighting, apart from limited humanitarian aid through normal channels, gives the lie to these allegations.

I again visited Timor, with two parliamentary colleagues, in mid-September of 1975. This was soon after Fretilin had taken control following the abortive show of force by UDT. I understand that the report on that visit may have been seen by members of this Council, and I would merely reiterate briefly that we visited four widely separated centres of our own choice by chartered aircraft, and inspected prisoners at Dili, Baucau, and Viqueque. Wherever we went Fretilin was in full control and there was not the slightest evidence of continued conflict. We were completely satisfied that there was not, in fact, any civil war taking place in East Timor in mid-September 1975. The only conflict was in minor border clashes with forces operating from West Timor, near Batugade.

We found the Fretilin administration to be responsible and moderate, and it obviously enjoyed strong support from the East Timorese people. The prisoners were being well cared for, and it is worth noting that the prisoners included some Fretilin supporters, who had been apprehended for breaches of discipline. The Fretilin party member with whom we travelled always impressed on the gatherings and on his troops the need for discipline, claiming that 'independence is more important than revenge'.

Although the Fretilin administration faced serious supply and economic problems, order had been restored and the people were going back to the villages to tend their crops. The civil war had ended, and there was no need or justification for Indonesian intervention to restore order. Like all other Australians who visited Portuguese Timor during this period, I came away full of admiration for the Central Committee of the Fretilin party. I was tremendously impressed by their moderation, by their integrity and by their intelligence in dealing with a very difficult situation.

I wish to comment briefly on the elusive question of casualties. From my inquiries and observations during the September visit, I was satisfied that about 400 people had died in Dili and possibly up to 1500 in other areas during the civil war. Even at that stage, the presence of mass graves was known to International Red Cross and other aid personnel in East Timor. They were believed to contain the bodies of victims from both sides of the conflict. With the Indonesian reports of more recent mass graves, there is no evidence whatever to show whether they in fact died by Indonesian or Fretilin bullets. With regard to the Provisional Government's brochure, which many members may have seen, it should be noted that some of the victims listed as being killed or missing are reported to be still alive, and it should be noted also that many names are said to be misspelt, which I suggest casts serious doubt on the credibility of that publication.

Lopes da Cruz told a news conference on 12 February 1976 that 50,000 to 60,000 people had been the victims of the fighting, and added, 'Excesses often occur now as revenge for Fretilin cruelty'. Sixty thousand included 40,000 refugees, but soon after that statement, Lopes da Cruz again repeated the original figures, claiming that 50,000 to 60,000 people had been murdered by Fretilin, and without making any reference to refugees.

There have also been a number of press reports from Jakarta that some particular units of the Indonesian army have been withdrawn from East Timor because of excesses in the field of battle.

I should like briefly to refer to statements made by Mr Sydell. I never met Mr Sydell when I went to East Timor, but some of my colleagues did. At that stage he was bitterly opposed to Indonesian interest and concern with East Timor. My colleagues say that he never impressed them as a reliable or satisfactory witness. He was certainly not in a position to follow or to judge events from his isolated situation under house arrest. He appears to be a person with vested interest in the attainment of Indonesia's objectives, and I believe he is merely repeating information fed to him from Indonesian sources.

In the limited war, there were undoubtedly excesses on both sides, but in considering the casualties, it should not be forgotten that the UDT started the blood-letting, and not Fretilin. In this situation there were bound to be reprisals before Fretilin established full control and enforced a strict discipline. After the Indonesian invasion, there would have been no point in indiscriminate killing by Fretilin, when they needed the goodwill and support of the ordinary people to survive against vastly superior Indonesian forces.

I should like to mention that I would like to bring to New York a film of the conflict around Balibo. This film was taken by an Australian television news crew, all of whom were killed shortly after the film was taken. The film is available to the Security Council to use as it sees fit.

From my observations during my two visits, five most important points emerged.

First, I am convinced there has been a serious and persistent misperception of the strength of the mass support for the Fretilin party. There has also been misperception of the strong desire for independence by the large majority of the East Timorese people.

Secondly, I believe that this misperception led to grave errors of judgement by Indonesia, by the UDT and by Apodeti, and possibly by other nations, in assessing their attitudes towards the conflict.

Thirdly, the civil war was started by UDT and some Apodeti supporters and encouraged by Indonesia. It was not started by Fretilin.

Fourthly, there was no civil war in progress after mid-September 1975, when Indonesian forces began their aggression in the border areas.

And, lastly, the Provisional Government of East Timor does not represent the will of the majority of people in East Timor. It represents minority groups that are concerned with the people of East Timor who, even now as we speak, are fighting and dying for their independence and national liberation.

Part D

REPORT ON VISIT BY KEN FRY TO THE UNITED NATIONS SECURITY COUNCIL TO PARTICIPATE IN DEBATE ON EAST TIMOR

I arrived in New York on Sunday 11 April and contacted the Democratic Republic of East Timor (DRET) group on Monday 12 April. The group was led by José Ramos Horta, assisted by one other Timorese (a senior engineering student on leave from a

Swedish university), two Australian post-graduate students study-ing in New York and one Australian teacher/part-time journalist. The group operated from an apartment not far from UN headquarters.

The following is a list of the current members of the United Nations Security Council:

China (Chairman)	Panama
Benin	Romania
France	Sweden
Guyana	Tanzania
Italy	UK
Japan	USSR
Libya	USA
Pakistan	

The Council can be divided into three distinct groups—Western, communist, non-aligned. Their basic position in relation to support for DRET was as follows :

	Pro-DRET	Neutral	Anti-DRET
Non-aligned	Benin* Tanzania** Guyana**	Panama	Libya Pakistan
Communist	China* USSR Romania		
Western		Sweden Italy	France Japan United Kingdom USA

* China and Benin were the most committed to DRET to the extent of opposing the weak non-aligned draft, China considering the use of the veto power.

** Tanzania and Guyana were co-sponsors of the draft resolution; both very firmly committed to DRET.

Mozambique sponsored the request for permission for me to address the Security Council.

This division of the members of the Security Council doesn't tell very much in terms of support for particular motions. A country's position on East Timor was dictated by its interests in terms of commitments and allegiances, based on trading links, resources, colonial history, as well as ideological and religious links. For example, Algeria, a non-member, was supporting DRET not only for reasons of solidarity, but because Algeria is involved in a similar situation with regard to Spanish Sahara.

The most important groupings of the Council were the non-aligned as opposed to the 'rest' (internally, China and Russia were very involved); and the 'Asia-Pacific' countries as opposed to the rest of the world.

Asia-Pacific

The general attitude of the European states was that East Timor is an Asian affair, and they preferred to take their cues from that region. For example, France stated privately that they were following the Japanese example, and suggested that the British were also impressed by the Japanese. This was so to the extent that, at one stage, the French delegate said the veto (France is a permanent member) might be used if the Japanese were sufficiently upset. In the Asian non-aligned bloc, Japan was quite openly acting as an agent and a broker of Indonesian interests. Pakistan and, to a lesser extent, Libya were favouring milder resolutions.

It is in this context that the Australian role, or lack of it, first becomes relevant. The Australian Ambassador's speech said very little, and in no way provided a constructive lead. Many delegates remarked either unfavourably or with distress on the Australian low profile. European nations, as well as unaligned Third World countries, expected a far stronger, more definite and more informative stand by Australia. In the circumstances, the Western capitalist nations felt bound to accept the lead of Japan; there is no reason to think that, except in the case of the USA, an active Australian presence would not have been welcome.

The change in Government in Australia was well known; it was the lack of initiative as much as the particular line followed that dismayed members. The Russian delegate could not understand the difference between the Australian activity last year, in the Fourth Committee, and the present performance.

Timor was considered (at least by the Europeans) to be an Asian matter as well as an unaligned one. Again, the powerful pro-Indonesian speeches by the Philippines and Malaysia, although grossly lacking in truth and integrity, were more influential than they should have been.

Non-Aligned

The non-aligned group in the UN as a whole is now quite dominant; this is the single most important fact about the organisation today, as opposed to the colonial and great-power dominance up to the 1960s.

The draft resolution, and the bulk of the lobbying, came from the non-aligned group. The USSR did very little but certainly made its support for Fretilin known. China was closely involved in the non-aligned lobbying, but was extremely cautious.

As everyone knew, the problem for DRET, and the hopes for a tough resolution, lay in the internal divisions in the non-aligned. Of course, Indonesia itself is a member of the group. Timor and Spanish Sahara were both commonly used examples of Third World aggression and sub-imperialism. Some non-aligned delegates see much more of this in the future.

DRET's most constant and active supporters were with the African former Portuguese colonies: Mozambique, Guinea-Bissau. Tanzania and Guinea and Benin were also very strong supporters, and Guyana took on the heavy and very long task of organising the lobbying effort. Algeria, while not a member of the Council, was also a very effective supporter. Tanzania, which is very highly respected in the UN, was hampered by the absence of its Ambassador, Salim Sebim, who is regarded as a very influential figure. However, the sponsors of the resolution had to accommodate the extremely principled stand of Benin on the one hand (having recognised DRET, Benin was under instructions to accept nothing less in the resolution) and doubts and pro-Indonesian feeling, on the other hand, of Pakistan, Libya and Panama. In the case of Pakistan and Libya there were ties of religion with Indonesia, but these did not seem to have been as important in Pakistan's case: simple regional and political identification was enough for that country.

Once I had addressed the Security Council, I intended to speak to as many delegates as possible or who wanted to speak to me. It was several days before it became clear how this should best be done. I said in my speech that I came to the Security Council at the request of the DRET, but that I was speaking as a private citizen. Throughout the lobbying I continued with this approach. In almost all cases I made my own contacts with missions. I was not associated with the Australian mission at the UN though I was in touch with them on most days. Over the next week I visited almost all of the delegates on the Security Council (only Romania, a safe vote, and China, also safe, were missed out).

The main subject we discussed with the missions we visited was the inadequacies of the early versions of the draft resolution of the non-aligned group. In the event, the major points that were taken very seriously by all delegations in these discussions were the suggestion concerning the admission of the International Red Cross, and the need to delete the early reference to the Indonesian Ambassador's statement that Indonesian troops were being withdrawn.

I think that, ultimately, it was on this point that our discussions were most productive. By Tuesday, this clause had been altered to omit this reference, and merely noted the statement of the Indonesian Ambassador in general. In every discussion we had, we emphasised that from the Australian intelligence sources, it appeared that the Indonesian Government's claim was quite untrue except in a technical sense: a small number of troops were being removed, but many more were still going in. The whole thrust of my activities had been to appear impartial, but to disseminate as much verifiable information as possible. In the event, it was on this very issue that the final successful resolution was challenged by Japan, though unsuccessfully. When we began our discussions, the Indonesian statement was widely accepted.

We consulted closely with the delegates from Guyana, who co-sponsored the resolution and who did the bulk of the lobbying, and the delegates from Algeria, who were very well informed on the various alignments and the subtleties of the process; but they encouraged us very enthusiastically to continue our efforts.

After several days, we realised that what we had to do was create a consensus on the importance of these questions. While not pretending to be anything other than outsiders, or amateurs, it was clear that all the non-aligned countries, who were the most import-ant in this issue, were very interested in the information we had, and each one appeared to encourage us to talk to all the others, using us to create a consensus about the importance of the issues. Clearly, the information they received from us was new, and was not the same information they received from the Australian mission.

AUSTRALIAN MISSION

It was apparent from our discussions that most European and non-aligned countries were looking to Australia both for information and for leadership. On these counts, they were disappointed and did not hesitate to express their disappointment.

The Australian mission adopted a low-key profile throughout, and did not appear to take an active part in the lobbying to strengthen the resolution against Indonesia. They did not appear to be up to date or well informed (for example, they did not have the Hansard on Senator Gietzelt's speech on Timor ten days after it was given).

On the floor of the Council, the Australian mission was seen to be in frequent consultation with the Indonesian mission. On a personal level, the Ambassador and all the officers of the mission extended to me every courtesy and assistance during my visit.

PGET

The Provisional Government of East Timor (PGET) delegation played a minimal role, apart from their two set-piece speeches. In contrast to Horta, who worked effectively and constantly with all the delegations (including the Indonesians), the PGET delegates (the older Goncalves, Carrascalao and Soares) never moved from their seats at the rear of the chamber, and were rarely active in the lobbying sessions. They were almost always taken about by the Indonesians. Very few delegations had much to do with them. This fits with the probability of their coercion both in Dili and New York; Richard Tanter interviewed all four prior to the debate; at that stage about ten days before the debate they had not read Gucciardi's report. Their defences of the Indonesian invasion were quite pathetic. They placed a great deal of reliance on the atrocity pamphlet, which in the event didn't carry much weight. I spoke on this matter in the speech, mainly testifying to what I had seen and commenting on the well-known fact that after the UDT coup and the brief civil war, there were known to be mass graves containing the victims from both sides.

The only hostile reception was from the Japanese Ambassador, Mr Kanazawa, who was rather rude and aggressive. He expressed surprise at the idea of a non-government citizen or someone outside the diplomatic corps coming all the way to the UN to speak in the interest of another country. He questioned my role and the basis of my interest in Timor. My response was in diplomatic kind, and he became more reasonable. However, he conceded nothing and tried to keep the discussion to matters of information.

The only disappointing interview was with a delegate from Panama. Due to the Easter break, we were able to speak only to an officer who was not dealing with the matter, and who, consequently, knew little about it.

We tried to arrange an interview with the representative of Papua New Guinea, but this was not possible. Non-aligned countries could not understand the low profile of this delegation, but other delegates claimed that this was a deliberate posture based on fear of Indonesia.

The opposition of Benin to the weak draft resolution and to the final resolution, adopted 12–0, was that as a Government that recognised the DRET under the leadership of Fretilin as the Government of East Timor, they could not accept or go along with a resolution that said less than that. This was an extremely carefully thought out and principled decision. In his brilliant speech during the voting session on Thursday morning, the delegate from Benin, Mr Paqui, carefully explained his country's position.

The four major speeches supporting DRET (Benin, Mozambique, Guinea-Bissau and Guinea) were all excellent. That of Mozambique was the most critical of the role of Indonesia and Portugal (Mr Lobos). The speech from Benin on the last day drew the question of East Timor and the aggression of Indonesia into the wider context of the UN's determination to execute its long-standing resolutions on self-determination in the proper spirit. It was a firm, intelligent and powerful speech, appealing against compromise and hypocrisy. Coming when it did, it was probably not influential so much as it was an expression of attitudes. Its power and frankness, however, I think surprised everyone, and probably strengthened the resolve to defeat the Japanese amendment. In the final vote, 12–0, the USA and Japan abstained, and Benin 'declined to participate', as it had explained in its speech.

To summarise the positive achievements of the work of the DRET delegation:

1) After lobbying fifteen delegations, we succeeded in having the reference to Indonesia withdrawing troops deleted from the original draft resolution.

2) By persistent lobbying of the Swedish delegation, we considered that we had some influence on their decision to oppose Japan's amendment, which sought to insert the word 'remaining' before 'Indonesian forces' in the body of the resolution.

The vote on this amendment was, in fact, a vote for or against the credibility of Indonesian statements to the Council. Sweden's vote was vital. They were the only Western nation to vote against the amendment. There was obvious disappointment in the Western camp, including the Australian delegation, when the amendment was lost.

To conclude, I would say that my trip was well worthwhile, and succeeded in mobilising opinion towards a stronger line against Indonesia on the Timor question. Whilst this does not provide any real help to the Timorese people in the short term, world opinion will be significant in building on the opposition to Indonesian aggression which is continuing to develop both inside and outside East Timor.

Part E

CLANDESTINE CORRESPONDENT

Anonymous letters were received by Ken Fry during 1977. It is believed that they came from someone inside the Department of Foreign Affairs. The allegations made within the letters formed the basis of Mr Fry's questions to the then Foreign Affairs Minister, Andrew Peacock, concerning Mr Peacock's visit to Bali in September 1975 (while Opposition Foreign Affairs spokesperson) during which Mr Peacock met with senior Indonesian officials who were themselves involved in the operation to invade East Timor.

*'Earlier this month I received information from a source which I believe to be credible and accurate,' stated Mr Fry in the Federal House of Representatives on 31 March 1977 (*Hansard, *page 807). He then outlined the allegations raised in these letters. For his part Mr Peacock denied all the allegations in the House of Representatives on 3 May 1977 stating: 'As to what purports to be the "record of interview" of that conversation, it is simply a travesty of a report. What is not outright falsehood or invention is drastically distorted.' (*Hansard, *page 1439).*

That week's National Times *newspaper (May 2–7, 1977) published similar allegations as disclosed in a purportedly Indonesian intelligence document which had been leaked to the newspaper. For the record, the* National Times *Jakarta correspondent, Hamish McDonald, interviewed one of the Indonesian officials who had met with Mr Peacock in Bali. Mr Harry Tjan of the Centre of Strategic and International Studies is said to have stated that 'the document accurately reflected the views of Mr Peacock on TImor and on Foreign Affairs as he recalled them from the Bali meeting' (*National Times *May 2–7, 1977, page 3), but Mr Tjan went on to deny that 'Australia's domestic politics, in particular any scenario for the dismissal of the Whitlam Government, had been discussed in any detail'.*

*Again, Mr Peacock denied the allegations, stating to Parliament on 3 May 1977 that the allegations 'amounted to nothing more than a farrago of fanciful fiction' (*Hansard, *page 1453). Mr Peacock may have been the target of an elaborate hoax set up in order to embarrass him. Whether fact or fabrication, the 'meeting' achieved this purpose. However, the one aspect that strikes solid footing is the alleged description of the Liberal Party's plan of accommodation with Indonesia over the invasion and the annexation of East Timor. It was the incoming conservative Prime Minister, Malcolm Fraser, who gave de facto recognition to the illegal annexation in*

January 1978 (with de jure recognition following in 1979). This recognition was given at a time when the slaughter in East Timor was at genocidal proportions. Seen from the perspective that this political recognition, de facto and de jure, was granted to criminals who had been, and were still, committing crimes against humanity, then I believe it matters very little whose account in these letters— Peacock's or the Indonesians—is faithfully accurate. Neither one has any saving grace. Reproduced here are the anonymous letter recieved by Ken Fry.

Received 11 March 1977

Dear Mr Fry,

In Parliament last year Mr Whitlam asked a question about Mr Peacock's meeting in Bali in September 1975 with two Indonesian officers. Nothing came of it. He doesn't realise how close he came to catching the biggest fish of all in this terrible Timor episode.

Peacock met two of the most important Indonesians on this occasion (before, you will note, Indonesia intervened!!). They were General Ali Moertopo's key advisers Harry Tjan and Liem Bian Kie.

Peacock said to them that:

a) A Liberal Government would not complain about Indonesian incorporation of Timor.

b) The Australian Liberal Party gave highest priority to relations with Indonesia.

c) Suharto was a 'wise statesman' and much admired by the Liberal leadership.

d) [this line has been deleted—Editor]

e) Peacock said he hoped Indonesia would act swiftly and efficiently.

On top of this he went on to inform Suharto's close adviser's men that it was planned to deny Supply to the Whitlam Government in November 1975 and that the scenario would be for the GG to dismiss Whitlam!! He, Peacock, would then be Foreign Minister. Naturally, their written report dated 26/27 September 1975 to President Suharto said that there would be a new Government in Australia within a matter of months, and that the Foreign Minister 'to be' strongly supported Indonesia's taking over P. Timor!!!!

This report—and this above all else—was instrumental in Suharto's reluctant decision to use force in Timor, and to move when he did. Indonesian forces attacked Timor a few weeks later after the Peacock meeting.

There are copies of this report in existence.

There is enough in this story to cause the downfall of the Fraser Government.

If you do not press this one you will never get another opportunity like it.

Do not reveal to anyone how you came by this information. Other information will follow if you handle this correctly.

Received 24 March 1977

Dear Mr Fry,

Further to my letter it is vital for you to know that only one matter prevented President Suharto from intervening in Timor during all those months leading up to early October 1975. He was under enormous pressure from his Generals and other advisers to move in and settle the issue once and for all. What was this one card he had up his sleeve? It was

67

the firm promise he had given to Mr Whitlam in Wonosobo and Townsville, that Indonesia would never intervene using force in Timor. He quoted this ad nauseam to his advisers, to the point where rumours began to circulate that they were moving to force Suharto's hand!

The Foreign Affairs files are full of evidence to this effect ie. that it was the promise to Whitlam that prevented Indonesian intervention. If the truth does not come out now, it will when future historians have access to the files!

When Suharto learned that a leader of the Liberal Party had informed his two key advisers that a plan had been devised to overthrow the Whitlam Government and that this Liberal leader had given an assurance that the next Government would support the Indonesian action in Timor, Suharto had no option but to agree to use force. Since Whitlam was about to go, the card up Suharto's sleeve went with it!

At this time (September/October 1975) Tjan & Liem Bian Kie openly told Australian diplomats and journalists in Jakarta that Australia would have a new Foreign Minister soon!

Wittingly or unwittingly, the boastful and arrogant Mr Peacock in Bali—showing off to key Indonesian officials— set in train a chain of events Suharto himself had tried so hard for so long to avoid!! The responsibility rests fairly and squarely on Mr Peacock's shoulders.

To express it in another way, there is no question that Indonesia had invasion plans for East Timor dating from late 1974. Why did she not move then (India/Goa)? The answer is simple. Suharto is basically a constitutional man. He wanted to proceed legally. His Generals disagreed. It was only the promise he had given Mr Whitlam that kept the Generals at bay. For the Generals, Peacock's amazing Bali performance was a heaven-sent opportunity. Suharto had nothing to stand on from that point. A fortnight later the intervention began.

Mr Peacock has much to answer for. Historians will judge Mr Peacock poorly.

Received 2 May 1977

Dear Mr Fry,

You must now realise, you have hit upon the most important story concerning the timing of Indonesia's invasion of Timor, and of Mr Peacock's role in it.

Paul Kelly in the *National Times* of 2 May need not have been so tentative and on guard. The document (translation) he published is authentic. Let there be no doubt about that whatever! The author was Harry Tjan himself!!

I notice Peacock in defence is saying that:

a) Tjan (and Liem Bian Kie) do not acknowledge authorship of the document nor vouch for its accuracy.

b) Adam Malik has said recently that Whitlam, not Peacock, supported Indonesian intervention.

As for (a), Tjan told Hamish McDonald (and others in Jakarta) 12 months ago in Jakarta when Tjan's document first began to circulate that the record was 100 percent accurate. He is now holding back a little to earn Peacock's gratitude. The fact is that Harry Tjan was one of the principal authors of Indonesia's Timor policy.

It is ironic—almost grotesque—that the Australian Foreign Minister must now ask one of Indonesia's Timor policy initiators to cover up for him to save his political skin. The Australian Foreign Minister will thus be beholden to the Timor invaders!

As for (b), the truth is that Malik had no role whatsoever

in Indonesian Timor policy! He was never present when the key decisions were made. The only people involved (in making recommendations to Suharto) were General Benny Moerdani, General Yoga Sugama (Bakin), General Ali Murtopo and Harry Tjan (an intellectual of the Centre for Strategic and International Studies). Peacock knows this, yet is so dishonest as to quote Malik (in all Malik's wonderful ignorance on Timor) to save himself.

To return to the beginning. Before he went overseas in September 1975, Peacock told the then Indonesian Ambassador, Her Tasning, that he was going to Bali and would welcome a meeting with some key officials involved in Timor. He told Her Tasning at the time (in Canberra) that the Liberal Party would support Indonesia—or, rather, not protest—if Indonesia intervened in Timor. Her Tasning, a General and member of Bakin, the State Intelligence Organisation, immediately alerted Yoga Sugama, Ali Murtopo, Harry Tjan. This was a chance the Indonesian intelligence had been waiting for. For months Suharto had turned down their pleas for direct Indonesian intervention in Timor. Each time Suharto had said *inter alia* that he had promised Whitlam that Indonesia would not use force in Timor. When he was confronted with Tjan's record, which shows not only that the shadow Foreign Minister and his party would cause no problems for Indonesia if she decided to use force but that Whitlam himself was on the way out. This was pressed home by the Generals, and Suharto had nothing to stand on. He agreed to a limited armed intervention in early October 1975. Five Australian journalists died days later (16 October). It is one of the ifs of history ... If Peacock had not been so stupid those men would have been alive today.

Peacock and Peacock alone was responsible for the timing of the Indonesian intervention. It is also just possible that Suharto would have held his bloodthirsty Generals at bay indefinitely. Who knows?

In this entire episode, Peacock had better remember Profumo, whose lie to Parliament was the greatest sin.

Peacock was set up by Indonesia's intelligence machine (the same OPSUS people who planned the West Irian campaign). He even requested a meeting! He spoke foolishly and carelessly. But he did say what is in Tjan's record. Peacock should remember that Indonesian intelligence officers usually carry tape recorders. They probably have him on tape! If he lies to Parliament he can be blackmailed by them.

One point: if the Tjan record was circulating in Jakarta one year ago, did the Australian Embassy know about it? If so, was Peacock informed? What did Tjan have to say about the record then?

To return to the Profumo point, Peacock knows that the Tjan record is authentic. As for the 'scenario' part, that is also authentic. Peacock had said much the same during a visit to Jakarta in April 1975. It is absurd for him to claim that because he had been out of Australia for 2 weeks in September 1975 he was out of touch with developments—laughable.

After the Bali meeting Tjan and Liem Bian Kie invariably referred to Peacock (when talking to Australian journalists and diplomats) as 'Your Foreign Minister' (as though he was Foreign Minister then). Peacock had convinced them in Bali (and they convinced Suharto).

You must persist with this. The more you push it, the more likely—inevitable—it is that the Truth will prevail.

Received 29 July 1977

Dear Mr Fry,

What you said on 31 March 1977 in Parliament about Mr Peacock in Bali was correct!

There are tapes in existence (in Jakarta) which confirm what Mr Peacock said in Bali. It follows that what Mr Peacock told Parliament on 3 May 1977 was not true. The documents published in the *National Times* were incredibly accurate, especially the Timor part ... (*the rest of this final letter is missing—Editor.*)

Bruce Juddery has spent more than thirty years as a journalist in Canberra. In 1975/76 he covered the East Timor tragedy for the Canberra Times *and his investigative reports helped to expose the extent of the collusion between the Australian Government and Indonesia in the invasion in East Timor. The advice given by Australia's Ambassador to Jakarta, Mr Richard Woolcott, to the Whitlam and Fraser Governments became public knowledge due to a series of leaked Government cables, subjecting the Government and Mr Woolcott to angry protest over indecent haste at accommodating Indonesia to secure commercial interests. One such cable was leaked to Mr Juddery in mid-1976. Mr Juddery remains a freelance journalist in Canberra.*

4

MY TIMOR STORY

BRUCE JUDDERY

It was dry, under high cloud, and cooling fast in the car-park off the Australian National University's North Road tennis courts at around seven o'clock on the night of 30 May 1976: about eight degrees then, down from seventeen at three in the afternoon and plummeting to minus two a couple of hours later and an overnight minimum of minus five. There had been a smoky haze in the air all day, the Canberra Meteorological Office recently reminded me.

The haze, I recall now, diffused the lights above the tennis courts as the man whom I had agreed to meet approached me *across* them. I had imagined he would pull up alongside my green Volkswagen. Of course, then I might have taken his car's number.

He would not let me take the small sheaf of papers—clearly telex cables—away with me. I was permitted to scan them, and take notes, for only about ten minutes. He later told me, via telephone, that he was surprised I had copied as much as I had.

They harked back to 29 October the year before, and were from Australia's Ambassador to Indonesia since the previous March, Dick Woolcott, to his then Minister, Senator Don Willesee.

They recorded that Woolcott had submitted all save the first paragraph of a statement Willesee planned to make to the Parliament on 30 October to the Indonesian authorities. In that paragraph, Willesee was to say that he had seen reports suggesting 'a degree' of Indonesian military involvement in East Timor, and that he 'regretted' the development.

'If the Minister says publicly that he regrets the degree of Indonesian intervention in the affairs of Portuguese Timor, will he not stir up a hornets' nest in Australia itself as well as producing a cold reaction here?' Woolcott inquired.

'Would not the first paragraph of the statement in its present form invite headlines of the type "Willesee Accuses Indonesia of Intervention" and would not this lead in turn to increased pressures on the Government to act against Indonesia by stopping the defence assistance program and, possibly, by cutting aid? Such a statement at ministerial level would also stimulate hostility to Indonesia within the Australian community, which it has been our policy to minimise.

'Although we know it is not true,' continued the 'telegram', as Woolcott calls his cables, 'the formal position of the Indonesian Government is still that there is no Indonesian military intervention in East Timor. If the Minister said, or implied in public, the Indonesian Government was lying we would invite a hurt and angry reaction.

'We would also be the only country in the region, probably including New Zealand, to make such a statement and we would then be regarded by Indonesia as having acted in a way which could stir up international opinion against Indonesia.'

That was what I have since thought of as the 'Woolcott cable'.

There were others, some fresher when we had published them earlier in the *Canberra Times*—but none providing such evidence of premeditated collaboration, no matter how understated, with the Suharto regime's programme to invade, by stages, East Timor.

Willesee, of course, went to water, if not with enthusiasm. From knowledge of what his Ambassador had acknowledged as a lie, he noted only that 'the Government has viewed with concern widespread reports that Indonesia is involved in military intervention in Portuguese Timor' and would be 'extremely disappointed' if this turned out to be the case.

So the Australian parliamentary system was suborned. A Minister was persuaded, by an Ambassador, if not to lie then to deny knowledge of a (privately) acknowledged lie. The layman might think that a lie!

Willesee, a decent man if not a strong one (as his response to Woolcott's cable suggested), and who had been under the thumb for most of his term of a Prime Minister, Gough Whitlam, who imagined he knew everything about foreign affairs (and proved through that highly polarising farce the Regional Community, not to mention his Indonesian 'initiatives', that he knew virtually nothing), had the decency soon afterwards to withdraw from Federal politics.

Back at the offices of the *Canberra Times*, then conveniently situated at Mort Street, near the ANU campus, I was asked only one question by the paper's then editor, Ian Mathews: was I sure the cables I had so briefly sighted were genuine? 'Yes,' I told him, and he went with the story, all over the middle of the front page.

There were reasons that we need not go into here why Ian took my word for it, even though (like anyone else in the journalist trade) I had got it wrong occasionally in the past.

There were reasons I was sure I had got it right this time. I had not been able to scribble notes of all of the 'telegram', but a couple of phrases stuck out as a Woolcottian mantra: the need to draw a line between 'Wilsonian idealism and Kissingerian realism' was one.

The distinction had been drawn a few months before, in a 'telegram' also exclusively reported by the *Canberra Times*—all right, by me—and addressed to the post-Whitlam Fraser Government.

But it had also been incorporated in private correspondence between Woolcott and people in Canberra, months before then, to which I had had access but could not use. The phraseological coincidences—I had no doubt of the age of the tennis-court cables, and as it turned out I was right—made their origins plain.

Woolcott's 'telegrams', of course, were transmitted before William Shawcross published *Sideshow*, the so-far definitive account of the application of 'Kissingerian realism' to Cambodia and so to its effective handover to the Khmer Rouge and consequent murder of maybe a couple of million people. Arguably, the slaughter in East Timor after December 1975 was even greater.

His invocation of 'Wilsonian idealism', for that matter, was of only limited historical accuracy. That American President's Latin American policies would suggest that Wilson reserved his idealism for the eastern side of the Atlantic.

However appropriate his allusions, Woolcott's intervention was part of a seamless operation through which Australia's Department of Foreign Affairs connived (conspired?) to smooth the way for what it considered the inevitable (desirable?) takeover of East Timor by Indonesia, during 1974–75 and to brush under the carpet the consequences of that operation in succeeding years.

Nature entered into that plan on Christmas Eve 1974, when Cyclone Tracy wrecked Darwin, whose airport was Australia's only direct, ready access to the Portuguese colony whose future had suddenly become moot with the officers' revolution in the 'mother country' earlier in that year.

For three months the airport was closed to the weekly two-way flights, via turbo-propped Fokker Friendship aircraft, between the Northern Territory and Dili.

Timor was plainly one of the emerging 'stories' of 1975. There was a lot of interest in seats on the Friendship when the service resumed. But there was a Catch 22 that limited direct access by the Australian media. I was told by Foreign Affairs that it was impossible.

To stay overnight in Darwin, one needed a permit. Permits were strictly limited. But the Friendship departed at about 6 am. The first flight in from the south arrived at about 10 am.

I got around that technicality by getting myself appointed a consultant to the Darwin Reconstruction Commission (DRC), which after a rocky start had just been given Tony Powell, coincidentally head of Canberra's National Capital Development Commission, as its chair; incensed by an article in the *Canberra Times* mildly lampooning his dual role, Powell bought the suggestion of a journalist in his Canberra office, Bruce Brammall, that he send *both* of us to Darwin to advise on DRC public relations.

We flew there at the weekend, spent a few days looking over the scene—and meeting Roger East, then trying to talk Powell into setting up a newspaper with himself as editor, another of the romances that, in December, was to lead him to believe he could wait out the Indonesian invasion, self-supporting with a fishing-rod, but instead got himself machine-gunned on the Dili wharf—gave the DRC some limited advice, and on the Wednesday, I caught the flight to East Timor.

My credentials as a foreign, let alone a war, correspondent were (are) limited; being the first person to arrive from Australia claiming that capacity (though a one-time colleague from Canberra had found his way overland a few weeks before) probably helped gain me access.

The Governor gave me a reluctant audience, and said very little, as did the Indonesian Consul in the colony, Mr Tomodok. Leaders of Apodeti, formally the Popular Democratic Association for the Integration of Portuguese Timor into Indonesia, and the Timorese Democratic Union (UDT) parties, ditto.

But the only Timorese politician to go out of his way to cultivate me was José Ramos Horta, who was running the organisational side of the Revolutionary Front of Independent East Timor, or Fretilin.

His organisation might have chosen a more tactful title: it certainly lent itself to Indonesian/Apodeti allegations of communist sympathies. But its leadership was mostly Jesuit-trained. Horta, certainly, was eclectic in his tastes. In the several hours I spent whiling away my time between interviews in his Dili waterfront flat, I did, indeed, read much of a biography of Karl Marx (from a bourgeois perspective), but also a warm biography of President Suharto, *The Smiling General*.

Later, we would laugh about what Indonesian intelligence would have made of a book of mine, *At the Centre*, an account of Australian bureaucracy, which I gave José when he visited Canberra later in 1975, and which was in his home (as he, fortunately, was not) on 7 December. By that time, he (and one or two other impecunious Fretilin exiles) were occasional overnight occupants of my couch and/or spare room, in Canberra.

I joined him on a trip to Baucau, where the Portuguese had recently completed a massive, economically questionable, airfield, engendering who knows what sort of paranoia in the neighbourhood.

A flat tyre stopped us and for about an hour the serried ranks of the Timorese intelligentsia and local Australian journalism (jumping up and down on an immovable spanner) failed to dislodge the spare wheel from the back door of his four-wheel-drive, until a local in a clapped-out Bedford, carrying firewood for Dili, turned up to point out that the thread on the restraining nuts ran in the direction opposite to that we had assumed.

We lunched on curried goat at Maniatuto, a beautiful village. José somehow blamed his brother for the earlier disaster, and made him patch the punctured tyre while he and I ate, and drank, I think, some of the excellent (and very cheap) Portuguese red wine available in the territory, or perhaps it was some of the ditto Mozambican beer.

The point of the above few paragraphs is that Fretilin's leadership, through Horta, did seek to woo me. I spent most of the next year or so consciously seeking to weigh my subjective assessments of East Timor with objective facts.

Subjectivity, of course, won out on issues like return of hospitality. The cynic might object that José's to me in Timor was in hope of friendly coverage, and mine in Canberra in expectation of inside stories.

The cynic might have part of a point. But the spare bed in Canberra produced few advantages, other than two now grown-up children who remember with pleasure an 'uncle' who pretended the dark glasses perched in his frizzy hair were a second pair of eyes; their mother was never less than totally hospitable, and rarely more thrilled than when she re-encountered the (by now) Nobel Peace Prize winner at the National Press Club in Canberra in early 1997.

The year after my visit to East Timor was heavily larded by coverage of the subject. Mostly, it was dominated by engagement with the Department of Foreign Affairs' deliberate campaign to (a) obfuscate what was going on in the territory and, as the crisis mounted, to (b) actively mislead the Australian Parliament and people as to what was going on.

It also produced some fairly personal abuse. Professor Heinz Arndt wrote to the *Canberra Times* a couple of weeks after the overt, 7 December invasion, asking where I, as a critic, had stood when India took over Goa in 1961. Reporting football matches in the New Zealand back-blocks, I retorted. I never got a reply.

The Foreign Affairs front was not impregnable. Australia's policy, which it progressively appeared was one of supine accommodation of whatever Jakarta determined, had its critics. Jim Dunn, who had been Australian Consul in the territory, increasingly spoke out against the drift of national policy.

I referred to him as a 'senior diplomatic' figure. I received a vicious call from the department, denying that Dunn had ever been anything more than an administrative officer. Maybe, but he had been acting Ambassador in Moscow when the Russian tanks ran into Prague. And the distinction between 'political' and 'administrative' officers had been abolished years before.

It later transpired, courtesy of a libel case against the *Canberra Times*, that the source of that piece of misinformation was not the low-life administrator who had passed it on to me, but the Secretary of the department of the time, Alan Renouf. I had previously imagined that the pettier manifestations of the department's prejudice against dissenters on the East Timor front emanated from pettier levels.

The same official who told me Jim Dunn was not a 'diplomat' told me not long after that the department had decided not to talk to me any more. 'We see little value in the present circumstances, in having dealings with journalists who accuse us of providing misleading information,' he said.

The 'accusation' to which the department objected referred to a discrepancy between its consistent assertion that it knew of no Indonesian military intentions with respect to East Timor—and this late in the month that Woolcott acknowledged that Australia knew the Indonesians were lying—and its warning to some aid workers who were proposing to move in for a month that this could be dangerous.

Foreign Affairs ran, for several months, what Freedom of Information tells me was called the 'Juddery line', that if I wouldn't take their word, they wouldn't talk to me. In fact, of course, during that period—Andrew Peacock told them to stop being silly a few months later—I had some of my most productive conversations ever with the department.

As you gather, I am not attempting to record a blow-by-blow account of coverage from Canberra, or mostly, of the protracted East Timor crisis of 1975; space does not permit.

There were some personal high points, where I did not necessarily shine. I took up the issue with Gough Whitlam at the Malaysian High Commission on their national day at, I think, the end of August. Should not Australia be intervening, somehow? I wondered.

'Do you think we should send Australian troops in?' demanded the Great Man.

'Well, no,' I allowed. Lately, particularly in the light of evidence that Suharto pondered late and long over his invasion, and might have been dissuaded by a less than totally hands-off (if not encouraging) Australian policy, I have sometimes wondered if I responded appropriately.

Through 1975, I remained engaged with the East Timor 'story'—both as a reporter and as the main editorial writer for my newspaper, the *Canberra Times*, on that and related subjects. Never once was I given less than 100 per cent support by my editor of the time, Ian Mathews.

He did, though, deny me the opportunity to be in at the denouement of this exercise in Australian diplomatic and political pusillanimity. I had a seat reserved on a four-seater aircraft, from Darwin to Dili, in mid-November 1975. In the meantime, I took a trip down the Murray on a houseboat, with three bachelors.

At Morgan-on-Murray I learned of the sacking of the Whitlam Government. Mathews told me: Forget about Timor; come back and help us cover the election.

So I missed out on the opportunity to share poor, silly Roger East's martyrdom, if that was what it was. I would have been on that last plane out that took, for instance, Jill Jolliffe.

I got to call Gough Whitlam a 'Pontius Pilate' for washing his hands of an invasion that he had, tacitly and not so tacitly, been encouraging for months. That didn't save any lives, or national honour or interests.

What I also got was the first of the 'Woolcott cables', in January 1976, urging the new Fraser Government, to 'let the dust settle' over the recent invasion.

Indeed, he said, the Indonesian leadership had decided to take over East Timor months before he had taken up his office the previous March. He did not mention how long before the invasion—for Indonesian troops were in the territory months before 7 December, killing Australian journalists injudiciously lodged at Balibo, among other things—this information had been available. Or how great was the consequent extent of the cover-up, pre- and ante-invasion.

Woolcott's message to the Fraser Government was that Australia should smooth the carpet, if not necessarily roll it out. 'The Indonesian Government will be looking to the Australian Government to help in redressing what it regards as an anti-Indonesian bias in the more vocal elements of the Australian community,' he telegrammed.

'We believe the emphasis should now be on accepting the inevitability of Timor's incorporation into Indonesia, letting the dust settle and looking ahead while taking what steps we can in Australia to limit the further growth of hostility towards Indonesia within the Australian community,' he added.

Then he invoked the Wilson-Kissinger dialectic. Woolcott's analysis went down well with his colleagues. Whether, in retrospect, it stands up as a testament to Australia's commitment to its own self-interest—which includes its proclamation of its liberal and democratic nature—is another matter again.

Rob Wesley Smith is a spokesperson for Australians for a Free East Timor in Darwin, Australia. He is an agricultural scientist and the founding secretary of the Council of Civil Liberties (Darwin). Mr Wesley Smith pioneered the Vietnam Moratorium in Darwin, has spent many years actively supporting indigenous rights and has been committed to the East Timor cause since 1974, ensuring a voice for the East Timorese struggle in the city closest to their country. In Part A of this chapter Mr Wesley Smith outlines the story of the radio transmitter used to receive news of the fighting after the invasion. This link was closed down by the Fraser Government. Part B highlights several of the broadcasts sent by Alarico Jorge Fernandes, the Minister for Communications and Security in the Democratic Republic of East Timor.

5

RADIO MAUBERE AND LINKS TO EAST TIMOR

ROB WESLEY SMITH

Part A

'**A** luta continua' on all fronts. In a letter to Xanana Gusmao in February 1997, I reminded him that I had heard that phrase for 21 years, starting during the monitoring and two-way use of Radio Maubere between 1976 and 1978. The long struggle takes its toll of supporters as well as participants inside East Timor, and some of the tensions and disagreements from that time still have an impact, though the struggle for freedom continues on all fronts.

Communication with East Timor in the early years of the Indonesian invasion, from 7 December 1975 to near the end of 1978, was almost entirely dependent on the use of probably just a single radio transceiver in East Timor in the hands of the Resistance. This radio had two crystal-controlled frequencies, 3804 MHz in the 75m band used for Radio Maubere, and 5270 MHz for two-way use. We never heard anyone else on it that I can remember, apart from during peculiar circumstances at the end, except the Fretilin Minister Alarico Fernandes.

This is utterly amazing. Could there be a parallel in history where a whole nation could be so completely isolated? A population of around 700,000 on 7 December 1975 is thrown to the wolves by the rest of the world. This world included democratic, industrialised, freedom-loving Australia, the land of 'a fair go', the land of 'looking after your mates', on whose northern shores I live, in Darwin, situated only 600 kilometres from where the genocide is taking place.

The sense of shame and disgust at Australia's attitude has fuelled my activism to try to help East Timor, the other main thrust of course being the knowledge of the atrocities and genocide going on so close at hand.

During the Second World War, in late 1941, Australia technically invaded the then-neutral Portuguese East Timor in order to pre-empt the possibility of the Japanese landing first. Of course this ensured that the Japanese did land, in February 1942, a few days after they bombed Darwin to prevent air counter-attacks. This caused over 240 deaths in Darwin, but at the time that was denied by the authorities—the first casualty of war is truth, et cetera et cetera!.

What happened then is perhaps best summed up by ex-Aussie commando from the 2/2nd Independent Company, the inestimable, inimitable Paddy Kenneally, in a piece he wrote in 1995 for Australians for a Free East Timor (AFFET) in Darwin, called 'The Friends Australia Abandoned'.

'On the 17 December 1941 Australian and Dutch troops landed

near Dili in neutral Portuguese East Timor. It was a hastily planned operation, as apart from their weapons and ammunition the troops had few supplies. Their stay in East Timor was expected to be short, they were to withdraw to Atambua in West Timor when Portuguese troops arrived from East Africa.

'Within a few weeks of their landing, 76 percent of the Australian troops had contracted malaria. Strategic areas in the mountains were selected for new camps. One section remained on the aerodrome in defensive positions. That was the position in East Timor when the Japanese invaded on the night of the 19/20 February 1942. By then Ambon and Rabaul New Britain were in Japanese hands. Singapore had surrendered. Australia was in a desperate position.

'The men in East Timor refused to surrender. They were short of everything except weapons, ammunition and fighting spirit. Prior to the Japanese landing contact between Aussie and Timorese was minimal, but all this was to change. The Australians were entirely dependent on the Timorese and Portuguese for food, shelter and guides. The Timorese carried the wounded—they were directly responsible for saving the lives of the badly wounded men. The 2/2nd Independent Company fought a successful guerrilla campaign in the mountains of Timor until they were evacuated on 16 December 1942.

'The unit could not have survived had it not been for the help so freely given by the people of East Timor during that campaign. The 2/2nd unit returned to Australia, but the people of East Timor had to brace themselves to face a vengeful Japanese force. The price they paid was staggering! By the time the war was finished in 1945 about 60,000 Timorese had died through reprisals, slave labour, disease and starvation (that is 10 percent of the whole nation).

'How did a grateful Australian Government repay them for their loyalty, aid and faithfulness to Australia's fighting men during a most critical period in Australian history? From Whitlam in 1974 to Keating in 1995 Australian Governments have abandoned and betrayed the people of East Timor. Through our governments we have waded through a sea of Timorese blood, and climbed over a mountain of Timor's dead, to sign the Timor Gap Treaty for economic gain with Timor's invaders. That is how we repaid the people of East Timor.'

On 17 September 1917, the then Australian Prime Minister Billy Hughes claimed that, 'on entering the world conflict in 1914 it was my Government's policy to protect our national integrity, to safeguard our liberties, and those free institutions of government which are essential to our national life, and to maintain those ideals which we have nailed to the very topmost of our flagpole—including White Australia'. (Quoted from 'Songs of Australia' 1988 by Peter and Martin Wesley Smith.) We can see now that it was our tradition that the brown people of Timor could be sacrificed. And we don't bother about other people's liberties, integrity and institutions!

Precisely! So what happened? A few concerned Australians had tried to help East Timor in 1975, fearful that time would run out before a full-scale Indonesian invasion. Denis Freney (deceased) from Sydney and Brian Manning from Darwin, both members of the Communist Party of Australia (CPA), had visited East Timor in 1974/75. In his book *A Map of Days* Denis tells of his early meetings with José Ramos Horta and the trips to Timor by himself and some others. These included two delegations led by Federal MP Ken Fry, soon to become a great friend of mine, and important in the radio contact. Denis wrote that Brian had organised the supply of some radio transmitters to Dili, keeping one in Darwin for contact should an emergency arise, which was very prescient.

After the murders of the five media crew in Balibo on 16 October 1975, Indonesia pulled back, expecting a strong protest from Australia. Whitlam did not protest, and neither has any Australian leader to this day. Had Whitlam done so, the full-scale invasion would not have taken place. Whitlam is rightly a hero for his stand on Aboriginal rights, but a dingo to the East Timorese (sorry dingoes!). We all knew an invasion was probably imminent;

I remember sending telegrams to Whitlam and Peacock, asking them to block it.

The last planes flew out of Dili as the invasion gathered. The International Committee of the Red Cross got advice on 2 December to evacuate, and Andrew Peacock personally intervened to arrange for a plane to pick up José Ramos Horta and other Timorese leaders. As people arrived in Darwin there was a lot of emotion and angst, and some competition, not the least for the control of future sources of information. Jill Jolliffe wanted to have a pooling or shared fully open access to future information, which would likely come by radio, but this was not the plan of those who controlled it.

I, personally, also was committed to trying to get aid to East Timor. There was a need at that time to chase this, in case it could get through, so I drove a Government truck to Kununurra to facilitate and hasten the loading of 100 tonnes of rice to go on the next ACFOA chartered barge from Darwin. I was legally able to visit Kununurra, in Western Australia, if it was not an overnight stay, so had to get from border to border within 24 hours, in a speed-limited seven-tonne truck. I was also to bring back coated seed rice for Timor, and new varieties for my own work as an agronomist. Exhausted, feeling desperate and lonely, with hours of driving to go, I heard the news of the full-scale invasion as I returned.

The first receiver was set up in the office of the North Australian Workers Union (NAWU), soon to become part of the Miscellaneous Workers Union (MWU), with the help of a strongly committed union organiser, Warwick Neilley. The office happened to be across the road from my flat, and all buildings still bore the scars of Cyclone Tracy, from Christmas Eve the year before. Reception was not good; it was on the wrong side of Darwin city. It took a while to get better locations and to improve techniques.

I moved to a new bedsitter flat, closer to the coast and with less electrical interference, so set up an antenna on a high pole strapped to the top of the external stairs rail, with two wires extending down on either side of the driveway. This gave pretty good reception, but once I even received on my portable tranny, jumping with excitement on the top stairs. Another time when recording a broadcast, I noticed the Catholic Bishop wandering outside the adjacent cathedral. He was a right-wing conservative but agreed to visit the bedsitter and listen. Dressed in his white robes, he was sitting on the bed in the gathering twilight when two Aboriginal kids came by, peered in, thought they saw a ghost and frantically fled. The Bishop must have thought he heard ghosts, because he never supported the rights of the East Timorese people in their time of dire distress. Another visitor, brought in 1978 by our loyal ALP Senator Ted Robertson, was the future Governor-General Bill Hayden. He was then a fierce supporter, but from 1983, he betrayed the East Timorese right to self-determination and freedom from Indonesian genocide.

The Union office receiver was a perfectly legal device, and we encouraged Timorese and the general public to come and listen and help. Carlos Pereira, whose father, Henrique, had been trained near Darwin as a paratrooper in the Second World War, was one who helped. Another was José Franco. The Pires family was brave enough to consistently get involved during these years. Rumours were spread that this radio was illegal, so I took a Commonwealth cop, incognito, to see that it was not subversive, though she was later sent for retraining! There were some who were not happy with the attention and demands the radio attracted, and this added pressure to find new locations.

Alarico Fernandes, as Minister for Internal Affairs and Security in the Democratic Republic of East Timor, had been broadcasting desperate messages asking for support, but none was to come. Northern Territory users of the Outpost Radio system, such as nurses, heard this material too. The messages initially were sent from their Marconi Centre, where Roger East apparently sent his last despatch to Australian Associated Press (AAP) as the paratroops rained down, but his transmission mysteriously disappeared. AAP has never explained what happened to this last message.

From then on Alarico used his portable radio. For most of the year his telegrams were received at the Outpost Radio in Darwin, and passed on to the addressees, but on 17 November 1976, the Fraser Government ordered this to stop. Telecommunications Union members were very supportive of the Timorese, but could not prevent this betrayal and denial of the right to communicate. They even received one message from Alarico to his mother in Sydney, and told him, 'message received but it will not be passed on', which was probably heartbreaking not only for Alarico but also for the operators. We later broadcast a message to Alarico from his Mum, to which he responded, after a pregnant pause: 'received with great emotion'. East Timor supporters campaigned on this for some time, with a petition and a 'Let East Timor Speak' funding campaign. In Darwin we also campaigned, but of course had to concentrate on the radio reception.

For initial two-way communication from December 1975 a young East Timorese man, Tony Bello, used an Australian-made Traeger transceiver, usually carried openly on the seat of a 'Moke', having to go out of town to throw up an antenna and get away from electrical 'noise'. The Australian Government secretly listened to the information and did not interfere. The UN Special Representative Winspeare Guicciardi came to Australia, and rang Bello on 24 January 1976, asking him to seek information from East Timor. It was then the Australian Government decided to interfere, and so this radio was seized by Post and Telecom officers from Tony as he drove along on Sunday 25 January. This anti-UN action, apparently, was directly authorised by Prime Minister Malcolm Fraser.

Winspeare Guicciardi came to Darwin on 2 February 1976 and stayed at the Travelodge. I went to see him and he was happy to chat as I think he was isolated and bored. José Ramos Horta was there

89

too, and I helped him do a press statement which was front-page
NT News when he left. Guicciardi insisted he would only visit areas
of East Timor declared safe by Fretilin, and insisted on radio
verification. Of course, he was told that was foolhardy, but he
insisted. As Bello's radio had been seized, they tried to use the radio
of the Portuguese corvette tied up at Darwin wharf, but did
not make useful contact before being jammed. They then were
'graciously' allowed to use the Government Darwin Outpost Radio,
and so, on the evening of 5 February, Alarico named four airstrips
at Same, Suai, Viqueque and Con, but by the next morning,
6 February, they were all being bombed. Surprise, surprise.

Winspeare Guicciardi left Darwin complaining of lack of
support from the Australian Government, but later denied this.
(Such tends to be the behaviour of Government and UN officials.
One wonders why it has to be this way, who taught them, and where
do they go to eventually. The contrast with the morality of the East
Timorese in Timor is vast. But do I digress?) On 11 February, the
Government stopped Bello using their radio. On 19 February, Bello
announced that he would leave Darwin and set up a radio in Macau,
but instead, the CPA comrades in Darwin set him up at a farm about
70 miles away, a site they cheerfully called Mount Macau. They
installed a new Australian-made Wagner 50-watt SSB transceiver.
After a couple of months Abilio Araujo and Estanislau da Silva
arrived, used the radio, and decided Estanislau should take over its
use, and also to make it a more mobile operation. This went OK
until the radio was located and seized on 27 September 1976.
Ironically, the stolen Wagner was later donated to the NT
University. The overall radio picture is quite complex, as there were
various radios involved: the public receiver; the 'secret' public one
(Radio Maubere two-way); and the 'Secret Secret' one, for Fretilin
radio traffic only.

I was involved in the first two, and gleaned a bit about the other,
although in general terms, only members of the CPA were trusted
with that knowledge. Despite my years of dedicated service,

loyalty, financing of facilities, lending my car (and having to replace its motor as a result), and local knowledge of the bush, I was never really trusted into the bosom of the CPA operation, nor ever had control even for a moment of the two-way gear. All the two-way Radio Maubere stuff was done with me driving to bush spots in my trusty Subaru 4WD, with Brian Manning and sometimes with guests. We had a pretty good hiding spot in the car for the radio and antenna, which was never breached.

At one stage we had a revealing brush with the authorities. Brian and I had set up overnight in hills near 'my' research station, 100 kilometres from Darwin, but Alarico had not come on air. We explored around a bit and, going up a bush track, saw wires strung between the trees. We eased away, and the next morning I came back and photographed what turned out to be a full-on radio direction-finding station. The operator called for help, and within one minute Radio, Police and Australian Security Intelligence Organisation (ASIO) officials smugly appeared, wanting to search my car. I prevailed on them to take some literature about the East Timor struggle. We found out that even the army had helped set up three radio direction-finding locations to try to trap us, a special effort before Prime Minister Fraser made another trip to Jakarta, but—dare I say smugly—they were unsuccessful.

Meanwhile, Denis Freney coordinated setting up a new 'secret' Radio Maubere, on 7 May 1976, done as a public challenge, with Ken Fry, friends and journos attending. The drive to the site was hilarious, in a serious sort of way, as they managed to elude Telecom and Police pursuers. Delegates lay motionless in the long grass as the pursuers hastened past. Denis had to rugby tackle a rather large, slightly inebriated, Aboriginal lady who really didn't see why she should lie down—at least Denis cushioned her fall with his own ample body. This radio was never seized, but was used in a rather conservative manner, in my view. Sometimes there were indications of extra Government interest in seizing it, and there was one period in 1977 when Brian refused its use for transmission for months. I was never allowed to take it on my own even if going a long way away to allow safe use, such as on my declining number of trips now possible to Wattie Creek, Yarralin and Bulla, in the Victoria River District, around 800 kilometres from Darwin, far from where it could be seized on site.

All this time, the grind of having to tune in at least three times per week at 6.30 pm to record Radio Maubere created its own tensions. We did not have a good spot for it in a house or whatever, and at one stage a suitable house had to be left due to personality problems. Sometimes when reception was crook, such as in the wet season, we would be reduced to recording from the back of my car parked in bushland. We could never be sure that a broadcast might not be made in the morning, or it might be expected at various times due to weather or pressures, and eventually, I used to tune in whenever possible before going to work. We tried to involve volunteers, but it was hard to get reliable workers. I got into trouble for querying a comrade's failure to monitor one night, but in even more trouble when he discovered I was covering his shifts from home on my 'Realistic DX-160 Receiver'!

At the same time people had families or partners to look after, or to seek, and all manner of activist stuff to do like demos, meetings, lobbying, newsletters, bookstalls (which Bill Day managed), and liaison with the East Timorese. I would have gone to the Pires family home more than once a week for three years, ostensibly to discuss the radio news, but I also got a pretty good feed (their son Quito later became the subject of my brother's prize-winning CD 'Quito'). Of course, everyone had to earn a quid, which in my case as an agricultural scientist was quite demanding in itself.

By the way, in 1976 attempts were made by former commando Cliff Morris, myself and other right-wing activists to use a boat to take over not only medical supplies and food, but also communications equipment, advice, codes and so on. The attempt on 16 September 1976 was captured by the brave Australian Navy and Customs, and Malcolm Fraser personally ordered us to be charged with attempting to take 'guns and drugs' to East Timor. On 14 February 1977, after ten days in court, we were duly convicted of gun and drug-running, and placed on small bonds. The dangerous weapons were mainly four Darwin-registered shotguns, and the drugs included Vegemite and thousands of dollars worth of Camoquin, financed by Community Aid Abroad. The return of the medical supplies was delayed until they were out of date by our current Prime Minister John Howard who was then the Business and Consumer Affairs Minister in the Fraser Cabinet (a post which also saw him in charge of customs duties). These convictions were later overturned on appeal to the Northern Territory Supreme Court, the Government's purposes having been served.

The results of Radio Maubere were always publicised, and when we had 'public two-way', then attending journalists would assist. Valuable messages in English would be transcribed by myself or Brian, sometimes having to listen to phrases five or ten times to understand if the static was bad. Denis did amazing work with the production of the comprehensive *East Timor News* and other liter-ature for many years. We had to cope with plenty of disbelieving journalists, who preferred to publish known lies from the Indonesian-Government 'accredited' Antara news agency, than the palpable truth from battlers in the bush, without 'accreditation', or even a radio licence. This is still a problem sometimes. Mind you, both then and now, there have been some decent journos too.

Brian sent the original tapes on to Denis in Sydney for 'official' use, including forwarding to Fretilin in Maputo. Whilst I worked closely with Brian, and whoever, the lack of trust meant that in late 1978 I bought my own Codan 6801 transceiver, more power-ful than currently being used. The struggle to get the necessary 3804 MHz crystal required a threat issued by local TV station owner, John Lewis, to invoke trade restriction laws. John, a conservative but fair-dinkum bloke, was living evidence that it is not whether you are left or right-wing that counts, but your decency and your belief in fundamental human rights for all!

Estanislau da Silva 'sat in' in a Government office in Sydney to try to force resolution of threatened charges against him relating to the seizure of the radio on 27 September 1976. Two large cops flew to Sydney to escort this diminutive 'urban or bush guerrilla' to Darwin. On 3 December 1976, Estanislau (currently a Fretilin leader in Australia) and Andrew Waterhouse (a very decent and technologically competent activist) were convicted in Darwin Magistrates' Court for 'use of an unlicensed radio'. The magistrate was aware of thousands of unlicensed CB radios, and the repeated refusal to give us a licence. He thought political influence was involved, and Estanislau was operating from the highest patriotic motives, so set the very low penalty of a $100 one-year good-behaviour bond. He set the same penalty for Andrew, but without the kind words.

Another secret radio was set up soon after, in late December 1976, and this remained in place and 'secret' until communications ceased, in December 1978. We had established some sort of bond with tough man Alarico, who spoke Portuguese, Tetun and English and also had radio technical skills. Thus, it was very difficult when the sole radio link was broken, actually by the Darwin operator calling Alarico a traitor, due to the belief that he was attempting to betray the Resistance leader in 'Operation Skylight'. I suspect the radio had been in Indonesian hands for a while. I would like to know more about that time. Soon after, Timorese hero Nicolau Lobato, the leader of the East Timorese nation, was killed by the 'brave' Indonesian military.

Nicolau's death gave great pleasure to the Indonesians, as he joined over 100,000 of his fellow country-people killed since late 1975. By the time Xanana Gusmao clearly took over the leadership of the Resistance, in March 1981, more than another 100,000 had been killed by assassination, sickness and starvation in a situation worse than that of Biafra, whilst the world did almost nothing. In 1977, the peace-loving USA President Jimmy Carter had author-ised the supply of Bronco OV-10F ground attack aircraft. With terrible effect on civilians, these aircraft dropped bombs and napalm indiscriminately, on a population defenceless against this assault. Broadcasts of the screaming sounds of engines from the dive-bombing aircraft provided some of the more dramatic recordings. An English-speaking (presumed US) adviser was reported killed. The attitudes of the USA, Australia, the UK and Japan in support of the Indonesian genocide in East Timor have changed only a little since then. Thus the killings have continued, sometimes more intense than others, to this day.

In early 1985, a transceiver was bravely taken into East Timor, and a link with Darwin was re-established on 26 May 1985, again orchestrated by Denis and with Ken Fry and journalists present, and our locals, including Agio Pereira, Abilio Araujo, Brian and myself. Agio and Brian did the radio contacts, but interest from the media flagged. After a few months the link ceased, and I heard that a part was required for the radio inside, but the request for it fell on incompetent ears.

Since 1989 there have been physical contacts, and usage developed of phones, faxes, mobiles, e-mail, audio and film tapes et cetera. Since the Dili Massacre of 12 November 1991, many more people have assisted the struggle for a free East Timor. One useful development, for example, has been that information collected on East Timor is often posted on an Internet conference called reg.easttimor, to which most activists subscribe, even some in Dili.

In 1992, we sent Xanana a computer, a Toshiba T1000SE, with word processing installed on the ROM, but no hard disk, so that the information lost would be minimised if it was seized. It was seized at Xanana's arrest on the 20 November 1992, but did not get mentioned at his trial, being safely ensconced with some corrupt Indonesian officer.

In 1997, the brutal Indonesian occupying power has particularly targeted outside communications, and information is very hard to come by. None is easy. Independent journalists, Australian politicians, UN and aid organisations still are barred from East Timor.

To complete the story, another bad and two more good ones. The Howard Government, elected in 1996, is ultraconservative and hypocritical, pretending to seek engagement with Asia, but restricting Radio Australia and closing its powerful transmitters across the harbour in Darwin. Although Radio Australia's Indonesian translators sometimes used derogatory terms for the Timorese Resistance, such as 'GPK', at least some news and comment got reported. I tried, to no avail, to interest the Portuguese in these facilities.

In 1994, the valuable Southeast Asian service of Radio Netherlands was under threat of closure, but public outcry saved it. I passed on the story of how it was used to good advantage in Timor in 1983. A local Indonesian military commander in the border region asked his Resistance counterpart for a local cease-fire, and was told to prove his bona fides by having certain information broadcast on Radio Netherlands. This was done, and the local cease-fire spread to the whole of East Timor for much of 1983.

In 1997 at last the Portuguese Radio RTP is now broadcasting weekdays to East Timor from 8.30 to 9.30 pm Darwin time on frequency 17.595 MHz in the 16m band. This is in Portuguese and Tetun but, of course, only one way. Full communication requires Indonesia to withdraw its troops and controls, and Indonesia should be subjected to severe sanctions until this happens. Meanwhile ... a luta continua.

Part B
TRANSCRIPTS FROM RADIO MAUBERE

On 31 May 1976 the Indonesian military convened a 'Popular Assembly' in Dili. This body issued a petition calling for the full integration of East Timor into Indonesia which President Suharto accepted and enacted on 17 July 1976. During this period Canberra confiscated one of the transmitters used to receive messages from

Fretilin in Darwin as well as confiscating a boatload of medical supplies that well-meaning Australians were trying to take to the civilian population of East Timor. These humanitarians were also prosecuted by the Australian Government and this process involved the current Australian Government leader, Prime Minister John Howard, who was at the time the Minister for Business and Consumer Affairs in the Malcolm Fraser conservative Government. Indonesian relief workers who visited East Timor in November of the same year reported that 100,000 people had been killed in the invasion. On 19 November 1976 the UN General Assembly rejected Indonesia's annexation of East Timor calling for the immediate withdrawal of Indonesian soldiers and for a genuine act of self-determination.

Received 20 July 1976

The Suharto Government in flagrant contradiction of the United Nations Charter and the General Assembly and the Security Council resolution on East Timor has announced the forced integration of the Democratic Republic of East Timor into Indonesia. The Political Committee of Fretilin on behalf of the people of East Timor convened an extraordinary meeting where the following resolution was unanimously approved.

'The Political Committee of Fretilin met on 18 July 1976, in the areas controlled by Fretilin forces and publicly denounced the Jakarta Government colonialist policy and reaffirmed to continue the war to drive out the Javanese colonialist aggression and for the consolidation of the national independence and the achievement of total liberty of the people of East Timor. The Political Committee on behalf of the Fretilin also condemns all countries who collaborated in the gamble of the Jakarta colonial fascist government by participating in the faked meeting of 31 May 1976, in Dili.'

> Political Committee of Fretilin, 20 July 1976. Nicolau Lobato, Vice President of Fretilin and Prime Minister of the Revolutionary Front of East Timor.

Received 22 July 1976

Intense fighting is going on in East Timor and Indonesian invading forces are starving. The captured population are daily escaping from the Indonesian concentration camps and have reported that the Indonesian troops are highly demoralised and complaining about the shortage of food.

From yesterday the Indonesian troops are making new attempts to take over the village of Quelicai. The enemy are advancing on four fronts and supported by five tanks and two armoured cars. Fretilin guerrillas are resisting strongly and inflicting heavy losses to the enemy.

In Maubara on 20 July 1976, Fretilin guerrillas carried out an assault to an enemy position killing 23 Indonesian soldiers, wounded many others and captured some enemy rifles.

The people are organised under the Fretilin Central Committee leadership and decided to fight the Indonesian aggression to the final victory. Independence or death. The people of East Timor will win. High regards. Alarico Jorge Fernandes, Minister for Internal Affairs and Security.

Received 26 July 1976

… Indonesian Government is sending more military units and increasing military operations in the territory. The captured population and war prisoners are submitted to torture, heavy labour and execution.

Completely unable to control the territory, the Indonesian forces are using incendiary bombs to destroy houses and crops. In Baucau, during the last week, over 450 houses and a large quantity of rice crops were destroyed by the Indonesian troops.

We call on the UN Commission of Human Rights, the UN Security Council and all Human Rights Organisations to take action against Indonesia in order to stop this vandalistic and barbaric aggression being carried out by the Indonesian troops over the people of East Timor. Independence or death. To resist is to win. The fight is still on. Highest regards. Alarico Jorge Fernandes, Minister for Internal Affairs and Security.

Received 28 July 1976

Independence or death. Timor's history is written once again with the blood of its heroic sons. Fierce fighting is going on in many parts of the territory against the Indonesian invaders.

In Tapo Mountain, in the area of Bobonaro, there was fierce fighting between Indonesian forces and Fretilin guerrillas. Fretilin guerrillas defeated the enemy killing 53 Indonesian soldiers, wounded many and captured three bazookas, nine automatic rifles and a big quantity of ammunition and other war materials. Six Fretilin guerrillas were wounded.

In Bazartete, on 21 July, Fretilin guerrillas assaulted one enemy camp, killing 45 Indonesian soldiers, destroyed 20 tents and rescued 307 captured population. In revenge of their losses, the enemy is systematically torturing and executing the war prisoners.

Once again, we bring our appeal to the UN Commission for Human Rights and UN Security Council and all nations, lovers of peace and progress to stop the Indonesian vandalistic aggression over the people of East Timor. To resist is to win. The victory is certain. Highest regards. Alarico Jorge Fernandes, Minister for Internal Affairs and Security.

Broadcast on 4 March 1977. An open letter from Alarico Jorge Fernandes, Minister for Internal Affairs and Security of the Democratic Republic of East Timor to the Indonesian people.

To Indonesian soldiers and Indonesian people.

Brother Indonesian soldiers, on behalf of the people of East Timor we want to ask you again: what are you fighting for? What are you seeking for in the beloved country of your brother Maubere people?

Brother Indonesian soldiers in East Timor—nothing, nothing, you are dying for nothing, you are fighting for nothing! Maubere people are not your enemy. Maubere people are essentially your brothers.

Indonesian people are essentially our brothers, and you are dying, ingloriously dying in East Timor, fighting for nothing, fighting just in the interests of the corrupt murderer Suharto, Adam Malik, Murtopo, and the other corrupt Indonesian officials.

Brother Indonesian soldiers, we want to call to your attention that Maubere people, that the glorious Fretilin revolutionary forces, don't want to kill you, but if you insist remaining in East Timor with rifles, then we have to kill you. We have to defend our own liberation, the liberation of the entire people of East Timor, that was oppressed over 400 years from the Portuguese shameful colonialists.

But now we are free and independent, a sovereign country already recognised by many countries all over the world. And you, what are you doing here? Go back to your country! Exactly in this moment, when the situation is deteriorating in Indonesia.

Look at yourself, you are poor, you have nothing, you have lost your liberation, your freedom.

Comrades, brothers, sisters, Indonesian soldiers in East Timor, go back to Indonesia and help your brothers, your families, and help the brother Indonesian people to fight the corrupt Suharto and other corrupt elements over there.

You have the obligation to help your brothers that in this moment are fighting for the brother Indonesian people's liberation in Indonesia, in Irian Jaya, in South Moluccas, in Sumatra and South Kalimantan.

Comrades, we should be brothers and not enemies. We are fighting each other for nothing.

> Alarico Jorge Fernandes, Minister for Internal Affairs and Security of the Democratic Republic of East Timor.

Received 29 June 1977

The enemy is still shelling with mortars Deto Tolu but no damage caused. On June 3 Fretilin forces rescued two comrades from the vandal Indonesian concentration camps. They said Indonesian troops are still raping women. Indonesian warships are still patrolling and shelling continuously the coastal areas from Suai to Betano.

On 6 June Fretilin forces rescued a couple and their three children, who were in very bad physical condition due to starvation and brutal treatment. They said that many of the captured population are dying due to lack of medical care. Mortar fire continually shelling Lebos area.

Intense shelling of Metinaro and Kaimauk on 12 June from Hera and Fatu Ahi. No damage. On 13 June the enemy advanced over some Fretilin positions at Kaimauk, but were repelled with heavy casualties. Fretilin also clashed with the enemy at Mamgkaka, two enemy killed and several wounded. One Fretilin guerrilla died. The captured population are forced to do heavy hard work. Women continually raped.

In 1975, at the time of the invasion, José Ramos Horta was Minister for External Relations and Information in the first Provisional Government of East Timor. He has been at the diplomatic centre of East Timor's struggle for independence and remains the Special Representative of the National Council of Maubere Resistance (CNRM) and the Personal Representative of Xanana Gusmao, leader of East Timor's Resistance. In December 1996 Mr Ramos Horta was awarded, jointly with East Timor's Bishop Carlos Filipe Ximines Belo, the 1996 Nobel Peace Prize. In Australia, Mr Ramos Horta has been invited to address the National Press Club on the issue of East Timor on three occasions. Reproduced here for the first time is the 1984 address.

6

JOSÉ RAMOS HORTA
31 MAY 1984

NATIONAL PRESS CLUB SPEECH, CANBERRA, 1984

It has been almost nine years since East Timor was invaded by Indonesia. Timor has not buried the time, has not buried the issue and has not made legal an act of naked armed aggression, for East Timor continues to be an issue of self-determination, a sacred principle and legal right established in the various United Nations declarations, and incorporated in the body of modern international law. As much as many good people in the Foreign Affairs Department in Canberra might wish the issue to be forgotten, as much as they may not care about the fate of a small mountain people, the issue of East Timor refuses to go away. It will continue to hound their consciences; it will continue to stand up as good evidence of the hypocrisy and double standards that have characterised Australian diplomacy.

The issue of East Timor will linger on as a human rights embarrassment for those Western Governments that claim to uphold the principles of self-determination, let's say, for the two thousand settlers in the Malvinas Islands, but choose to ignore the fate of more than half a million people just three hundred miles from Australia. As an East Timorese at the United Nations often watching the debates on the Malvinas/Falklands issue, the interest, the formulas with which the British, the Australians and other Western powers support the right of the Falklanders for self-determination, I wonder why those 2000 settlers have more rights to self-determination than the half-million people of East Timor, and when the television screens of ABC, CBS and so on, showed the terrain of the Malvinas, showing the penguins, the goats, et cetera, I could not stop thinking: maybe these wild penguins, these lazy goats, have more rights to self-determination than myself and the people of East Timor.

The issue of East Timor lingers on because the people of East Timor continue to resist with an amazing courage the brutal occupation of their homeland. How many people have died in East Timor since 1975? It is difficult to estimate, for there has been no census; there has been no independent body that has been to East Timor to count, to compare statistics of 1974, before the invasion, with the current population. But all available evidence from Government sources in Jakarta and Catholic sources in East Timor indicate that at least between 100,000 and 200,000 people have died. People have died from the war, famine, lack of medical care, mass executions, torture, disappearances. Hundreds more are dying right now and many have died already since August 1983, when the Indonesian army launched a large brutal operation. Sources in East Timor, Jakarta and Macau report that another offensive involving 14,000 troops is under way at this very moment.

The cancellation of the visit of an Australian diplomatic mission to East Timor is further evidence of this, just as it is further evidence of Jakarta's contempt for Australia. One thing that strikes me, as an observer of Australian-Indonesian relations, is how the leaders in Jakarta can afford to cancel an official Australian delegation from going to East Timor. And they leave it to Canberra, they leave it to the Australian Government, to put on the best possible face. The Indonesian leaders don't even bother to explain or to apologise; it's up to Canberra to make the best explanation possible for Australian public opinion.

The International Committee of the Red Cross has also been unable to operate in East Timor since July 1983, shortly before the 1983 offensive. East Timor is the only case in the world where there is not one single independent humanitarian organisation operating there. One look at the Middle East, the problem in Lebanon—there are hundreds of humanitarian organisations, government agencies, that render assistance to the people of Lebanon. We look at other areas of the world—Central America, where there are no restrictions on humanitarian organisations from performing their mandated duties. East Timor is the only case where a government—the occupying power—has succeeded in blocking the more fundamental rights of the people of East Timor to receive the minimum medical care, the minimum food supply. The laws of war, the provisions of the Geneva Convention governing the conduct of governments in times of armed conflict, are grossly trampled upon by the Indonesian generals.

Australia has turned a blind eye to the tragedy of East Timor, a territory very close to Australian shores. While a vicious war is going on just 300 miles away, and another potential conflict is boiling on the island of New Guinea, Australia chooses to ignore these problems, and engages in a human rights crusade in a far-away capital. I do not want to single out a particular government minister or a particular government of this country. The bankruptcy of Australian diplomacy, the policy of appeasement, is not a monopoly of the present Labor Government. We recall how the previous Government engaged in a frantic diplomatic campaign at the United Nations in support of Indonesia. The scene of Australian diplomats running around the conference rooms of the United Nations chasing African delegates, Latin American delegates, Asian delegates, using arm-twisting tactics to persuade and to vote with Indonesia was, if not tragic, amusing.

During my years at the United Nations I have often wondered whether these Australian diplomats are on the payroll of Canberra or Jakarta, and often, as an East Timorese, I ask myself, and I ask Dick Woolcott, 'what have we done wrong to you Australians?' The ratio of support for the East Timorese cause at the United Nations was due in large measure not to Australia's pathetic attitude; rather, it was due to Australias' active lobbying on behalf of Indonesia.

Madam Vice-President, ladies and gentlemen, I have come to Australia not to engage in an anti-Indonesian campaign, let alone to engage in a war of words with the Australian Government. I greatly admire the Indonesian people, their culture and history. Australia is also a country that I most admire and respect. We are fascinated by Australia. Its heroism during World War II, its greatness in territory and wealth, its people—a generous people, simple, informal and friendly. If one is asked why the people of East Timor helped Australians during World War II, I would say, not because the simple mountain people of East Timor look at the map, study the whole political situation of the region and say, 'for the interests of East Timor, let's help the Axis powers'. The simple mountain people of East Timor were not aware of the complexities of World War II. When they decided to help the Australians, it was precisely because they saw the Australians, in general, as generous, friendly, informal, simple and courageous. For the selfless help they gave, the East Timorese paid with tens of thousands of lives.

Australia is a leading power. It is a leading power in this region. Its industrial wealth, democratic institutions, its heroic people make it an important element of the region and of the world.

Australia must assume with courage and vision a role commensurate with its status as a medium-sized power in the world. Regrettably, Australia surrendered its independence to its giant neighbour. The result is there for all to see: a measured industrial democracy toeing the line dictated by a Third World junta. East Timor is only the by-product of a certain malaise that has hampered Australia's approach to the region. The Australian Foreign Affairs Department seems to be transfixed by the Jakarta generals and they fantasise about an Indonesian invasion of Australia, economic sanctions, banning of Qantas overflights, et cetera, et cetera.

Australia is second only to Japan in industrial wealth in the region; militarily it's unmatched. However, Australian diplomacy seems to be geared only towards appeasement of the Indonesian generals. This policy of appeasement has resulted only in more arrogance, more militarism and disdain for Australia's views and interests. We do not advocate any radical shift in Australian attitudes and policies in regard to Indonesia. Both countries must live with each other, as geography imposes a cooperative relationship on the two countries. We do not advocate a termination of diplomatic and economic relations with Indonesia. We are not asking Australia to send troops and weapons to East Timor for the Fretilin guerrillas, though I guess the Fretilin leaders, the East Timorese leaders, would welcome such a gesture.

We are proposing for Australia the role of an honest broker, a peace-maker. It is high time that a political solution be found for the ongoing conflict in East Timor. We understand the process and nuances of the policy-making decisions: when a government considers the various policy options put before it by its experts, it weighs the pros and cons of each proposal. Friends of East Timor, what will be the elements that an Australian Government would consider? These elements, I believe, would be: (a) domestic implications (public support, electoral reactions, et cetera); (b) international implications—would the countries of the region support such a policy, and if they do not support it, what would be the cost to Australia?—and (c) moral and legal aspects (if Australia were to undertake a diplomatic initiative with a view to resolving the East Timor problem, would the Australian people support such a move, and will Australia be able to rally the support of other Melanesian countries in the South Pacific region?

As much as former Prime Minister Malcolm Fraser was able to force certain countries in the South Pacific region in 1982 to vote against a resolution for East Timor, as much as Australian diplomats at the United Nations were very enthusiastic in lobbying for support against East Timor at the United Nations, I believe they have considerable leverage to reverse the situation, at least in regard to the South Pacific region and other countries in the Caribbean or within the Commonwealth. The People's Republic of China will certainly support Australia's initiative; Portugal would be only too anxious to have Canberra undertaking such a peace initiative. Several European countries, we believe, would follow suit. If not the American administration, the US Congress would endorse Australia's initiative. Australia would be operating from a position of moral and legal strength, and should undertake a diplomatic initiative with the utmost urgency and determination.

The Fretilin leaders, and other East Timorese leaders not necessarily involved with Fretilin, I believe, are willing to sit down with Indonesian leaders. We all should go to the table of negotiations without preconditions, without a fixed agenda. The first objective, to be achieved as a matter of urgency, would be a complete cease-fire. This cease-fire would not affect the status quo in the territory at the moment of the cease-fire. The cease-fire should enable a speedy and massive programme of relief, assistance and rehabilitation. The cease-fire should be observed and guaranteed by United Nations observers. A cease-fire will create a climate of relaxation and trust that would facilitate further talks to take place as to a comprehensive process of peaceful settlement of the current conflict.

We are not suggesting that it is going to be easy. We do not know of any diplomatic undertaking that has produced quick results. The Namibian question has been on the United Nations agenda since World War II. The contact group, made up of the Federal Republic of Germany, Canada, France, the USA, and Great Britain, has been functioning for several years now and the question of Namibia lingers on. The Palestinian problem is as old as the state of Israel. The Iran/Iraq conflict is dragging on, in spite of strenuous efforts by the United Nations Secretary-General, the Non-Aligned Movement and the Islamic Conference to bring an end to the war.

The East Timor problem is a problem created by a small group of generals in Jakarta, among them a psycho-killer, General Benny Murdani. President Suharto is known to have opposed a military venture in 1975. Benny Murdani (a Catholic—not all Catholics are good), an ambitious general who climbed in the ranks by stabbing other more senior officers in the back, wanted a war to justify his rank of general, and to prove that, although a Catholic, he is loyal to the Islamic Republic. We believe, that apart from the Benny Murdanis of Indonesia, there are decent people in the army, in the intelligentsia, who do not agree with the present policies of the Central Government in regard to East Timor. The Indonesian people do not support the war in East Timor. The Government tries hard to hide its military adventure from the Indonesian people, unlike the Konfrontasi-Malasi in the early 1960s and the West Irian campaign, of which Benny Murdani was a great commander—the only problem was that he dropped in the jungle, was almost captured by the Dutch, and was saved only when the Netherlands and Sukarno reached an agreement in New York. Nevertheless, he became famous, because Indonesia needed a national hero at the time.

East Timor has not become, has not been made, a nationalistic *cause célèbre*. It is therefore relatively easy for any government in Jakarta, it is relatively easy for President Suharto, to extricate himself from the East Timor mess without great loss of face. The alternative to a peace effort by Australia is the continuation of conflict that has reached the dimensions of genocide. The conflict now boiling in West New Guinea and in Papua New Guinea itself is a warning to those who advocate appeasement against assertiveness, diplomatic inaction against bold peace initiatives. I thank you very much.

Ian Davis from the Age *newspaper, Mr Horta. Your visit to Australia comes some six weeks before the ALP national conference. There is a possibility that the ALP's platform commitment will be diluted at that conference in July. I wonder if you could tell us what the consequences for East Timor would be if the ALP reduces its support for East Timor or drops East Timor entirely from its platform?*

First, I understand that Mr Ian Davis is a person whom Bill Hayden defined as very dangerous when he writes on foreign policy issues, but I have read Mr Davis' articles and I do not think he is very dangerous in national affairs—maybe dangerous to the State Department, I'm sorry, to the Foreign Affairs Department. To answer your question, yes, it would be a tragic event. It would be a serious moral setback to the East Timorese people, and I believe it would be a betrayal of the Labor movement, its ideals, if the Labor Party Convention was to drop, to delete the question of East Timor from the agenda. We are not asking the Labor Party Convention, as we are not asking the Labor Government, to cut off relations with Indonesia, to come out and condemn Indonesia and to impose sanctions. We hope that the ALP Convention would unanimously recommend a bold diplomatic initiative to be undertaken by the Labor Government.

Kitti Anna King—UNC News Service. Given Australia's record on East Timor, or at least the one you've described today, how likely is it that Canberra will change its tune and start playing the role of a peace-maker or an honest broker?

Well, I cannot predict the response, the reaction from the Foreign Affairs Department, from Prime Minister Hawke and Foreign Minister Hayden, but I hope that the Australian Government realises the dimensions of the human tragedy in East Timor, the dimensions of its inaction, not only in regard to East Timor but in regard to the situation in Papua New Guinea, a situation which is becoming explosive, not because I believe Indonesia is going to intervene in PNG, but a whole process of destabilisation, of tension, of mistrust, that is the result of the consequence of Canberra's appeasement of the Jakarta junta. We believe that the Australian parliament, those elected people who reflect Australian values, would call upon the Government to undertake a new initiative, a new look at the whole situation, and we believe that it is feasible.

As I mentioned, there is no easy solution to any conflict in the world—there has simply not been attempted any solution, any diplomatic initiative, in regard to East Timor on the part of Australia. Quite the contrary—Australia has undermined other modest efforts initiated by the Secretary-General of the United Nations, an honourable man, a skilful diplomat, who has committed energy and effort to solve the East Timor problem. The Portuguese Government has also indicated seriousness, its willingness to solve the problem of East Timor, but the Australian Government has basically torpedoed every effort undertaken either by the Secretary-General or by the Portuguese, but that was the previous Government. Now we have a Labor Government that has been in power for a bit over a year and I hope that the Labor Convention, its own party, will be able to persuade the Government to undertake a new initiative.

Jane Eyre from Australian Associated Press, Mr Horta. Several years ago, Fretilin sold some of its crops and the revenue from those sales went into the Commonwealth Bank in Darwin, and I understand that that money has now gone into 'consolidated revenue' and that you are one of the signatories to that account. Could you tell us whether you intend to make representations to the Government to get that money back in any way?

Well, in fact, in 1975, in the period that Fretilin was in control of

East Timor, there was a transaction of coffee. We export some coffee to Australia and show that an independent East Timor would look to Australia for trade, for cooperation, but the result of this several years later is that the Government, not content with its diplomatic sabotage against us, expropriated our coffee. I have read some reports to the extent that the Federal Treasury, the Federal Government, has—I do not say confiscated this money—but we intend to contact lawyers in this country to challenge this. There were two signatories to the account: myself and the then Fretilin Finance Minister. He was unable to withdraw the money with me—it required two signatures. He was in East Timor—we don't know whether he is dead or alive—and so I made a statement, an exposé to the bank, and I was told that it required two signatures. The reason for the freezing or confiscation of the account is that there has been no claimant. Well, at least, there has been one claimant, and he's alive. So, I don't understand why the banks say that there has been no claimant—I have claimed this money for several years. I am not an expert in Australian banking laws, but we intend to contact some lawyers in this country to help us to clarify this matter.

Ken Davidson, the Age, *Mr Horta. Given Australia's official attitudes, do you think those attitudes are based on a belief, a belief held by both the previous Government and the present Government and the Department of Foreign Affairs, that Timor should be absorbed into Indonesia, or are our attitudes really based on fear of Indonesian military might? In relation to the second question, I was wondering if perhaps you could explain to us how, what I believe to be a few hundred Fretilin guerrillas, can manage to hold down now I think about 14,000 Indonesian troops, and this has been going on now for nine years. Specifically, where is Fretilin getting its arms and ammunition to carry on this fight?*

Well, I read your piece this morning in the Melbourne *Age* and you, better than me, define the reasons for Australia's inaction, Australia's certain malaise that paralyses Australian Governments and Australian initiatives. As far as Fretilin's strength, the guerrilla strength in East Timor, the prospects of the Resistance, I must say, quoting a Pentagon official with whom I met in New York a couple of years ago (a top Pentagon official), and after I briefed him on the situation in East Timor, he says: 'the experience in Vietnam, in Cambodia and other places, shows us that a guerrilla army doesn't need to win the war in a clear-cut military victory.' He says 'as long as you survive, as long as you keep bleeding the enemy army, the enemy will be forced to come to negotiations at one point or another'. I believe his expert opinion applies to the question of East Timor, and the experience of the past nine years has shown precisely this.

When Indonesia invaded East Timor, I remember General Ali Murtopo boasted that in three weeks' time, the question of East Timor would be solved, that the Resistance will be finished, the territory pacified. It has been nine years now and the Resistance is quite active, and the evidence of this is the fact that the Australian Embassy delegation's trip to East Timor was cancelled because of the ongoing operations in East Timor undertaken by the Indonesian army. The International Committee of the Red Cross has also seen its visit to East Timor cancelled—it shows that there is a considerable resistance on the part of the East Timorese.

After your question concerning Fretilin's supply of weapons and ammunition, first, most of the weapons in Fretilin's possession are weapons that were left behind by the Portuguese army. It was a substantial amount of weapons that were left behind by the Portuguese—modern sophisticated weapons used by the NATO forces in Western Europe. The second source has been a substantial amount of weapons captured from the Indonesian army itself. We have hundreds of photographs taken in the liberated areas of East Timor sent to us as recently as last year, showing a wide variety of weapons in Fretilin's use, from American sub-machine guns to Israeli sub-machine guns (the Uzi sub-machine gun). So, Fretilin is quite well supplied in terms of light weapons.

Can Fretilin hold out with 2000 to 3000 troops against the Indonesian army? Yes, we believe so. The terrain in East Timor is very suitable for guerrilla warfare—the nine years has shown this. The history of World War II, where there were only 300 to 400 commandos in East Timor fighting 20,000 Japanese, well armed, well equipped, at the cost only of 40 Australian losses, shows that the guerrilla warfare in East Timor can continue and can force Indonesia to come to negotiations.

In March 1983, there was a dramatic development in East Timor. There was a meeting between the Fretilin leaders and the Indonesian military commanders. It was the first time that the two sides ever met, and it was at the initiative of the Indonesian top military commanders. Later on, the military people in Jakarta denied that such a meeting took place, but of course it took place— we have abundant evidence, with photographs of this. The result of the meeting was a cease-fire agreement agreed upon by both sides which lasted between March and August 1983. Why does Indonesia, Benny Murdani and other generals, claim that there is 'no war in East Timor, that Fretilin was only a bunch of 50, 100, 150 terrorists', quote, unquote. Why then did the military commander in East Timor need to go to Fretilin-liberated areas to meet with Fretilin leaders? The meeting took place in Fretilin-liberated areas—not in Dili, not in Baucau.

So, we believe that Indonesia, pressurised by the continuing losses on its side in East Timor, and by a combination of diplomatic effort, world public opinion and growing dissension in Indonesia itself, will be forced to come to terms with the problem. We believe that Indonesia has possibilities to get out of the situation in an honourable fashion. We will be most flexible, willing to work out with the Indonesians a formula that would help them save face, a formula that will guarantee their own interests, their own security.

Ken Davidson. Just to come back to a specific point which you haven't answered—munitions. Sure, you've got weapons left over from the Portuguese and so on, but if you're shooting guns, you

Jakarta has always boasted about its 'special development' of East Timor. These photographs illustrate the meaning of this 'special development' for the East Timorese. I have not censored them because to do so would be to act according to our Government's compliance with the murderers. In spite of our Government's claims of an improving human rights situation, these photographs show the brutal daily reality of life in East Timor.

The photographs were taken during the current Indonesian military campaign code-named Operation Annihilation. Its purpose: to eliminate the guerilla resistance. Innocent youths are arrested, tortured and murdered in order to gain information about the locations of the guerilla resistance. The two victims shown here are young East Timorese women; one is, in fact, a schoolgirl. They were arrested during the public celebration in December 1996 on the return of Bishop Belo from Oslo after receiving the Nobel Peace Prize.

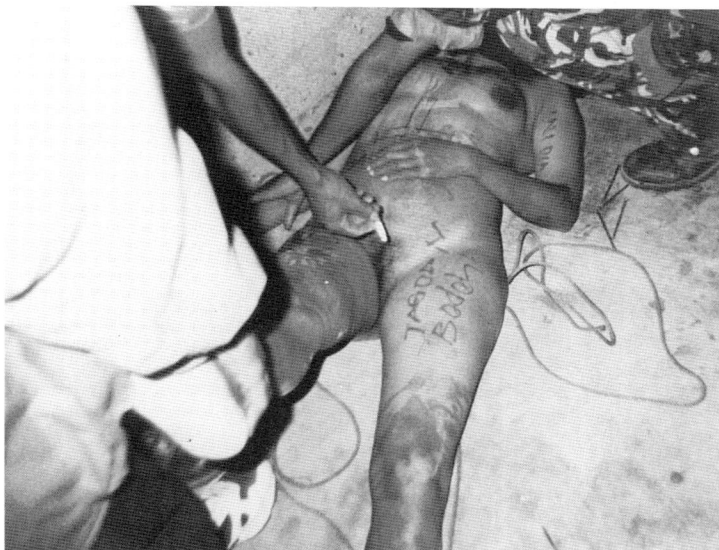

One victim is tortured with nails hammered into various parts of her body, and as well with cigarette burns and beatings. The other victim, the schoolgirl, is raped, knifed and tortured to death.

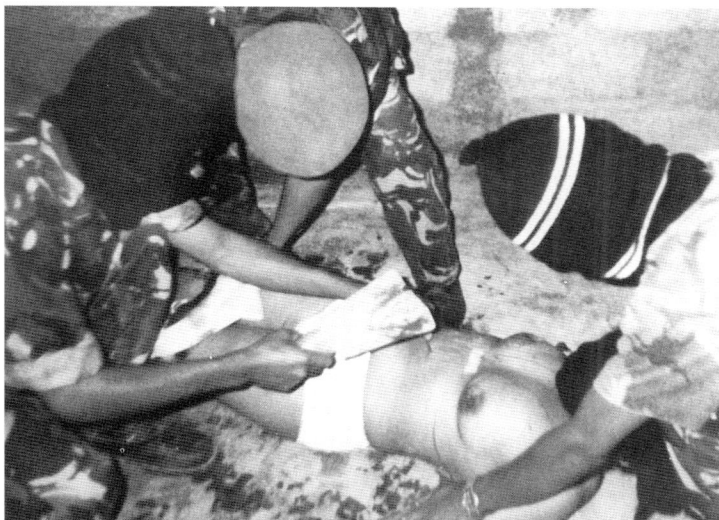

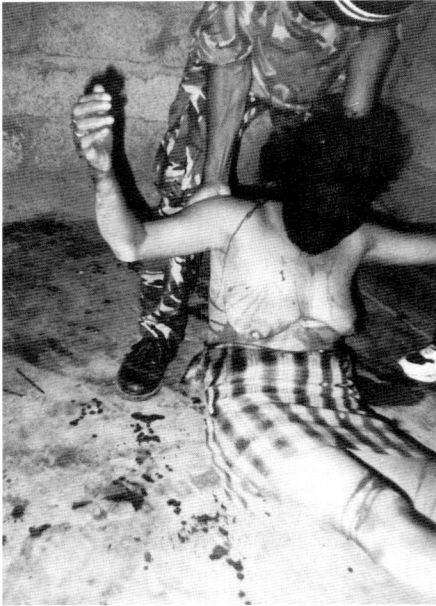

In the photo containing the transfigured picture of Jesus, the killers have mockingly written, 'If you really are God, come down and bring her back to life.' These killers continue to be trained by Australian and American Armed Forces.

have to have munitions. Where are they coming from and how are you obtaining them?

The ammunition used by the Timorese army, the Fretilin army, with the Portuguese weapons, is the same ammunition that is used by the Indonesian army, and it's easier to acquire ammunition than rifles and so on. I know of instances when Fretilin leaders in East Timor, they control certain sections of the rich coffee area, and they exchange coffee for ammunition in West Timor or in Dili itself among certain Indonesian military groups. It is quite understandable—they are not winning and they are not motivated to fight in East Timor. We know of instances when units of the Indonesian army in East Timor have agreements with Fretilin units in other areas not to fight each other. They go for a three-month, six-month rotation to East Timor and they want to return home safe to their families, to their relatives. For them, the war in East Timor means nothing. Of course there are exceptions—there are the top commanders, the other units that are professional and trying to do the best job they can.

Uri Tamal, Public Radio 2XX. Mr Ramos Horta, if you were in the seat of our Foreign Minister, what would you do in practical terms in order to get to the stage which you describe: that a) Australia becomes a broker, a peace-maker, and b) that Australia changes its foreign policy within the region and specifically towards East Timor?

Well, if I were to be in the seat of Foreign Minister of Australia, I would agree with Bill Hayden in relation to Ian Davis. I would be extremely dangerous for Australia, because I would have in my mind East Timor and not Australian interests. But if I, as an East Timorese, were to propose something to the Australian Government, I would propose taking into consideration the possibilities, feasibilities of any proposal. Having studied the pros and cons of an undertaking by Australia, such as the diplomatic initiative that I outlined, we do not believe that the negative implications outweigh the positive effects.

There is no way that Indonesia can impose sanctions upon Australia. It would be the first instance in the world where a Third World country with about twenty billion dollars debt, a net importer of food, imposes sanctions on one of their major aid donors. At this point in time, because of the oil glut in the world, the dropping of oil prices, not even the countries in the Middle East, not even Saudi Arabia or a combination of Arab countries are in a situation to impose sanctions on the Western countries, let alone Indonesia. So, we do not see in economic terms what the losses are for Australia. If the losses were really great, tremendous, we would understand such a situation and we would not want to drag Australia into a diplomatic and economic nightmare. But we understand that this is feasible; it has simply not been attempted.

Australia's Foreign Affairs Department simply finds it more convenient to leave the East Timor issue under the carpet. They are not willing to confront the Indonesian generals in a firmer fashion. There are no losses, as I explained earlier. The Melanesian countries in the South Pacific region, and lots and lots of African countries, would immediately support Australia. I can mention countries—such as Zimbabwe, a Commonwealth country, Zambia, Kenya, moderate countries in Africa, Algeria in north Africa, and all the countries in the South Pacific region—Australia would be able to convince to support. Countries in Western Europe, Portugal definitely, and other countries, the Scandinavian countries, the Netherlands, the Norwegians. I have discussed with numerous delegations at the United Nations—they always ask, 'But what is Australia's position? Why doesn't Australia do this or do that? If Australia were to undertake such an initiative it would make our job easier; we would go along with Australia.' The problem is simply lack of interest, or a policy of resignation, of surrender, which I cannot really understand, and I got some of the Australian attitudes, its psychology, from an article today in the Melbourne *Age*.

Warwick Beutler from ABC Public Affairs. I'm interested in how much influence these days people like you, yourself from outside

East Timor, how much influence you exert over Fretilin's activities inside East Timor? What is your command structure? How much influence and input do people like yourself have in events in the territory and can you guarantee a cease-fire on Fretilin's side in East Timor?

First I would like to say that we have regular contact with the Fretilin leadership in East Timor. Almost the entire leadership is inside the country and not outside, and I would like to set the record very straight, because there has been some speculation, particularly spread by the Foreign Affairs Department, that Fretilin leaders are in Mozambique. In Mozambique we have one delegation. In Portugal we have one, in Australia, in New York we have another one. We have a total of four or five people overseas. The rest of the leadership is inside East Timor, and we have frequent contacts with them.

In studying the communiques, the instructions that we receive from the Fretilin leadership, I am 100 per cent certain that, first, they understand the complexities, the nuances of the politics in the region. When they welcomed the Indonesian delegation in the liberated areas, very warmly, very cordially, it was the best evidence of their willingness, of their readiness, to solve the problem. We received their instructions to pursue the matter with the Secretary-General and with the Portuguese President, and we have had evidence that they take into consideration our views.

In regard to other areas, other problems that they might not be aware of, complexities of the situation in other parts of the world, I must also tell you they follow events outside East Timor very closely. I have been struck when receiving the communiques from East Timor how they knew my whereabouts. They knew I was travelling somewhere and I received a criticism, 'why haven't you been to Australia?' Of course, they did not know that I have been banned from Australia for seven years. They even advise us which Governments to contact and we were criticised for not having contacted other countries. How do they follow it? Various radio stations, Voice of America and, our most important listening post in East Timor, Radio Australia or ABC. They follow events, they monitor them, and they know what is happening outside their world. And I can assure you that, yes, we can give guarantees as to the implementation and the strict observation of any cease-fire.

Peter Reith, Melbourne Sun. *Government documents leaked earlier this year show that Australia regards Indonesia as the only serious threat to us, as well as raising a possibility of potential conflict over Papua New Guinea. How much of a factor do you think this has been in the reluctance of successive Australian Governments to get involved in East Timor, and do you think those fears of possible conflict over Papua New Guinea are justified? And secondly, you mention a political solution—what do you regard would be a realistic solution?*

First, concerning Australian attitudes, fears of an Indonesian invasion, of course I believe, and most experts in this matter would agree, that it's absurd. I think Australian fears of Indonesia are not objective, they are subjective. These fears are fantasised by certain elements in this country, particularly in the Foreign Affairs Department, to justify bankrupt policies. Can anyone in his or her right mind think that the Indonesian army, which cannot handle East Timor, cannot handle West New Guinea (a group of guerrilla fighters with few weapons), can even handle Darwin? So it's totally out of question in a pure military sense. In a political sense it's completely out of the question, so it is simply subjective reasons concocted by the State Department—I'm sorry, by the Foreign Affairs Department—in order to justify its policies of appeasement.

As far as the proposal that I put forward, Fretilin's position has been firm from the very beginning, since 1975, and it continues to be today. Self-determination for the people of East Timor, an act of self-determination to allow the people of East Timor to exercise their choice—independence, continuation with Portugal, or integration with another independent state. Various United Nations resolutions, particularly Resolution 1541, provide for three alternatives: independence, free association with a colonial power, or integration with another state. Fretilin subscribes entirely to these alternatives.

When I propose talks through an Australian initiative, I mention no agenda, no preconditions—everything and anything can be talked about and negotiated at the round table. If the Indonesian leaders are able to persuade the Fretilin leaders to drop certain demands, or if the Fretilin leaders are able to persuade the Indonesian leaders to withdraw from East Timor, or Australia can intervene in the process of the talks and come up with a new proposal satisfactory to both sides—well, all these elements are to be considered in such a round-table conference. We are not anticipating anything, we are not proposing any definitive solution—it can be negotiated at a round-table conference. The important thing is for all of us to sit down, and the priority to be achieved during such a meeting is a complete cease-fire to improve the situation in East Timor.

John Lombard, Radio Australia. Could I take up the point that other questioners have talked about—your proposal for an Australian initiative—and play a devil's advocate role on what the response is likely to be, in that the Indonesians are likely to say that such a round-table conference is not on. As far as they're concerned, the issue has been settled and the position of East Timor as the 27th province of Indonesia is non-negotiable, and they've already said this several times, both to Australian leaders and to others. I put that proposition to you, and secondly, where you raise the question of being a long-running issue in the same context as Namibia, Palestine and the Iran/Iraq war—you remember that in 1962, Indian troops marched into Goa, another Portuguese territory, and nobody hears today about an act of self-determination for the people of Goa.

Well, starting from the end, in relation to the question of Goa, I believe there are major differences between the question of Goa and East Timor. For expediency and convenient reasons, Indonesia always tries to draw a parallel between India's intervention in Goa and its intervention in East Timor. Historical, legal aspects of it indicate there are substantial differences, as well as there being differences between the question of East Timor and the question of the Malvinas and the others. The question of India intervening in Goa—well, there was no resistance, there was no liberation movement, no independence movement that claimed independence for Goa at the time.

With the situation in East Timor, there is continuing resistance, and Indonesia never claimed East Timor as part of its Republic. One can debate whether, even before the pre-colonial period, or during the pre-colonial period, if Timor, East Timor, was part of the ancient Indonesian empires. For 300, 400 years, Indonesia was colonised by the Dutch, East Timor by the Portuguese. This alone marked the difference between East Timor and Indonesia.

Turning to the more present-day question, yes, the Foreign Affairs Department might say negotiations or an Australian initiative are not on—we, again, would point to the continuing conflict in East Timor, to Indonesia's inability to win the war, to the continuing and growing suffering of the people of East Timor, and this is a moral obligation for Australia to do something to stop this, the suffering of the people of East Timor. We would again insist, remind Australia, that the politics of appeasement of the Indonesian Government have not produced any positive result for Australia.

The question of West New Guinea and Papua New Guinea should be a reminder that unless Australia stands up now in support of the small nations of the South Pacific region, in support of the Melanesian community, the situation in West New Guinea and Papua New Guinea will get worse. And the implications of this, the repercussions of this, I believe, will be far greater than the negative effects in the Australian-Indonesian relationship resulting from a possible Australian intervention. We understand also that it's not easy to convince the Australian Department of Foreign Affairs, but we have patience working with the Australian people, with the

Australian politicians—Labor, Liberal and the Country Party. We will bring them around. It is not a radical proposal. It is a modest, flexible proposal that we believe is very much the soul of the Australian people.

Bob Reed, last clerk at the Australian Consulate in Timor. Mr Horta, what was Dick Woolcott's answer to your question, 'What have we East Timorese done to Australia?' Two, we sometimes hear allegations of Indonesian troop defections to the Fretilin nationalist side. Do you have any information on this matter?

Well, Dick Woolcott did not answer. He was embarrassed. I respect Dick Woolcott as a skilful Ambassador. I have no personal antagonism towards Dick Woolcott, we keep talking at the United Nations, although fruitlessly. Concerning your second question, yes, there has been a substantial number of defections, not so much on the part of the Indonesian army itself, but East Timorese who are conscripted into the Indonesian army. Last year alone, at least 200 East Timorese in the Indonesian army defected and took away their weapons and ammunition. The previous year, information that we received from Fretilin indicates a total of 300 to 500 hansips of East Timorese in the Indonesian army defected, and we know, of course, of cases of Indonesian soldiers simply refusing to fight.

In 1981, around August/September, in Baucau, a whole unit refused to fight. They left abandoned their weapons and returned to Dili. We know they were arrested and taken to Bali, including their commander. We know their commander was badly tortured; his leg was amputated in a hospital in Bali. We follow developments with the Indonesian army very closely, and we have friends in the Indonesian army who do not agree with the war—they consider it a waste of time, a waste of energy.

Robert Domm is a long-time labour advocate and human rights activist. He is co-author, with Mark Aarons, of East Timor: A Western Made Tragedy. *In September 1990 Robert Domm was the first 'outsider' to make direct contact with East Timor's guerrilla headquarters and he recorded the first ever interview with the Resistance leader Xanana Gusmao, the most wanted man in East Timor. The interview, achieved with courageous determination, singlehandedly smashed the Indonesian illusion of the Resistance being a voiceless, insignificant handful of 'terrorists'. The eloquence and sensitivity of Xanana Gusmao's thoughtful responses to Robert Domm's questions were in themselves a reflection of the heroic and inspirational struggle of perhaps the greatest freedom fighters the world has seen since the Viet Minh. Robert's story on his encounter is memorable and shares a conviction that we all have—* 'the just nature of their cause will ultimately win the East Timorese their freedom'. *In Part 2 are extracts from the Xanana Gusmao—Robert Domm interview.*

7

EAST TIMOR: 'TO RESIST IS TO WIN'

ROBERT DOMM

Part 1

Streams flowing together become rivers
Rivers increase, whatever opposes them

So must the children of Timor unite
Unite against the wind that blows from the sea.

Francisco Borja da Costa, East Timorese poet, penned this nationalist call to arms shortly before the Indonesian air and naval attack on Dili on 7 December 1975. Only 30 years old, the poetry ceased when he was tortured and executed by invading paratroopers, along with many of his compatriots, on that terrible day. Thus Indonesia set the pattern of its rule.

It was a hot mid-September morning in 1990 as I stood on one of the wide, dusty streets of the capital, Dili, facing a one-legged man dressed in old and filthy rags. Supported by a crude wooden pole he stared at me blankly, graphically gesturing how Indonesian soldiers hacked off his leg with a machete. An elderly woman, observing the scene nearby, added that the man had also been bashed about the head with rifle butts. The Timorese seemed determined that this story be told to an outsider, though their anxiety at doing so in a public place was all too evident.

It had been fifteen years since the invasion and forcible integration of East Timor into the Republic of Indonesia. For most of that period, the territory had been closed off to all but carefully selected visitors. While the United Nations continued to regard Indonesia's occupation as illegal, this did not trouble the security forces, to whom rigid control and manifestations of public obedience were the things that really mattered. The Timorese had waged a determined armed resistance throughout this time, but it had gradually waned under the weight of the occupier's military advantage and the lack of outside material support. The human costs of the overall conflict had been horrific; the one-legged man's story was by no means unique. In the tightly knit familial structures of East Timor, every local was related to a victim.

I had been commissioned by the Australian Broadcasting Corporation's Radio National to travel to East Timor to conduct an exclusive interview with the guerrilla commander Xanana Gusmao, hiding out deep in the mountainous interior. Xanana had been Resistance leader since the late 1970s, when repeated Indonesian military offensives had shattered Fretilin's organisation and destroyed much of its earlier leadership group. He was significantly responsible for rebuilding the scattered remnants of the organisation into a credible military and political force. As such, he was the number one person on the Indonesian military's most-wanted list. Incredibly, given the territory's small geographical area and the extensive network of secret police and informers, Xanana Gusmao had evaded capture or death for the fifteen-year duration of the war. No outsider had ever made direct contact with the guerrilla headquarters.

It was obviously necessary to conceal the true journalistic intention of my visit. Connecting up with the underground or Clandestine Resistance in Dili, a major operation was organised by the locals to smuggle me past the many Indonesian troops and security personnel, whose oppressive presence permeated everything. To meet the elusive Xanana, we had to secretly leave Dili by car early one morning and travel slowly for a few hours up the winding mountain roads. At a pre-arranged point, an unarmed guerrilla guide met our civilian party and we set off on foot through the forest where, after a short period, we were joined by an armed security unit despatched by Xanana for our protection. The guerrillas wore a combination of Indonesian army camouflage gear and civilian clothing. Most were carrying United States army M16 semi-automatic rifles, which they claimed were captured from the occupying forces. In contrast to their somewhat ragged appearance, the guerrillas moved swiftly through the rugged terrain with military skill and great care. Along the way, they were actively assisted by passing locals and look-outs with information on enemy troop movements.

The most striking aspect of travelling through the mountains was the harsh contradiction between the forest's natural beauty and tranquillity, and the all-encompassing atmosphere of insecurity associated with the military occupation. Arbitrary executions and torture were commonplace and the rule of law was non-existent. A sickening, ever-present fear and apprehension gripped the Timorese, influencing all components of their behaviour.

After traversing some considerable distance at an exhausting pace, our party reached a very steep mountainous peak, covered in forest and seemingly inaccessible. The struggle up via a natural pathway gouged by centuries of monsoonal rain epitomised the difficulties the guerrillas faced in surviving and, paradoxically, the difficulties the Indonesians faced in hunting them down. Eventually we reached the guerrilla camp, which could not be seen even from a short distance away. A distinctive-looking Xanana suddenly materialised, dressed in a crisp Portuguese army uniform, gazing anxiously down as we literally crawled up the last few metres. The bearded commander, quite tall for a Timorese, greeted us confidently in fluent Portuguese.

During our interview, and speaking pensively in a slow, subdued voice, Xanana accused the Indonesians of adopting a 'bestial attitude' towards his people. 'They are assassins, inhuman, and everything that is Timorese is to be destroyed, violated, oppressed and killed.' Defining a military strategy conditioned by the occupier's strategy, Xanana claimed his guerrillas had reached the stage where they intentionally confronted their enemy only if an opportunity arose to capture arms and equipment. The Indonesian military were pursuing a campaign of 'territorial counter-insurgency', the launching of small units of twenty or more soldiers in all possible directions in a given zone. This campaign had been effective in restricting operations and causing difficulties for the Resistance. 'We feel that the enemy is everywhere,' Xanana said somewhat wearily, 'we even say we carry them in our bags.' While seeking to preserve men and materials by choosing the time and place for combat, Xanana claimed that armed clashes occurred every day across many parts of the territory, from Tutuala, at the eastern end of the island, to the border region with West Timor.

Exemplifying the resilience which had characterised their long war of resistance against far superior military odds, Xanana vowed to continue the struggle indefinitely. 'We are prepared to continue to resist for as long as necessary, as long as Jakarta does not adopt a more flexible attitude, more just and more responsible.' Believing that the tide of history was on the side of his people, Xanana's motto, 'To Resist Is To Win', summed up the incremental nature of their campaign.

Indonesia and its apologist allies in the West had long argued that integration had brought significant development and material improvements for the local population, freeing them from the stagnating shackles of Portuguese colonialism. Rejecting this contention, Xanana asserted that there was a 'confrontation at all levels of these improvements'. Indeed, there were no material benefits that could compensate the Timorese for their sacrifices, he said. The infrastructure projects initiated by the Indonesians did not benefit the local population and were part of a 'strategy to sub-jugate the people'. According to Xanana, the true beneficiaries of the development projects were the Indonesian military, especially corrupt generals, Indonesian civil servants 'exploiting economic conditions', and Indonesian transmigrants brought in by the government and 'to whom the most fertile land is offered'.

'We would not deny that in the Western countries, there is a supremacy of political rights over economic rights,' Xanana explained. 'But they consider that in East Timor, economic rights should prevail over political rights. We consider that they are treating us as animals to be fattened. We are human beings like all others in the world. We do not think that politics is a question of being able to read and write, but of feeling that freedom is a natural right, something that always existed.'

The Indonesian occupation and its economic developments, Xanana said, violated the traditional Timorese cultural attachment to their land. 'Our people are essentially rooted to their culture and traditions. They have their own concepts of life, of existence, and live to realise them. They are impregnated spiritually and existentially with the concept. They conceive their passage through Mother Earth as a temporary time, ephemeral, in which they have to realise their traditional concepts. Our people are fondly attached to Mother Earth. All their acts, cultural manifestations and even life, are destined to consecrate, to honour, to worship Mother Earth as life.' The occupiers prevent the Timorese, he argued, 'from realising, from living, from practising their traditions, their customs, and this is what essentially offends our people'.

Armed resistance is but one aspect of the organised opposition to Indonesian authority. The opening of East Timor to outside visitors in 1989 created a new opportunity for the underground or clandestine organisations comprised of civilian Timorese living in cities and towns under Indonesian rule. The major driving force of the clandestine organisations was the students who had grown up under the occupation and, ironically, had received an education in Indonesian schools and universities that was generally not available to them under the Portuguese. For Xanana and his colleagues, the seeming paradox was easy to explain:

'The difficult situation in which the people live under enemy control necessarily has to create in the children that were born after this occupation a perception of the injustice of the situation, of a criminal situation, which affects their own relatives, their neighbours and friends ... The youngsters, both those born before the invasion and those since, are children of the people ... who under 400 years of Portuguese domination always knew how to keep alive the patriotic consciousness ... The schools established by the Indonesians deny them their own language, their own culture, their traditions, their way of seeing things. The Indonesians tried to impose on them a way of thinking which they know is not theirs, yet they receive a transference in terms of continuity, a transference of their Maubere (East Timorese) identity and culture, customs and traditions. A Maubere goes to a school in the Bahasa language, where they teach another history, another way of seeing, another concept of life. Evidently, a people which knows itself cannot be reduced, cannot be subjugated.' For Xanana, this was the fundamental lesson of the fifteen-year war.

Most Timorese understood that they could not hope to defeat

Indonesia militarily. Jakarta, however, had lost the political battle for legitimacy from day one of its invasion. The occupier had no realistic hope of winning the hearts and minds of the Timorese as far too much water had flowed under the bridge. The trauma of more than 200,000 deaths in a country of 700,000 could not be forgotten, nor forgiven, even over many generations. An uneasy, sullen and depressing political stalemate hung, therefore, like a heavy cloud over Jakarta's inflexible East Timor policy. Xanana Gusmao himself remained 'interested and ready to debate and discuss any project for a solution without preconditions, under United Nations auspices'. His calls for a cease-fire and a negotiated solution to the conflict predictably fell on deaf ears in Jakarta.

After eighteen hours at Xanana's mountain hideout, our party began the gruelling trek back to Dili, once again travelling some distance by vehicle. Along the way, Resistance members pointed out areas where major battles or massacres by Indonesian troops had taken place over the years. At each location, local people had previously lived in villages for generations. Now there was nothing—no people and no obvious trace that the villages ever existed. The Indonesian military are adept at the clinical eradication of evidence of their crimes. For the Timorese in our group, with their strong attachment to the land, these ghostly locations were invisible monuments, to be honoured and remembered as symbolising their essential traditions and identity.

In the capital city, the agonised concrete and steel monument erected by the Indonesian Government to commemorate integration and to honour its war dead stood starkly visible but totally ignored by any passing East Timorese; a silent, lonely sentinel symbolising a tragically failed policy.

Postscript

This chapter has been adapted from an article first published in the French daily *Le Monde* on 28 December 1990. Twelve months later, the Indonesian military opened fire on hundreds of unarmed

Timorese demonstrators and mourners in Dili's Santa Cruz cemetery. The ensuing massacre, with its large death and injury toll, was witnessed by foreign observers, and sparked outrage and revulsion throughout the world. It graphically exposed the true nature of Indonesia's occupation to many who previously knew little of the issue. Western Governments came under enormous pressure to censure Indonesia and to press for a genuine negotiated solution to the conflict. Jakarta, however, remained as intransigent as ever in respect to any substantive policy change. In late 1992, Xanana Gusmao was captured alive in Dili and was subsequently put through a farcical, political show trial as a so-called 'common criminal'. His initial sentence of life imprisonment was commuted to twenty years in a cynical piece of manipulation by Indonesia's President Suharto, himself the architect of the illegal invasion and brutal occupation of East Timor. At the time of writing, Xanana remains incarcerated in Jakarta's notorious Cipinang prison. Despite international awareness of East Timor being at an all-time high, with the awarding of the 1996 Nobel Peace Prize to two prominent Timorese, and the more recent and unprecedented diplomatic efforts of South Africa's legendary President Nelson Mandela, an internationally acceptable, just and comprehensive solution still awaits. There is little doubt, however, as Suharto's long reign nears its end, that a political settlement will eventually come about. Although it is over seven years since I interviewed Xanana Gusmao, the determination, resilience and courage of the East Timorese that I witnessed during that visit remain as evident now as they were back then. It is these qualities that have kept their cause alive for twenty-two extremely difficult years. These qualities, and the just nature of their cause, will ultimately win the East Timorese their freedom.

Robert Domm
Sydney, Australia
5 February 1998

Part 2

Excerpts from the interview by Robert Domm with Xanana Gusmao, 27 September 1990. (Robert Domm—RD; Xanana Gusmao—XG.)

RD: Interview with Mr Xanana Gusmao, Thursday 27 September 1990, East Timor. This is Robert Domm reporting for the Australian Broadcasting Corporation from the Military Headquarters of the Armed Resistance to Indonesian occupation of East Timor. The Headquarters is situated deep in the hills of East Timor, and for the first time in fifteen years since Indonesia invaded in 1975, I'm talking to the commander of the Falantil, the Armed Forces of the Resistance. Good evening, Mr Xanana.

XG: Good evening.

RD: My first question to you, sir, is if you are able to do so simply, describe the current military situation in East Timor?

XG: In the current situation the guerrillas try to minimise their great difficulties. After fifteen years, obviously everyone understands that without any support from outside, Falantil cannot think about great military successes against the enemy. The current situation on the enemy's part has been constant military action to suffocate the Resistance. What we do is to try to neutralise, to accommodate each coup that the enemy unleashes against us. This is something of a lesser military impact. This is the current situation, in which the guerrillas try to soften the attacks of the enemy. We note that the impact of the enemy's engagement is not so strong as before.

RD: So you are saying that the scale of the military activity by the Indonesians has been reduced in recent years?

XG: Not exactly the activity. What has been reduced is the impact—this has been lessened.

RD: Can you explain what you mean by the effect has been reduced? Are you saying that they are meeting more and more resistance from the Timorese people, and therefore being less effective?

XG: When we refer to effect we mean the level of difficulties that they cause. The more we feel that the situation is difficult, that's what we mean by the effect being bigger. This is to say that the effect means that the more difficulties the Indonesian troops impose on us, the more the impact we feel from their activities. The less the difficulties, the less impact they have.

RD: May I ask you some basic questions? How many Indonesian troops are there normally in East Timor?

XG: Normally we count between 10 and 15 battalions. Previously, when they wanted to launch a major offensive, they would then increase the number of troops, depending on the level of the offensive. So, at the moment we could count between 8 and 10 battalions.

RD: How many is that who are under arms?

XG: It's 10 to 15,000. When they want to launch a big offensive, they increase the number of their effective troops, depending on the level of the offensive.

RD: The number of Indonesian troops in East Timor now, how does that compare to before? Are there less troops than before?

XG: Indonesian troops as such, no. If we consider the term 'Indonesian troops' as Indonesians themselves, then I must say, no. If we add the number of other military forces, we could say that they have been kept in the last two to three years at the same level.

RD: How do the Indonesian troops conduct their operations against the Resistance?

XG: It depends on the nature of the offensive. Obviously, every type of offensive which the enemy launches is aimed at our extermination. It does not have any other purpose. If we go back to the period which we consider to be essentially the guerrilla warfare period, in 1981, Indonesia launched an offensive in which it used almost all the people of East Timor. This is one type of offensive. In 1983–84, they launched another type of offensive, with their entire armed arsenal —warships, tanks, airplanes, mortars, cannons—in battalions which we counted, and we simply became tired of counting. Later, in 1986–87, they used elite troops, special forces in counter-insurgency warfare, where they began to practise, as Benny Murdani said, 'territorial guerrilla warfare'. Such a strategy does not involve a great number of military personnel, but well-defined planning and well-defined periods of time. It involves a complete spreading out of their forces, which they reduce to small groups. From 1988, they launched a new offensive, again with a big military force. Since then, from 1989 until today, Indonesia has reduced the number of military personnel, and as a priority, it uses Timorese troops for counter-insurgency.

RD: How in fact did they use the population?

XG: To occupy all the terrain. They cover an area with the people, and then attack another area. Then they move, and in this way they practically cover everywhere. The population is used to cover the terrain, so that they push us into Indonesian forces. The Indonesian troops are ready. They are covered by the population; they push us, they force us to clash with the troops. If we enter into their circle, then we would not be able to leave safely in time.

RD: Are you saying to me that the tactics the Indonesians used were to forcibly relocate the population to areas where Fretilin support or Falantil support was strong, and then they would surround the population with troops? Is that what you are saying?

XG: Men, children, the elderly.

RD: When you say forcibly, what would happen to the population if they resisted the Indonesian tactics of relocation?

XG: The offensive I wanted to describe is this: for instance, if they think we are in this mountain, they mobilise all the population of the local concentration camps and they make a ring from the concentration camps and they all begin to advance from there. The Indonesian troops then begin to push, and if we don't know how to escape in time, then we clash with the Indonesian troops.

RD: Can you continue to explain the forcible relocation of the population?

XG: I would like to explain the forced mobilisation of the people into military operations. This is different. The displacement of the people in favour or against—against in one sense, because they think they don't participate in the areas under the control of the guerrillas. These are the two aspects of the policy of forcing the population to participate directly or indirectly in the extermination of the Resistance. When Indonesia mobilises the population into military operations, we say that this is a direct participation—where the population, which does not want to be involved, is forced to be. Another aspect is the displacement of the people into the areas controlled by the guerrillas.

RD: What are the current tactics applied by the Indonesian troops? How do they conduct their operations now?

XG: Now they are using territorial counter-insurgency, based on this: they launch small groups, which go in every direction in a particular area. They spread into small groups throughout all the terrain, so that we are constantly in armed clashes with these small groups. Moreover, from time to time they use larger forces. They spread out by zones, in each region. Where there are bigger Falantil forces, it's there that they apply bigger numbers of troops, supported by counter-insurgency troops. This is the current military situation, the current tactic that the enemy applies. If you want to better understand counter-insurgency, I would say it has the following purpose: it spreads out throughout a large area; it has a fantastic capacity for mobility, so that they can detect very quickly the presence of the guerrillas. This method makes it very difficult for the guerrillas to take their own initiatives, because we don't have a permanent, a fixed enemy. It has no real volume or quantity, and we don't know what to confront. We feel that the enemy is everywhere; we even say that we carry the enemy in our bags. They have improved their technical knowledge of guerrilla tactics, and at the slightest sign of the presence of the guerrillas, they chase them until they provoke an armed clash. This is different from the previous tactics, where they used big numbers of troops within a fixed period.

RD: What is the behaviour of the Indonesian troops? In Australia we heard many reports of atrocities being committed by Indonesian troops in the past. Did the Indonesian troops adopt those tactics in your experience?

XG: Yes, particularly against the Resistance, we must say that the Indonesian troops do not behave in any other way. They chop off the heads of the guerrillas; they torture them on the spot. For instance, if a guerrilla is wounded and captured, he is killed. Recently at the beginning of September, a guerrilla in the eastern sector was wounded and taken to a village and killed …

RD: Can you explain to me what types of military equipment the Indonesian troops use against the Resistance?

XG: Lately, we have not seen the brand name which we saw on all the equipment and weaponry. On all this equipment, we used to see the brand name of NATO. They also use Bronco OV-10Fs, Skyhawks, Tigers and other types of armaments. The Indonesian troops use these. They use M16s and AR15s; we have these weapons but they are not here at the moment.

RD: I might just explain that Mr Xanana is showing me an automatic rifle and it has been captured from the Indonesian troops, and on the side of the rifle are the words: 'Property of the US Government, M16A1 Calibre 5.5, 6mm'. The serial number is 532 0696 and the rifle is made by Colts Firearms, Colt Industries, Hartford, Connecticut, USA. Actually, this is a semi-automatic.

XG: Lately they use this one, not AR15s. It is similar, but it's an M16—the others are AR15s. This is what the Indonesian troops use.

RD: Is this gun also US-manufactured?

XG: Exactly. One is M16, and the other is AR15 …

RD: What are the current strategies for fighting the Indonesian troops?

XG: In our action plans, in reality we have adopted corresponding strategies to the Indonesian strategies. When they use big military forces, we opt for a form of action which allows us to be resupplied with weapons and ammunition. This strategy has been quite successful. This is what led Jakarta to change its military strategy. Lately, with the counter-insurgency strategy, we are adopting a strategy to save men and materials. This means that today, we are only trying to neutralise our adversary's attacks. In the course of the years, we haven't changed our strategy very much, but we could conceive two fundamental strategies if we look at the whole fifteen years' war. The first phase was a defensive position, in fact we were defending positions: it was a positional war. We lost our support bases in 1977–78, and then we changed some plans. Initially, with the large number of troops, we tried to take advantage of it, by re-supplying ourselves by capturing weapons and ammunition. Lately, we have only been trying to save men and equipment.

RD: So, what you are saying is that your current strategy is not to confront the Indonesian troops, but if an opportunity exists for you to be successful and capture some equipment, you will do so?

XG: Yes. And this could not happen when they used a lot of forces. Now, because they use small groups spread out, we have not only one enemy, we have many enemies. The difficulty is always the same: to the extent that the enemy soldiers come with only one round of ammunition, and we have only one bullet in the gun. Obviously, when we go out and search for an opportunity, we are better prepared to achieve some successes. We have the conditions well prepared, both as regards the terrain, as well as the choice of men and their disposition. We can then set up an ambush with never less than five guerrillas and never more than ten, with two sections, a platoon or two companies. So, when we take an initiative, we have to take at least five arms. So when we go with five or ten arms we go out to search for an opportunity.

RD: I have noticed in your camp here a significant number of soldiers, all with Indonesian guns. Many, many of them with Indonesian guns, captured weapons. Is that where most of your weapons come from now? From the Indonesians?

XG: The majority of the weapons, which were from the Portuguese, are now greatly reduced, since we don't have the capacity to get ammunition for them. That's why our main attention goes on to the semi-automatic weapons which the enemy gives us, because they are the constant weapons that they use.

RD: Mr Xanana, what effect does the war between your troops and the Indonesians have on the civilian population?

XG: I would say a horrendous effect, a horrendous impact, since the war has caused many deaths, so much suffering to our people. All the atrocities you hear about outside are only a very, very small part of what actually happens in East Timor. It is really difficult to tell you the extent of the impact. But since we say that the people's Resistance continues, this is the true effect of the war.

RD: What is your estimate of the numbers of civilians who have been killed in the last fifteen years?

XG: We would not say a figure. I would say that the truth will surface one day after the war.

RD: My last question on this point. There have been reports in Australia that maybe 100,000 civilians have died through the fighting and through famine and disease.

XG: I believe that it is more than 200,000.

RD: You have given me an estimate of how many civilians have died in East Timor since the Indonesians occupied in 1975. Can you give an estimation of how many casualties the Indonesian troops have suffered during that time?

XG: I cannot give you an exact figure, because we cannot count the number of Indonesian soldiers. We don't know everywhere they are buried. To make an estimate, we could say between 25,000 and 30,000.

RD: Between 25,000 and 30,000, and you can estimate that from your experiences, fighting them, and also the number of people in the cemeteries—Indonesian troops, is that correct?

XG: It's essentially based on our experience over fifteen years.

RD: Well, conversely, what have been your casualties in your operations against the Indonesians?

XG: We must say that we enormously feel our casualties. Obviously, everyone understands that we are a small, weak army. If I say a number which is lower, obviously no-one will believe it, and if I give a bigger number, people will also say it's not true. All I can say is that we feel very deeply our casualties.

RD: Sir, you have commented before on your military strategies in the current situation, but could you comment in a bit more detail on your offensive capabilities. For instance, do you have the capacity to mount attacks on towns in East Timor?

XG: Militarily, we are very realistic. We don't dream of very great military offensives; we cannot do them. Our strategy is conditioned by the occupiers' strategy, and that is why our motto is: 'To resist is to win', and not, 'To annihilate them is to win'.

RD: You have waged a guerrilla war now for fifteen years, do you see this guerrilla war continuing to be a protracted one—a long, drawn-out guerrilla war in East Timor?

XG: I would first explain that if the world understands guerrilla warfare as an armed confrontation, then that understanding is wrong.

RD: The Indonesian Government's anxious to say to the world that the fighting in East Timor is now finished. Can you comment on that, and also give a general overview of the extent of the military confrontation between your troops and the Indonesian Armed Forces?

XG: The enemy propaganda has always been, since the loss of our bases in the mountains, that the situation is much more stable. That's the reason why it promoted the policy of 'openness' in East Timor. It's a pity, Mr Robert, that you are not able to go to some other parts of the country not far from here and see the following day a battle. It's a real pity, and we understand that this is one of the difficulties of our struggle. In a general appreciation or survey of the situation, I must say that the war continues from Tutuala to the border regions. In Lospalos, there is an intense presence of battalions Tu Jampa Humpat 744 with Indonesian forces …

RD: Can you explain how important to you are the Timorese students? Can you describe how they are organised, and can you indicate the importance to you of the recent demonstrations which they've organised?

XG: For the struggle, the role of these students is of great significance, especially the group that has graduated, which has the intellectual capacity that allows them to see the problems. They did not abandon the Maubere people. I am saying that the Maubere people are not disappointed with the position taken by their children—their sons and daughters. Their importance resides essentially in the fact that they better understand the foundation of the people's problems. The way they are organised is not very convenient for us to talk about. What we can say is that they are completely organised. All of them live up to their responsibilities to their homeland, and they are mobilised to enable them to take practical actions in the struggle. The importance of this practice for the struggle is based on the manifest expression of their patriotic consciousness, a consciousness which is in the blood of the Maubere people. Because it's in our blood, it's a consciousness that's not lost, and I think the whole world can understand the phenomenon of Maubere nationalism. It is not a phenomenon which is our propaganda, it's not an ephemeral, temporary phenomenon but it is part of our unconscious; it is part of the soul of the Maubere people which is transmitted from parents to the children, and its importance resides precisely in the continuation of this Maubere consciousness in the soul of the people.

RD: What do you think of the attitude of the young Timorese, that is, those who may have been born just before the Indonesian invasion or subsequent to it? Do you feel those young people are pro-independence?

XG: Yes, as I said earlier, the blood of the Maubere people goes from parents to children, and it could not be otherwise. The children of yesterday, at the time of the invasion, also directly suffered the horrors of the war. They saw their parents being massacred, they saw their mothers being maltreated, as well as their relatives and their friends, and they also felt the weight of the war against our people. Many of them lived in the mountains for the first three years. Others from the very beginning were under enemy control. It's inevitable that a youngster that sees his father massacred should feel hatred towards the assassin. It is obvious that a youth who witnessed these atrocities around him cannot disassociate and alienate himself from the whole situation in which we all live. He is directly or indirectly affected. Obviously, the children born before the invasion 'live' the war, and they continue to participate in it. The students today are organised from year three, four, or five, and they already participate in clandestine organisations. It's impossible that, in the course of so many years, the new generations would not have felt that it was their duty to participate in the struggle for the liberation of their home-land. As to those who were born during this criminal occupation, the situation might be a bit different, in that they did not witness the horrors of the war like the others, in the sense that they might not have witnessed the bombardments, or the battles, or the long marches made in the forests of the mountains. But the war did not end with the loss of our bases in the mountains. The difficult situation in which the people live under enemy control necessarily has to create in the children that were born after this occupation a perception of the injustice of the situation, of a criminal situation, which affects their own relatives, their neighbours and friends. And they are listening and understanding that, in the final analysis, it affects the entire Maubere people. It is really difficult to say that they are not in favour of independence when everything that feeds this struggle is the liberation of our country. The youngsters, both those born before the invasion and those since, are children of the people. They are not children of one people and children of another, and they are not children of the transmigrants: they are children of these people, who under 400 years of Portuguese domination always knew how to keep alive the patriotic consciousness. This is so clear, so evident in the last fifteen years of rough repression, of cruel oppression which could only teach the children to better love not only their country, but each other as a nation, as a culture, an identity—their Maubere soul. The schools established by the Indonesians deny them their own language, their own culture, their traditions, their way of seeing things. The Indonesians tried to impose on them a way of thinking which they know is not theirs, yet they receive a transference in terms of continuity, a transference of their Maubere identity and culture, customs and traditions. A Maubere goes to a school in the Bahasa language, where they teach another history, another way of seeing, another concept of life. Evidently, a people which knows itself cannot be reduced, cannot be subjected. They are a people which is conscious, which wants not to be alienated, and this is the case of the Timorese youth, and this is the fundamental problem of the war. If Indonesia thinks that by exterminating Falantil the war will end, they are wrong, because we would say that, in other words, the war will start again …

RD: What have been the main ways traditional life has changed?

XG: I would say that there have been a lot of changes, a lot of difficulties for the people to continue their customs and traditions. The Indonesian occupier has been exploiting what it sees as Maubere identity, presenting folk lore to tourists and foreign delegations. They think that the Maubere identity only resides in cultural manifestations. This is a failed policy, because the traditional way of living of our people changed radically, in the sense that it was radically prevented. Our people are essentially rooted to their culture and traditions. They have their own concepts of life, of existence, and live to realise them. They are impregnated spiritually and existentially with the concept; they conceive their passage through Mother Earth as a temporary time, ephemeral, in which they have to realise their traditional concepts. Our people are fondly attached to Mother Earth. All their acts, cultural manifestations, and even life itself, are destined to consecrate, to honour, to worship Mother Earth as life. There haven't been a lot of changes to this. What happened was a lot of obstacles to the realisation of these traditions. We can establish two levels: one situated in Dili, where there are less difficulties: people are better off on the economic plane, but more susceptible to be detached from their traditions. But the Maubere people are entirely in the country, and there they feel that they are prevented from realising, from living, from practising their traditions, their customs, and this is what essentially offends our people …

RD: It's said that women suffer more than men in East Timor. Can you comment on that, and on the role women play in the Resistance?

XG: The difficulties felt from the horrors of the war are felt particularly by the women, obviously because of their difference in relation to the men. We must say that Timorese women lived through so many difficulties—I don't know whether I should even say difficulties. The Timorese women felt even more oppressed than the men—there are so many cases that we could describe, and it would be too long. Of the number of cases of disrespect in regard to Timorese women—violations, abuses, threats—they are generally known and they take place from Tutuala to the border region. Many women gave their lives for their honour. Others were subjugated by force. An entire platoon raping a woman, sexually abusing her until she died. Many gave their lives. Others prefer a bullet to dishonour, while others who were weaker or pursued by a large number of troops—they could not resist. We can see a bestial attitude—they are assassins, inhuman, and what for them is Maubere is to be destroyed, violated, oppressed and killed. This is the situation of Timorese women. To specifically define the role of Timorese women in the Resistance would be like defining two very distinct fronts of struggle. We could only say that the only thing we do not allow is for our Timorese women to carry arms, because we still have men. But at the same level with the men, they have contributed in the most dangerous years of 1979 to 1981, and other difficult periods like from 1983 to 1985, when the enemy's reprisals were against men, and the Timorese women knew how to respond. They were the last stronghold of the Resistance when the men were not allowed to move about, and then it was the women who assumed the full role in the most difficult moments. So today, we cannot say clearly what is the role of the women as such, but they participate at an equal level with men ...

RD: What do you think of international attitudes towards East Timor? Firstly, the superpowers—America, the Soviet Union, China and Britain?

XG: Some of the attitudes are ambiguous, others are irresponsible. In regard to the United States, we think it is an attitude of selfishness. We understand that this derives from the economic interests the United States has in Jakarta. The United States considers itself to be the bastion of defence for universal values and human rights, yet it makes a distinction between peoples and rights. Today, the position which the United States takes in regard to Kuwait is totally contrary to its position on East Timor. The Soviet Union, in our view, behaved on the basis of its own world interests. In regard to East Timor, for the Soviet Union the United States was not the problem, so it was not even a case to be considered. In regards to China, which in principle supports the liberation movements, they also adopted a position which is somewhat inconsistent and incoherent about East Timor. The United Kingdom has a policy which is just duplicating the policy of the United States, and whatever the Americans say is what Margaret Thatcher does. And that's how we see the great powers in regards to our rights, which rights they say they defend. This is because of their interests which they don't want to lose.

RD: What about the attitude of Australia towards East Timor?

XG: We have to say that Australia has taken an attitude of an accomplice in the genocide perpetrated by the occupation forces. Accomplice, because the interests which Australia wanted to secure with the annexation of East Timor into Indonesia are so evident. The best proof is the Timor Gap agreement. It is inconceivable and unaccept-able that a democratic country with a Western way of life, a country which claims to be the defender of human rights, should profit from the blood of other people—a small neighbouring people who do not forget the important role they played in the defence of Australia, when many Timorese died so that the Japanese would not invade Australia. So it is an attitude of true betrayal. We feel hurt, we feel betrayed, that a country with Western values should help the Indonesian propaganda, covering up the tragedy, and then participat-ing in this rapacious exploitation in the Timor Gap, something that is, in fact, legitimately ours.

RD: You referred to the Timor Gap Treaty. What is your attitude towards the Australian-Indonesian agreement to exploit Timorese oil and gas reserves, the so-called Timor Gap Treaty?

XG: I think that it is a unilateral, illegal decision, illegitimate and criminal, in the context that we are being exterminated by a party to this agreement. Australia, with this treaty, becomes an accomplice. Australia talks loudly about international law, but we can only explain this agreement as a disrespect for principles. There is an international agreement which says that no acquisition by force is legal. As far as I know, Australia is also a signatory to this agreement —that no acquisition by force should be accepted as legal—and Australia denies this with its Agreement with Jakarta. It shows the dirty, cynical and criminal policies practised by the Australian Government in regards to East Timor.

RD: Can you think, sir, to comment on the attitude of the Vatican towards East Timor?

XG: I think that it is an attitude which betrays a corruption of universal principles. We see the role of the Vatican in the policies of Jakarta. We all know about the expulsion of Monseigneur Lopes, and the expulsion of the Portuguese priests, and we expect that one day, Monseigneur Belo will be expelled. I think that it is an immoral attitude on the Vatican's part, and that the Vatican is also acting in this world in the interests that move the attitudes of politicians. The statement by Father Tucci, who came to prepare the visit of the Pope, is very revealing of the Vatican's attitude. When he disagreed that the Papal Mass should be in Tacitolu, he merely stated that the Vatican should not sacrifice its interests only for the sake of a few hundred thousand Catholics. I don't think that is the most correct attitude. We continue to feel the influence which Jakarta has on the Vatican and, in consequence, the influence the Vatican exerts on the Church of East Timor. If the Church of East Timor rejected its role, its mission to defend the oppressed, to defend those who want justice and peace—I think that the Vatican would have had a very, very negative role in East Timor. What we said yesterday about the role of the Church in East Timor also comes up here, in the context of the Vatican's pressure on the Timorese clergy. The Vatican on many occasions intended to take up the role of mediator in the East Timor problem, and even today, we can say that the Vatican maintains this position. For us, it is a position not at all dignified.

RD: Mr Xanana, many people may argue that while what has happened in East Timor is unfortunate, it is now impossible for East Timor to be independent. Realistically, can you achieve your goals, and how long are you prepared to suffer the deprivations of a guerrilla life in the bush?

XG: Realistically speaking, I think that it would not be appropriate for me to tell you here whether I think it is possible for us to achieve independence. We are geared towards the defence of our rights, and realistically, all nations desire that. If many people argue that it is impossible for East Timor to be independent at the moment, I think that they see the question in a very simplistic way. The problem of East Timor is not a simple question for Indonesia and the rest of the world. We consider that we have that from good sources. We are prepared to continue to resist for as long as necessary, as long as Jakarta does not adopt a more flexible attitude, more just and more responsible. We already stated that we are prepared to accept our extermination, as long as Jakarta thinks that there is only one way to solve the problem, that there exists only the use of force to make us surrender. Surrender in terms of our people, in the sense that the problem is resolved through war, is only to resolve an important part of the Resistance. We are prepared for as long as necessary, as long as Jakarta does not change its attitude. In this sense, it is only after Jakarta shows more flexibility that I would realistically comment on how we could achieve independence.

Russell Anderson was one of several 'foreigners' who participated in the pro-independence rally on the fateful day, 12 November 1991 in Dili, the capital of East Timor. A media consultant, Mr Anderson had planned his visit to East Timor to coincide with the proposed visit of the UN/Portuguese Human Rights delegation. The following is a report of the massacre at the Santa Cruz cemetery submitted to Australia's Department of Foreign Affairs and Trade.

8

THE MASSACRE OF 12 NOVEMBER 1991

RUSSELL ANDERSON

I attended the Catholic Mass held at the Motael Church on 12 November at 6 am in commemoration of Sebastiao Gomes Rangel's death. Due to the large crowd, approximately 4000, the Mass was moved outdoors, to the west of the church but still within the church grounds. All was quiet. Open jeeps with military sitting in the back drove by and observed the crowd.

A demonstration was planned to start after the Mass. I believe the demonstration was organised because of the expectations held by the visit of the Parliamentary Delegation and the frustration felt due to its cancellation.

With the Mass over, people moved to the entrance way of the churchyard and onto the street.

Concealed banners were unfurled and hidden T-shirts with slogans were displayed. No military were to be seen.

As more and more banners unfurled into a sea of waving slogans, the crowd became vocal, with shouts of 'Viva Sebastiao, Viva Timor Leste, Independence, Viva Xanana'. The age grouping of the demonstrators was again mixed, but younger people were more visible in the front. The faces of the East Timorese lit up with an expression of life and vigour. Pent-up frustrations seemed to be released with a feeling of at last being able to show openly their cries for independence in the hope that the world was watching. I felt a nervousness, a sense of fear swell within me as I remembered I was in an occupied country. I also saw a nervous fear on people's faces as their eyes scanned the streets.

From the beginning, organised demonstration marshals were in attendance. It seemed the marshals were a youth group, distinguished by similar clothing. A marshal tried to operate a megaphone but had problems with feedback, creating a siren sound. Eventually he spoke to the crowd, who were still unfurling banners and starting to move along the planned route.

The march was led by two women carrying traditional baskets of flowers draped with knitted colourful cloth. From the beginning, marshals joined arms to contain the lead by slowing down enthusiastic banner wavers who wanted to run (not in any direction—it never looked like a riotous situation—they jogged and ran along the route). The marshals had a hard time, shouting at people to slow down and having to continually regroup.

I stayed in front of the march and had a hard time keeping up. In the simmering heat I was sweating and panting. The march proceeded along the harbourside. Ironically a military ship was preparing to dock. The seafront was lined with Indonesian ships, and the soldiers standing in the confines of the harbour looked on with disgust and hatred on their faces.

The demonstration went along Jl Gov. Alves Aldeia past the Governor's house and turned right into Jl Bispo Medeiros. Near the Resende New Inn Hotel, a road sign was banged about ten times by demonstrators as they passed. Marshals yelled and ran quickly to the spot and stayed there to make sure no-one else hit the sign.

The head of the march reached the roundabout and stopped (in front of the Telecommunication Centre). The marshals and others convinced a now exhausted lead to wait for the others.

While everyone waited at the roundabout, a man, hopping but supported by two others, approached me. I was eagerly shown his dripping bloodied calf and foot. A cloth had been tied around his upper calf. Not speaking the language, I could not understand their efforts to tell me what had happened.

The demonstration walked off again as one group. I found myself about 40 metres from the front. I had an audio-cassette recorder, and people were talking into the microphone.

I had noticed military at the barracks on the corner of Jl Av Sada Bandiera and Jl Bispo Medeiros.

Also near the Resende Hotel, I saw a lot of police at what appeared to be a main police station, on the right-hand side just after the roundabout. They had pistols in their pouches standing shoulder to shoulder with riot sticks at the ready. Every time I saw police or military, they stood well back from the crowd, between 30 and 50 metres away.

At this point the demonstrators, with a large Fretilin flag, waved and jumped enthusiastically, displaying their boldness.

I walked quickly through the crowd to get to the front again. By the time I got to the cemetery entrance, demonstrators were still climbing the wall for photographers to take pictures of the banners and their hands held high in a V-sign.

I gave a quick count as the crowd swelled in front of the cemetery. I estimated between 5000 and 6000 people. I remembered that at Sebastiao Gomes' funeral many people joined the procession at the cemetery. I put this down to the area being more residential and a safer place for more afraid people to join in.

In this residential area I saw a lot of people also standing beside the roadside. Some in government blue shirts and others in normal dress, while others stood further back near their houses. Very few offered gestures of solidarity or yells of support. It could have been a sign of what was to come. But it looked like the town of Dili was closed and everybody was there. A lot of school children still wearing their school uniforms joined in the march from a nearby school. School was coming out or it had closed because of the demonstration. Some children so small reached up and grabbed the microphone in my hand.

As the photos were taken of the people standing on the front cemetery wall, others moved inside to say prayers and lay flowers on Sebastiao Gomes' grave. Again the demonstration was organised. A marshal announced the ceremony of prayers and laying of flowers through a megaphone.

I stayed in front of the cemetery interviewing people in my broken Spanish about their feelings over the Parliamentary Delegation's cancellation. At the same time, I was noticing that most people were walking away continuing south down the road. I found out later that the demonstration was to continue in that direction to Bishop Belo's house and to Hotel Turismo, where UN delegate Mr Kooijman was staying. However, I felt that people were walking away through fear of the unknown. Of what might happen.

To the south of the demonstration the military were forming. The first truck was about 100 metres away from the diminishing crowd. These soldiers, in what I will call 'the first truck', wore a distinctive camouflaged uniform. These were the ones I saw methodically form the frontal assembly of the military attack and they were the ones who created the initial onslaught and deaths. Later that day this was confirmed by Americans Amy Goodman and Alan Nairn, who stood between the demonstrators and the soldiers during the massacre.

Two trucks stopped behind the 'first truck'. I noticed military marching down the road along the route the demonstration had just walked. The second truck, with a roar of its engine, drove towards the crowd but turned left. The crowd yelled. I felt there was excitement because the military were leaving. They, however, parked around the corner and started filing out of the truck.

I was frightened by the movement of the truck and noticed that most people had moved away. I walked through the crowd and stood at the back. At a quick count I estimated 1000 in front of the cemetery entrance way. More people were still inside the cemetery.

I observed the 'first truck' was almost empty, as the last soldiers unfiled and were forming a front line to confront the demonstration. More military were marching down the street, and I saw some military peeping around the cemetery wall from the north side. All of these military wore a green or dark-green uniform, except for the soldiers from the 'first truck'. It was clear the military were being commanded into a confrontational position.

From the back of the crowd I looked around for the others (the foreigners). I saw Bob Muntz. He stood just inside the cemetery. On seeing me he came out. We looked up to see the soldiers of the 'first truck'. They were now in three lines about fifteen abreast the street. From where I was standing, they looked quite close to the demonstrators, about 80 metres.

From the position I stood, I heard no warning to the crowd to disperse. Not that I would have understood the language, but any shout or order through a megaphone I would have heard and recognised. There was none. Not a single warning.

Bob Muntz and I decided we should leave. I had taken ten hurried steps north along the cemetery wall and was looking back to see the helmets of the military line bobbing up and down, jogging or marching towards the crowd. The crowd began to walk backwards, walk away. Some were already running.

Suddenly a few shots rang out, continued by an explosive volley of automatic rifle fire that persisted for two to three minutes. It sounded like the whole fifteen in the front row had their fingers pressed firmly on the trigger. They were firing directly into the crowd.

I ran, like everybody else. I took a quick glance around and saw people falling. I realised that I would be shot in the back if a bullet lodged into my body. Most people, especially in that initial burst of fire, would have been shot in the back, running away.

In my vicinity, most people ran around the south side of the cemetery to get out of the line of fire. Once around the corner I scampered through barbed-wire fences, frantically jumping over tin fences, following the rivers of people past houses and trees and more fences. I lost Bob Muntz early on, as I followed a different path. I was running in a zig-zag direction, going south-east.

My body began to convulse from fear and I was out of breath. I felt very sick and sat down, unable to run. There didn't seem to be as many shots being fired. Suddenly it started again from the direction of the cemetery, and some shots seemed much closer. I was up and running again. The soldiers were chasing us.

I changed direction many times as small bursts of fire went off, sometimes as close as 50 metres away. Others sounded further away. My eyes were wide open, watching the reaction and direction of the people running in front of and behind me. My eyes scanned any nook or cranny. I stayed alert for any movement that may have indicated soldiers with automatic rifles, possibly from any and all directions.

After at least fifteen minutes of running, I came to a bitumen road. The street was called Jl Belarmino Lobo and I wasn't far from the intersection with Jl Kuluhurr—I was so glad the military had not cordoned the whole area. I started walking as calmly as possible down the street. Hundreds of people were fleeing across the road. Not far from the corner, people stricken with fear sought my protection by walking with me. One person grabbed my wrist tightly and wouldn't let go, saying 'come house with me'. By that stage I was under no illusion that my white vulnerable skin could protect any of these East Timorese people. Nevertheless he was terrified, so I said I would go with him. We both approached the corner, shaking. We looked up and down. No military. We continued down the street.

Taxis drove past and people yelled at them to stop. As the taxis came to a tentative halt, my attached companion ran towards the taxi, like about twenty others. The taxi filled in seconds. People climbed on top and hung from the doors and rear bumper bar. As the taxi drove off, people were flung and fell to the ground. This happened three more times as I walked down the street towards my hotel.

Back at the hotel there was no-one. I was terrified, pacing up and down. I waited. I had a shower and changed my clothes, which had been ripped by the barbed-wire fences.

After waiting half an hour, I decided to ride around town on a motorbike. Looking back now, this was madness, but I had to know what happened to the others. I turned the bike up Jl Belarmino Lobo, the street I had walked down. Noticing there were no military I rode cautiously up the street. About three-quarters of the way, twenty soldiers rounded the corner. Thinking I would look suspicious turning the bike around, I continued.

The soldiers noticed me and glared. Some of them were looking in houses, around corners and over fences. Some had their automatic weapons in a position to fire and others had them strapped over their shoulders. I thought I would be safe: I'd changed clothes, was wearing a helmet and had sunglasses on. I gave a warm 'good morning' and a smile. The glare on most of them changed to a smile and I motored on.

Turning right, I saw soldiers all along the street. It looked like a mopping-up operation. They, too, were searching the area. I noticed but did not stare at three bodies in front of a house about 30 metres off the road.

Upon reaching the next corner, I gave way to two military trucks packed with soldiers. I again waved and smiled, but soldiers in the second truck started yelling and pointing at me. The driver didn't stop. Turning right again, I was close to the cemetery. There were three speeding trucks heading towards the cemetery so I diverted and went back to the hotel.

Bob Muntz was back. Bob had a wound on his arm. Blood seeped through his shirt. He told me that Kamal had been shot several times, and had been found bleeding profusely in the street. Kamal had been taken to the military hospital. There was no time for sadness. We had to think. We still feared for our lives. How do we get to the hospital to see him? What about the others? What about the East Timorese?

John Pilger, internationally renowned and critically acclaimed Australian journalist based in London, has been a war correspondent, filmmaker and playwright. His exposés during the Vietnam War, of the nightmare of Pol Pot's Cambodia and of the Indonesian genocide in East Timor have become causes célèbres. *Among his many awards are the International Reporter of the Year and the United Nations Association Media Peace Prize. The following is a reproduction of the chapter* A Land of Crosses *from John Pilger's book* Distant Voices *explaining how the documentary film* Death of a Nation *(John Pilger and David Munro) had been planned and actually made. The film* Death of a Nation, *shown on television in many countries from 1994, increased activism and interest in East Timor's struggle for freedom and remains a testimony of a 'largely forgotten history' and 'enduring evidence' of the culpability of those responsible, both as participants and as disaffected bystanders, of the genocide of more than one-third of the population of East Timor.*

9

A LAND OF CROSSES

JOHN PILGER

David and I flew from Sydney to Bali with a plane-load of happy Australian tourists. We caught an internal flight to Kupang in Indonesian West Timor. Not far from where Captain Bligh had sought refuge after the mutiny on the *Bounty*, we found 'Teddy's Bar'. We explained to Teddy about 'Adventure Tours', that we needed a four-wheel-drive vehicle and a driver who knew the mountains in the east. He could provide both, but reminded us that foreigners needed special documentation to cross the border. We paid him and left.

It was early Sunday morning as the road reached down to the sea, and the border came into view. The bags with the cameras were beneath the seats. We wound up the tinted windows, and I lay down in the back. Ahead of us was a minibus spilling out its occupants for inspection of their papers. 'Don't stop,' we directed the Timorese driver. 'Drive around it.' The police on duty had walked back to their cabin. We accelerated and were through.

Now the faces changed. In the west of the island people had smiled and waved; here, they almost never did. On the roadside they invariably looked away. The young and the old did not stare; young men consciously turned their backs.

Working with the aeronautical map and its blank spaces, we turned inland to get away from the military route. On the horizon was a line of black smoke and fire. This was the traditional method of agriculture known as slash-and-burn, wherein the burnt scrub temporarily enriches the soil. The effect was three-dimensional, a harsh, almost menacing landscape. Yet we had only just climbed away from the coastal belt, with its lines of sugar palms. Ahead was a plateau of savannah that looked like the vast outback of Australia. Ghost gums rose out of grass almost as tall, then this changed without notice to a forest of dead, petrified trees: black needles through which skeins of fine white sand drifted, like mist. On the edge of this stood the surreal crosses.

They are almost everywhere; great black crosses etched against the sky, crosses on peaks, crosses in tiers on the hillsides, crosses beside the road, overlooking white slabs. I have seen graves and crosses like these in the north of Portugal, where they are stark symbols of the rhythm of life and death in an impoverished corner of Europe. There, you pass them without comment. In East Timor they litter the earth and crowd the eye. Walk into the scrub and they are there, always it seems, on the edge, a riverbank, an escarpment, commanding all before them.

The inscriptions on some are normal: those of generations departed in proper time and sequence. But look at the dates of these, and you see that they are all prior to 1975, when proper time and sequence ended. Look at the dates on most of them and they reveal the extinction of whole families, wiped out in the space of a year, a month, a day. 'R.I.P. Mendonca, Crismina, 7.6.77 ... Mendonca, Filismina, 7.6.77 ... Mendonca, Adalino, 7.6.77 ... Mendonca, Alisa, 7.6.77 ... Mendonca, Rosa, 7.6.77 ... Mendonca, Anita, 7.6.77 ...'

I had with me a hand-drawn map of where to find a mass grave where some of the murdered of the 1991 massacre in the Santa Cruz cemetery had been dumped; I had no idea that much of the country was a mass grave, marked by paths that end abruptly, and fields inexplicably bulldozed, and earth inexplicably covered with tarmac; and by the legions of crosses that march all the way from Tata Mai Lau, the highest peak, 10,000 feet above sea level, down to Lake Tacitlou where a Calvary line of crosses looks across to where the Pope said Mass in 1989 in full view of a crescent of hard, salt sand beneath which, say local people, lie human remains.

We approached Balibo, where the Australian television teams had died. We could not see the whitewashed house on which Greg Shackleton had painted 'Australia' before the murders. Shirley Shackleton also has been unable to find it and believes it has been demolished. The main road wound past the church where Shirley had planted a tree for Greg in 1989. She had struggled to get permission for this, with the Indonesians saying no as it would, they said, admit liability for the murders. Finally, a priest offered the yard behind his church, and prepared a plot; and Shirley was allowed to plant a sapling with Indonesian troops surrounding her, sealing off the vicinity.

'They had not allowed any Timorese to be there,' she said. 'But as I kneeled, saying a few words to Greg, the most wonderful singing washed over me. On the other side of the road, a young people's choir had timed its practice to my being there. I shall never forget those beautiful voices. They came through the barrier the Indonesians had set up between us, and they comforted me. You see, that's how the Resistance works; everything is pre-arranged but never appears to be. They will never be defeated.'

The road out of Balibo snaked up through the mountains, with the four-wheel-drive easing us around the strewn tree trunks with inches to spare and boulders suspended above as if on invisible wire. 'Gerry', our driver, pumped the brake pedal and leaned back on the handbrake like you do on the oars of a dinghy. It was becoming clear why the untried Indonesian army had taken years to get the better of Fretilin. This was guerrilla terrain, as difficult for outsiders to negotiate as any I have ever known.

Coming down the spine of the mountains, we were swallowed by folds of baked eroded red earth and by the silence. People seemed absent; but they were there. From the highest crest the road plunged into a ravine that led us to a river bed, then deserted us. The four-wheel-drive forded the river and heaved out on the other side, where a boy sat motionless and mute, his eyes following us. Behind him was a village, overlooked by the now familiar rows of white-washed slabs and black crosses. We were probably the first out-siders the people here had seen for a very long time. The diffident expressions, long cultivated for the Indonesians, changed to astonishment. We had entered, without knowing, a kind of prison.

The village straddled the road, laid out like a military barracks with a parade ground and a police post at either end. Unusually, the militia were trusted Timorese. The remoteness might explain this; the Indonesians remain terrified of Fretilin. That week a patrol of nine Indonesian soldiers had been ambushed and killed. People were moved here from their homes so they could be easily con-trolled. The village was a 'resettlement centre', similar to the 'strat-egic hamlets' invented by the Americans in Vietnam as a means of separating the population from the guerrillas. To the Timorese, the 'control areas', as the army calls them, are little better than concentration camps, which they cannot leave without a 'travel pass'. As a consequence, their ability to grow food is extremely limited. In the late 1970s and early 1980s famine claimed many thousands of lives, on a scale likened by international relief officials to the war-related cataclysms that had hit Biafra in the mid-1960s and Cambodia in 1979–80.

Although we saw no starvation, many people were terribly malnourished.[1] Camps such as this are also known as 'model plantations' and produce mostly cash crops for an export trade controlled by an Indonesian company, P. T. Denok, which was set up by generals close to Suharto. P. T. Denok monopolises the trade in sandalwood, cumin, copra and cloves; all the coffee grown in Timor, one of the finest Arabica coffees in the world, is controlled by the generals' front company.[2]

After we had turned south, towards Suai, we saw other camps where many of the faces were Javanese: the product of the 'transmigration programme' designed to unravel the fabric of Timorese life and culture and eventually to reduce the indigenous population to a minority. Meanwhile, the East Timorese are themselves encouraged to 'migrate' to Irian Jaya, Sumatra and West Kalimantan, where there is work and where they remain permanently displaced. From a distance, I watched a flag-raising ceremony in one of these 'villages'. Javanese cheer-leaders led a motley group of farmers, who were forced to stand to attention and cry out their allegiance in Bahasa Indonesia, a foreign language.

In Suai, the centre for oil drilling on the south coast, militarism seemed to invade all life. Traffic stopped for marching schoolgirls, jogging teachers and anthem-singing postmen ('*Tanah Airku*: My fatherland Indonesia'). Billboards announced the 'correct' way to live each day 'in the spirit of Moral Training'. In an Orwellian affront to the Timorese, one billboard told them, 'Freedom is the right of all nations', quoting Indonesia's own declaration of independence. This is known as the 'New Order'.

'It is the Indonesian civilisation we are bringing [to East Timor],' said the Indonesian military commander in 1982. 'And it is not easy to civilise a backward people.'[3] 'Feeble mentality is still very evident among the Timorese,' explained the Indonesian Armed

Forces magazine. '[Such] low social, economic, mental conditions are the source of many negative features because they result in extremely inappropriate thought processes and experiences. The *Binpolda* [a kind of military brainwashing squad] have a great role to play in building village society if this is to proceed in accord with the programmes that have been decided upon. All the more is this so in East Timor where society so greatly yearns to be guided and directed in all spheres of life. Guiding the people is a process of communication whereas communication means conveying ideas or concepts for the purpose of creating uniformity.'[4]

Timorese occupy few jobs other than as drivers, waitresses and broom-pushers. In a café in Suai the Javanese owner, a portly young woman, flirted with lonely Javanese soldiers while a Timorese girl cooked, served and swept. As the Javanese emptied their bowls of noodles, they snapped their fingers and the girl cleaned around them, giggling nervously. On the wall was a gallery of posters of the Indonesian generals shot in the 1965 'communist coup'. They are the official martyrs of the New Order. 'If President Suharto hadn't rescued the nation, and beaten the communists,' we were told, 'Indonesia would have broken up into many pieces.' This is the state's line, repeated incessantly on television and in schools.

That the 'martyred' generals died in factional fighting within the military, leaving Suharto to mount a real coup and the extermination campaign that was the precursor to East Timor's agony, is a truth uttered only at great personal risk. In the New Order, Fretilin guerrillas are 'separatist delinquents' who 'threaten the break-up of the fatherland' and must be 'wiped out' by the 'heroic people's army'.

Thousands were massacred in Suai in the late 1970s, their bodies dumped on the oil-blackened coastline. The few Timorese who spoke to us publicly, drifting by the parked four-wheel-drive and muttering snatches of Portuguese and English out of the sides of their mouths, were terrified and, of course, extraordinarily brave. Every street has a military facade, with a variety of units, mostly special forces, housed in former Portuguese villas or prefabricated houses, announced by large signs and military insignia. Next to the hostel where we stayed were the 'red berets', whose record of slaughter is documented. In the heat I slept very little, covered in an insect repellent so strong it melted the plastic case of my watch. The sound of the night was the soldiers next door playing country and western tapes, accompanied by the melodic humming of mosquitoes that carried the falciparum strain of malaria, which can be fatal.

'Before the invasion we lived a typical island life, very peaceful,' said Abel.[*] 'People were always very hospitable to foreigners. Villagers would go about their daily lives, working in rice fields without constantly looking over their shoulders, worrying about the military or guns. I could get up at any time and come back home at any time, go down to the river, catch prawns or go hunting without any restriction. I had to go to school to learn Portuguese. We had to learn to lead a double life; you go to school to communicate with the Portuguese, but once you are in a village you are totally within the traditional village life. But if the Portuguese had done what the Indonesians have done, the whole of East Timor would have been populated by white Portuguese. That's not to say there was no brutality from the Portuguese. Of course any colonial situation is always brutal. But I think we were happy, yes I think so.

'It is difficult to describe the change since then, the darkness over us. Of fifteen in my immediate family only three are left: myself, my mother and a brother who was shot and crippled. My village was the last Fretilin base to fall to the Indonesians in 1979. There was a massive bombardment. People said that all trees were blown off the rocks, whole rocks became white. Because the land was very fertile; I mean you can grow almost anything there; lots

---

[*]The identities of most of the Timorese interviewed inside and outside East Timor are disguised, including those who insisted they could be identified, saying they had 'nothing to lose'. The interviews were conducted by myself, and Max Stahl and Ben Richards.

of people from the lowlands went up there for protection. So it was overpopulated and very soon there wasn't enough to sustain the number of people that were hiding there. Disease, and slow starvation, also took a lot of people. I told you about my family, but the estimate is that our clan has been reduced from 5000 to 500.

'Up until 1985 or 1986 most of our people were concentrated in what they called the central control areas, we lived in concentration camps for a long, long time. Only in the last three or four years have some of us been allowed to return home, but we can be moved again at any time. We are only allowed to go to specific areas to grow food. We have to go there at a certain time in the morning and come back at a certain time in the afternoon.

'Any step away from those guidelines is considered suspect. Indonesians use local people to spy on the others. So there's a constant fear of somebody always looking over your shoulder. People usually know who the spies are and they learn to deal with it. Certain things are not to be said widely even within the family. People have to be careful what they say about the Indonesians, they have got to pretend that everything is OK, just accept what the Indonesians are doing to them. That is part of finding a way to survive for the next day. But a human body and mind have limitations and can only take so much. Once it boils over, people must come out and protest and say things which mean they will find themselves dead the next day. I suppose you can compare us to animals. When animals are put in a cage they always try to escape. In human beings it's much worse. I mean, we the people in East Timor call it the biggest prison island in the world. You must understand that. For us who live here, it's hell.'

Was it Primo Levi who said that the worst moment in the Nazi death camps was the recurring fear that people would not believe him when he told them what had happened, that they would turn away, shaking their heads? This 'radical gap' between victim and listener, as psychiatrists call it, is suffered *en masse* by the East Timorese, especially the exiled communities. 'Who knows about our country?' they ask constantly. 'Who can imagine the enormity of what has happened to us?'

'I was born in Timor in 1963,' said Constancio. 'When Indonesia invaded I was twelve years old, and I went to the jungle. I was on the run all the time. Then I crept back to Dili to see my family, and I was caught. I was only fourteen. I was tortured, but I survived. In 1990 I helped an Australian lawyer, Robert Domm, meet Xanana Gusmao, our Resistance leader. After that they caught me again. It was my birthday; and they tortured me all over my body, so that blood came out from my mouth and my nose and my ears. There were so many of them, hitting me, in front and in the back, and down here in my genitals, many times, so many times. They'd start at nine o'clock in the morning and did not finish until midnight. They let me go; but I heard that I was supposed to be arrested again, at two o'clock in the afternoon. I had no chance to say goodbye to my wife. That was over two years ago.'

'Have you seen her since?' I asked.

'No, not once.'

'Do you have children?'

'When I went into hiding, my wife was six months pregnant. I have a son. But I have never seen him, except this one photo I have just received. I look at it all the time ...'

'What makes you keep on fighting?'

'Because of our *right* to independence. This is a universal right; and a third of us have died for this right. Don't pity me. Think of my wife. They keep on interrogating her, torturing her psychologically. This is her daily bread, and the daily bread of our people, and it is mine, too.'

From the day of the invasion Fretilin gave the Indonesians a shock. For two years those whom Jakarta had dismissed as 'primitives' held the interior to which most of the people had fled. It was only the arrival of Western military equipment, chiefly low-flying aircraft, that changed the course of the war. Otherwise Fretilin might have forced the Indonesians to negotiate their way out of East Timor.

Indeed, in 1983 Fretilin forces were in such command of most areas outside the towns that the Indonesians agreed to a cease-fire. Today, there are probably no more than 400 guerrillas under arms, yet they ensure that four Indonesian battalions do nothing but pursue them. Moreover, they are capable of multiplying themselves within a few days, for they are the locus of a clandestine resistance that reaches into every district and has actually grown in strength over years. In this way they continue to deny the fact of *integrasi*— integration—with Indonesia.

Domingos is 40 years old and has been in the jungle since 1983. 'My wife was tortured and burnt with cigarettes,' he said. 'She was also raped many times. She is now in Kraras. In September this year [1993] the Indonesians sent the whole population of the village to find us. My wife came to me and said, "I don't want to see your face because I have been suffering too much ..." At first I thought she was rejecting me, but it was the opposite; she was asking me to fight on, to stay out of the village and not to be captured and never to surrender. She said to me, "You get yourself killed and I shall grieve for you, but I don't want to see you in their hands. I'll never accept you giving up!" I looked at her, and she was sad. I asked her if we could live together after the war, and she said softly, "Yes, we can." She then walked away, back to Kraras.'

Kraras is known by the Timorese as the 'village of the widows' because of the slaughter that took place there. During the summer of 1983 a whole community of 287 people was massacred here. One of them was the man who saved the Australian Commando Steve Stevenson's life, Celestino dos Anjos, who, like most of them, was forced within his family to dig his own grave, then shot. I found Celestino's name on a list compiled in Portuguese by a priest who had passed it to Max Stahl. In a meticulous hand he recorded the name, age, cause of death and date and place of death of every one of these people murdered by the Indonesian army in the district of Bilbeo. In the last column he identified the battalion responsible for every murder.

Every time I pick up this list, I find it difficult to put down, as if each death is fresh on the page. Like the ubiquitous crosses, it records the Calvary of whole families, and bears witness to genocide ... Feliciano Gomes, aged 50, Jacob Gomes, aged 50, Antonio Gomes, aged 37, Marcelino Gomes, aged 29, Joao Gomes, aged 33, Miguel Gomes, aged 51, Domingos Gomes, aged 30 ... Domingos Gomes, aged 2 ... 'shot'.

So far I have counted forty families, including many children: Kai and Olo Bosi, aged 6 and 4 ... 'shot' ... Marito Soares, aged one year ... 'shot' ... Cacildo dos Anjos, aged 2 ... 'shot'. He must have been Celestino's grandson. There are babies on the list as young as three months. At the end of each page, the priest imprinted his name with a rubber stamp, which he asked not to be publicised 'in the interests of personal security'. Using a typewriter whose ribbon had seen better days, he addressed this eloquent, angry appeal to the world:

'The international community continues to miss the point in the case of East Timor. There is only one crime, only one criminal. To the capitalist governors, Timor's petroleum smells better than Timorese blood and tears. How long do the Indonesians think they can imprison, torture and kill? This is what the Timorese people in their concentration camps have asked themselves since 1975. It has always been a question without an answer.

'It even seems as if it is the United Nations itself that is easing the path of the aggressor, giving it the time and conditions necessary to execute the ethnic and cultural genocide of the Timorese people and, finally, declare that East Timor is definitely integrated into the Indonesian Republic. Unfortunately the UN and the international community are the only viable solution for this tragedy but they have to be consistent with their condemnation of the 1975 invasion, and not leave it to the following year, since each year the level of extermination increases.

'So who will take the truth to the world? Sometimes the press and even the international leaders give the impression that it is not human rights, justice and truth that are paramount in international relations, but the power behind a crime that has the privilege and the power of decision. It is evident that the invading Government would never have committed such a crime, if it had not received favourable guarantees from Governments that should have a more mature sense of international responsibility. Governments must now urgently consider the case of East Timor, with seriousness and truth. They must insist and advocate full Human Rights: the right of the Timorese people to independence.'

We drove into Dili in the early afternoon. It was quiet: not the quiet of a town asleep in the sun but of a place where something cataclysmic had happened and which was not immediately evident. Fine white colonial buildings faced a waterfront lined with trees and a promenade fitted with ancient stone benches. At first the beauty of this seemed uninterrupted. From the lighthouse, past Timor's oldest church, the Motael, to the long-arched facade of the Governor's offices and the four ancient cannon with the Portuguese royal seal, the sea was polished all the way to Atauro Island where the Portuguese administration had fled in 1975. Then, just beyond a marble statue of the Virgin Mary, the eye collided with rusting landing craft strewn along the beach. They had been left as a reminder of the day Indonesian marines came ashore and killed the first people they saw: women and children running down the beach, offering them food and water, as frightened people do.

At dawn the next day we walked the length of the beach to the stone pier where people were brought to be shot and their families and friends ordered to count as each body fell into the water. I wanted to record a tribute to Roger East, the Australian journalist who went to East Timor early in November 1975, and stayed to his death. East had been outraged at the killing of Greg Shackleton and his colleagues and sympathetic to Fretilin. Before leaving Darwin he told his sister, 'The people have been betrayed. Someone's got to go and get the truth out.'[5] His brother urged him to get a weapon, but East replied that he was 'too old for that' and had 'lived too long with just a typewriter'.[6]

Arriving in Dili he set up an East Timor news agency and made many friends among the Timorese, who appreciated his dry humour. When the Australian Government urged its nationals to leave Dili, he was the only one to stay, in spite of the fact that Indonesian propaganda had called him a 'communist' and promised that he would 'share the fate' of the television crews. As the invasion began and Fretilin withdrew to the east of the city, East remained in the Hotel Turismo, on the seafront, typing a despatch which he sent to Australian Associated Press-Reuter in Darwin. Inexplicably, it was never used.

Roger East was caught in the street by Indonesian troops, bound with wire and dragged to the pier where he could hear the executions taking place. According to two eyewitnesses, he kept up a stream of rich, Australian abuse until the point of his death. He was told to face the sea; he refused and was shot in the face. His body fell, with all the others, into the 'sea of blood'. An Indonesian report later claimed East was an armed revolutionary. After that, all knowledge of him was denied. Like the aftermath of the Balibo murders, an inquiry by the Australian Department of Foreign Affairs came to nothing, and not a word of protest was lodged publicly with Jakarta.

Staying at the Hotel Turismo, I could not get Roger East out of my mind. My room was a haven for cockroaches and spiders, and clearing a path through them was a prerequisite for a trip to the cesspit of a bathroom. I thought about him in this squalid and menacing place as he weighed up whether to stay or go. What would I have done? I would have got out. Roger East's memory deserves more than his Government's wretched obsequiousness to his killers.

Today, the Turismo is where Indonesian officers, their hangers-on and local informers can be found. 'Who are you?' we were asked at the reception. 'I see you are a company director. What is your company?'

'Adventure Tours,' I replied.

When I recorded a 'camera piece' that morning on the beach near the pier, under the noses of a group of Indonesian soldiers and with the camera only partly concealed, I could hear an echo of my words and felt deep inside me a cold fear I had not previously known.

We were now being watched constantly and decided to drive back into the mountains. Climbing the steep road out of Dili, we passed a war memorial built by the Australian veterans of the Timor campaign against the Japanese. Its dedication read, 'To the Portuguese from Minho [a northern Portuguese province] to Timor.' The memorial was intended for native Timorese who gave their lives for the Australians, but the inscription does not mention the word 'Timorese', because all Timorese were supposed to be Portuguese citizens.

Low cloud engulfed us, with crosses marking every bend, it seemed, all the way to Aileu. 'When they finally forced Fretilin to withdraw from Aileu in 1975,' wrote James Dunn, 'Indonesian troops, in a brutal public spectacle, machine-gunned the remaining population of the town, except for children under the age of four, who were sent back to Dili in trucks. These infant survivors were ultimately to be placed in an orphanage near Jakarta, where the "poor victims of the Fretilin terror" were to become the subject of the charitable indulgence of Tien Harto (Suharto's wife) and her coterie of bored wives of the affluent and powerful in the Indonesian capital.'[7]

In the centre of Aileu is the mass grave of victims of the Japanese in 1942. On the hill above are statues depicting God and Jesus, smiling and surreal, and more crosses leading to yet another Calvary. There is no sign of the Indonesian massacre. From behind the tombs of the 1942 memorial, we attempt to evade local spies while filming marching students; once again, a whole town seemed to be marching and honouring the flag of its executioners. I had yet to become accustomed to this irony; it was as if prisoners were taking their exercise in a prison yard hung with bunting and accompanied by a brass band. 'Welcome to Timor,' said an old Timorese man in English sitting on the steps of a café. He stood and lunged for my hand. 'Welcome to the land of *free* people!' At this, he gave out a fine, false laugh, like a cackle. The Javanese owner of the café tapped his finger to his head and said, 'He's okay, just a little mad.'

None of the shops in Aileu is owned by a Timorese; all seemed to be Javanese. As one of the principal sponsors of the 'trans-migration programme', the World Bank should be pleased with its success in transforming towns like Aileu. The World Bank is also the main backer of Indonesia's 'family planning programme' in East Timor. According to a senior bank official, 'there is no inher-ent contradiction between the Indonesian Government's population and transmigration programme. We believe that family planning is capable of providing important economic and social benefits to all concerned.'[8]

When the World Bank opened its 'family planning' head-quarters in Dili in 1980 the puppet Governor of East Timor, Mario Carrascalao, was more to the point. The aim of the programme, he said, was 'to prevent an increase in the population of the province'.[9] For the regime, there is, of course, no 'inherent contradiction' in reducing the East Timorese population while increasing the immi-grant population. A senior Indonesian officer told Bishop Belo, 'We only need your land. We don't need people like you Timorese.'[10]

'In the village clinics,' said Christina, 'anything is possible. You have to do what the Indonesian doctors say. Many of the women are injected with Depo-Provera without knowing what it is. Women have been sterilised when they come to the clinic for something else, even for medicine for their babies. They do not know what is happening, or they are told that it's okay by the *babinses* [the guidance officials, or brainwashers, in the resettlement camps]. We have lost so many people killed by the Indonesians, we must give birth in order to compensate or our population will fade away. We are not like any developing country. It's a mistake to think of us that way. We need to increase our population, just to survive ... Yes, we know what they are doing to us; we can't fight this kind of attack on us with guns.'

In 1989, General Suharto received the United Nations Fund for Population Activities Prize, which praised his 'support for family planning'.

We drove east, towards Baucau. It was here in 1981 that *Operasi Keamanan* ('Operation Security') had its most devastating effects. Timorese between the ages of eight and fifty were recruited to form human chains across the island, known as the 'fence of legs'. The object was to flush out Fretilin guerrillas, with Indonesian troops following on behind and pursuing them into 'human corrals' where they could be captured or killed. A man who survived one of those 'corrals' reported, 'It was a ghastly sight. There were a great many bodies, men, women, little children strewn everywhere, unburied, along the riverbanks, on the mountain slopes. I would estimate that about 10,000 people were killed in that operation.'[11] Two years later a 'scorched earth' policy brought repeated bombing raids. This was known as *Operasi Persatuan*, or 'Operation Unity'.

I was struck by the similarity of the landscape to parts of central Vietnam, between Quang Ngai and Song Tra, where the Americans dropped huge quantities of chemical defoliants, poisoning the soil and food chain and radically altering the environment. Indonesians also used chemical defoliants, most of which they made themselves. Today, as in Vietnam, the trees are twisted into grotesque shapes and there is no cultivation. This is known in East Timor as the 'dead earth', a place whose former inhabitants are either dead or 'relocated'.

We reached Baucau in darkness. Baucau is a former Portuguese resort that once proclaimed a certain melancholy style and where holiday flights used to arrive from Australia. ('Come and get a whiff of the Mediterranean!' invited a 1960 Trans Australia

Airways brochure.) Today the airport is an Indonesian air force base and Baucau a military 'company town', surrounded by barracks. In the town square are two enormous statues of Timorese in 'native costume', their hands raised towards an Indonesian flag. The statues, made from reinforced concrete, are crumbling in the tropical climate, their expressions unsmiling and wan.

Behind them stands the Hotel Flamboyant. We climbed the long staircase in darkness and called out. A Timorese man emerged from the shadows, limping and coughing terribly. 'What do you want?' he asked. 'A room?' we said. He turned and struggled along a deserted colonnade, and flung open two doors. There was no water, a fan that turned now and then, a mattress coated with fungus and a window without glass. 'There are no mosquitoes in Baucau,' he said mysteriously. He left us with our echoes. The Hotel Flamboyant was, until recently, a torture centre.

'I was arrested by the military command in Baucau, KODIM1628,' said Julio. 'They used electric shocks on me. They attached a wire at the top of my feet, toes, fingers and ears, then started operating the current. I passed out. Then they attached negative and positive wires at the top of my toe, finger and actually inside my ear. I passed out again.'

'My father was arrested several times,' said Alberto. 'He refused to join the new administration. They took him to the police headquarters, then sent for me and my sisters and brothers to see him being tortured. They said to us that if we followed our father's example, this is what would happen to us. They beat him with iron bars at first, then they did something to him that you learn in karate. They put their hands on his stomach and manipulated his organs and intestines. Indonesian soldiers are trained in these methods. They did this to him in four sessions. Then he got a disease in his stomach and vomited a lot of blood. That was 1983.'

'When I was young,' said Agio, 'the military came to my house, and killed my two brothers in front of my eyes. Before they killed them, they prepared a hole and persecuted them. When they did it, they pulled out a heart from one of them and showed it to us. "That's a guilty, dirty, filthy heart", they said to us. "You cannot be like this because this is the heart of a communist ..." '

Torture appears to have been systematic throughout East Timor. The Indonesian military publishes an erudite manual on the subject, entitled 'Established Procedure for the Interrogation of Prisoners'. Section 13 reads, 'Hopefully, interrogation accompanied by the use of violence will not take place except in certain circumstances when the person being interrogated is having difficulty telling the truth ... If it proves necessary to use violence, make sure that there are no people around ... to see what is happening ... Avoid taking photographs showing torture in progress [such as when] people are being subjected to electric current, when they have been stripped naked etc. Remember do not have such photographic documentation developed outside East Timor which could then be made available to the public by irresponsible elements. It is better to make attractive photographs, such as shots taken while eating together with the prisoner, or shaking hands with those who have just come down from the bush, showing them in front of a home, and so on ... If necessary, the interrogation should be repeated over and over again using a variety of questions, so that, eventually, the correct conclusion can be drawn from all these different replies.'[12]

As John Taylor has pointed out, the torture manual's definition of interrogation, of drawing a 'correct conclusion' from replies which constantly denied this conclusion's inversion of reality, could also have been taken as a guide for the Indonesian military's relations with its Western backers.[13] Foreign 'fact finding' delegations have occasionally visited East Timor under military sponsorship and have been accommodated in the Hotel Flamboyant, presumably in a wing undisturbed by the activities of its torturers. One such delegation was led by Bill Morrison, former Defence Minister in the Whitlam Government and later Australian

Ambassador to Indonesia. The Indonesians allowed the Morrison visit mostly on their terms, including the use of military interpreters. 'The delegation', wrote John Taylor, 'duly recorded that the military had invaded East Timor to quell chaos, that Suharto was reluctant to intervene, that the vast majority of people voted for the military in the elections, that food shortages were due to the long dry seasons and even that malnutrition was due to "a lack of variety in diet".'[14]

Morrison arrived during the cease-fire in 1983, which allowed him to meet a group of Fretilin representatives who had flagged down his convoy. The Indonesian interpreters so distorted his conversation with the guerrillas that all references to atrocities and a nearby concentration camp were omitted. That night the delegation stayed at the Hotel Flamboyant and recorded in their report: 'Back in Baucau the delegation leader informed other members of the delegation of the meeting [with Fretilin] before settling down to a night of bridge.'[15]

Morrison had promised the Fretilin group, 'Somehow we will get a message to you ...'[16] No message was ever sent; Morrison's report claimed that 'the [Indonesian] administration in East Timor appears to be in effective control of all settled areas';[17] yet his own encounter with Fretilin had contradicted that. On his return to Australia, Morrison was asked to comment on a report from Fretilin that the Indonesians were about to break the cease-fire and attack the population. 'We have just been there,' he said, 'and seen with our own eyes, and we have discussed with the military commander ... Certainly nothing we saw, nothing we were told there, gives any credence to that report.'[18]

A few days later, the Indonesian chief-of-staff, Benny Murdani, launched a new terror campaign, using American and British aircraft. 'This time no fooling around,' he said, 'we're going to hit them without mercy.'[19]

When David and I returned to Dili it was evident that our cover was wearing thin. At the New Resende Inn the same spook was waiting for us as we came and left. Perhaps it was David's highly convincing public conversation with a Javanese travel agent about the 'tourist potential of East Timor' that bought us extra time. Talking to any Timorese was extremely risky. A group of American Congressional aides had been and gone, aware that the streets had been 'cleaned' for their visit, as the Timorese say, with some 3000 arrests and expulsions from Dili. The nights now belonged to truck-loads of black-helmeted troops.

When an old man approached me in the hotel courtyard, asking me in a whisper to contact his family in exile in Australia, I walked away at first, then turned back and drew him into a passageway. 'All my children are in Darwin,' he said, 'I sent them out. It cost a lot in bribes. Now I long to see them.' I asked him if he had ever tried to leave. He shook his head and ran a finger across his throat. 'Will you take a letter for me?' he asked. 'Post it anywhere but here. They open everything. I have not had a letter for eight years.' I agreed to collect the letter that evening.

Across the road from the Roman Catholic cathedral three security policemen stopped a woman as she opened the gate, and demanded her name. She kept going to the bishop's door. Brave woman. The Church in East Timor is, to the generals, a greater enemy than Fretilin, in spite of the Pope's apparent silence on the genocide during his visit to East Timor in 1989. According to members of the East Timorese Church, the Pope was 'poorly briefed' prior to his visit. Once there, they said, he spoke generally about human rights and has since maintained the independence of the East Timorese Church by not recognising it as part of the Indonesian Bishops' Conference. Yet he also gave public commun-ion to General Murdani, who led the invasion and whose troops did much of the killing.

The massacre of hundreds of young people who marched peace-fully to the Santa Cruz cemetery on 12 November, 1991, remains like a presence in Dili. They had set out to place flowers on the grave of a student, Sebastiao Gomes, who had been shot dead at the church two weeks earlier. When they reached the cemetery, they were shot down by waiting troops, or they were stabbed or battered to death. There was no provocation. What was different about this massacre was that foreigners were present, including one with a video camera. However, it was after the foreigners had been arrested and expelled from East Timor (one, a New Zealander, was murdered; several others were badly beaten) that a more typical, unreported massacre took place.

'After the killings in the cemetery,' said Mario, 'I escaped being hit. So I pretended to be dead. The soldiers came and searched all the bodies and me, and hit me on the head so that I bled. They threw me with the other bodies on to a pick-up truck. They took us to the mortuary, locked the door and went upstairs. Some of my friends were still alive, crying. They were calling out for water. I told them the only water was dirty, so we must pray together. I saw with my very eyes that among the bodies were children and old people. Suddenly I heard steps approaching and I lay down again, pretending to be dead. Two soldiers came in. One of them picked up a big stone, and the other got a tablet from a jar. They then said out loud that if anyone was able to walk they had to stand up.

'When some of my friends got up, one of them was hit on the head by the soldier with the stone; he died later. I heard the blows, and it sounded like coconuts cracking as they fall from a tree on the ground. As they got close to me I stood up so suddenly that the soldiers were taken aback. I told them I was an informer, that I really worked for them. I didn't want to lie, but this saved my life. The soldier with the jar of tablets was making the injured take them, and he gave me one; I think it was yellow; it made me vomit.' (We passed several of these tablets to Scotland Yard's forensic laboratories in London, which found them to be paraformaldehyde. When vaporised this is a powerful disinfectant and must not, under any circumstances, be ingested.)

José, a Timorese orderly at the military hospital in Dili, took up the story. 'I was at the hospital receiving the dead and wounded,' he said. 'Most of them were dead, but some were pretending to be. The soldiers didn't unload the bodies one by one; they just pushed them down on the ground. If they spotted one that was alive they killed him by running the van over him. Some of the soldiers were afraid of killing more. So they ordered the Timorese who were there to kill them. People said no, or they ran and hid in the toilets. The Indonesians then tried to inject them with sulphuric acid. But the soldiers stopped doing this as the people screamed too loudly. Instead they gave each of them two pills and they got very ill.'

The hospital orderly described how Indonesian military doctors took part in killing the wounded. 'The doctors themselves went to get poison liquid,' he said, 'and they gave it to people to drink. I don't know if the higher ranks in Indonesia knew about this; anyway, they would deny it. This information is not hearsay; it was given to me by someone who was actually told to kill some survivors. We were forced by the Indonesians to do this job. If people didn't take the poison, they were stoned or beaten with sticks. One effect of the poison was that people started passing out one by one. You could see them struggling with their breathing. There was one soldier, a corporal; he was the most ferocious. He gave poison to people. Then he stoned them till they died. Up until now I have not told this to any foreigner. I am worried about my safety. The Indonesian intelligence follows everyone. That is why I have had to keep it secret.'[†]

While Indonesian officers and spooks sang maudlin songs backed by the Karaoke in the hotel dining-room downstairs, I attempted to shred my notes and stuff them down the lavatory. This succeeded in blocking it, and it then had to be unblocked; the rest David and I burned, almost setting the bathroom curtain on fire. An element

---

[†]This man and the other witnesses to the 'second massacre' in November 1991 are now safely out of East Timor. In February 1994 they gave testimony to the United Nations Human Rights Commission sitting in Geneva.

of black farce, which had underpinned 'Adventure Tours', was now reasserting itself. With the small videotape cassettes strapped to legs, bellies and crotches, we said farewell to Gerry, our driver, and set out to leave the country from Dili airport. Swathed in Timorese cloth and nursing a large wooden statue sold to me by a village *liurai* (king), we hoped we looked as 'travel consultants' might, although I doubt if this made as much difference to our fortunes as the wonderfully chaotic distractions at the airport caused by the melee of Indonesians desperate to escape from a posting most had come to dread.

I had met the old man who wanted to give me a letter to post. After all the years of separation, he said, with tears in his eyes, he had not been able to compose his thoughts and put them on paper in time for my departure. Instead he gave me a telephone number in Darwin for Isabella, his eldest daughter. I telephoned the number when I got to Bangkok. A recorded voice said it had been disconnected.

Endnotes

1 American journalist Rod Nordland reported the famine. See the *Philadelphia*, 28 May 1982.

2 Carmel Budiardjo and Liem Soei Liong, *The War Against East Timor*, Zed Books, London, 1984, pp. 103–5.

3 Ibid., p. 98.

4 *Angkatan Bersenyata* (Indonesian Armed Forces newspaper), 24 October 1985, cited by John G. Taylor, *Indonesia's Forgotten War: The Hidden History of East Timor*, Zed Books, London, 1991.

5 *New Journalist*, Sydney, May 1979.

6 Ibid.

7 James Dunn, *Timor: A People Betrayed*, Jacaranda Press, Australia, 1983, p. 286.

8 Letter from the head of the Indonesia Country Programme Department, East Asia and Pacific Regional Office, World Bank, to Carmel Budiardjo, *Tapol Bulletin*, 12 September 1985.

9 John G. Taylor, *Indonesia's Forgotten War: The Hidden History of East Timor*, Zed Books, London, 1991, p. 159.

10 *The New York Times*, 24 April 1993.

11 Interview with Christiano Costa by Carmel Budiardjo, Geneva, March 1988.

12 Instruction Manual No. PROTA/01-B/VIV 1982, 'Established Procedure for Interrogation of Prisoners', Military Report Command, 164 Wira Dama, 8 July 1982, p. 34 in translation.

13 Taylor, p. 144.

14 Ibid., p. 138.

15 Australian Government Printing Service, 1983, Appendix 24B, pp. 157–60.

16 Ibid., p. 160.

17 Ibid., p. 163.

18 Ibid., Appendix 35, pp. 207–13.

19 *Sinar Harapan* (Indonesian press), 17 August 1983.

The East Timor Ireland Solidarity Campaign has been one of the most productive solidarity groups on East Timor in the world. The group has been instrumental not only in alerting the Irish Government to the plight of the East Timorese, but as well, the European Union. The East Timorese diaspora has led to several young asylum-seekers being granted sanctuary in Ireland and these young exiles are now an integral part of the group. When in September 1993, the then Australian Prime Minister Paul Keating traced his family roots back to Ireland, he never expected his visit to be so important to Dublin and the Irish people. The visit gave them the opportunity to voice their disgust at Keating's pusillanimous position on East Timor. Both politicians and citizens confronted Mr Keating: 'Australia, where is your conscience?'

10

ISLAND TROUBLES: (PAUL KEATING'S IRISH VISIT)

SEAN STEELE

By any standards it should have been a triumphant, trouble-free visit. The great-grandson of Irish emigrants coming back to visit, a sure sign that the Irish had made it in Australia. That success was to be embodied in one man: Paul Keating, Australia's Prime Minister.

For Keating, the visit was billed as a pilgrimage of sorts. It was an attempt to profile himself as an international statesman of Irish origin returning to his roots in County Galway, on Ireland's Atlantic seaboard. It was there, in a harsh, rain-soaked land, that his ancestors eked out a living from poor soil, struggling against both climate and an unjust land system that forced peasants onto tiny plots of land while squeezing the maximum rents out of them.

Galway was one of the counties worst affected by Ireland's Great Famine of the 1840s, when one million died of starvation and disease and over another million emigrated. Although conditions improved slightly afterwards, the constant fear of starvation was never far from people's minds. It certainly wasn't far from Paul Keating's great-grandfather's thoughts when he left for Australia with his family, in 1855. This era marked the beginning of the Irish diaspora. Millions of Irish fled grinding poverty, uncertainty and, in many cases, political persecution for the chance of a better life and freedom in the USA, Canada, Australia or New Zealand. Here was the great-grandson of one of these emigrants returning to complete a journey that began a century and a half before.

Keating saw himself as following in the footsteps of other international figures of Irish origin, namely Presidents John F. Kennedy and Ronald Reagan. Kennedy's visit was a huge success. Reagan's, however, wasn't. It was marred by demonstrations against his administration's policies in Latin America. Most of the objectors could have been dismissed as a lunatic fringe were it not for the fact that one of the most vociferous critics of Reagan was a Catholic bishop. (Many Irish missionaries, priests and nuns—hardly the most radical of people—along with aid workers have worked in El Salvador, Guatemala, Peru, Nicaragua and Chile, and are only too aware of the role US policy has played in these countries' plights.)

Keating probably never imagined his visit would experience such trouble. After all, Australia has a reputation as a champion of the underdog, a place where everyone can get a 'fair go'. If the Irish could do it, anyone can. Keating was a living symbol of this. Bob Hawke had visited Ireland in 1988 and had spoken of Australia's commitments to the principles of justice and law, including the debt owed to Australian Aborigines. And he had not experienced the type of trouble that Reagan did. Certainly Keating would never have imagined that this triumphant return would founder on that tiny half-island 400 kilometres north of Australia: East Timor. Neither would he have ever imagined such an unlikely issue could have had its origins in an even more unlikely place.

A sprawling area of 50,000 people on Dublin's south-western periphery, Ballyfermot is no different to other working-class suburbs. Built in the 1950s to accommodate people relocated from the inner city, its narrow roads are lined with identical two-up, two-down red-brick terraced houses. Like other working-class areas, it has its share of social problems. Unemployment is 40 percent—over twice the national average.

Despite the problems, Ballyfermot retains a vibrant community spirit. People remain close, and think nothing of casually dropping in on their neighbours for a cup of tea or a chat. And they think nothing of helping each other out and sharing what little they have.

It was in Ballyfermot that Ireland's link with East Timor was forged. A group of friends gathered to play cards in the house of Tom Hyland, an unemployed bus driver. During the game, a neighbour who didn't have cable TV dropped in and asked if he could watch a programme on British television called *In Cold Blood: The Massacre of East Timor*. The group sat mesmerised as they watched scenes of Indonesian soldiers slaughtering hundreds of unarmed demonstrators at the Santa Cruz cemetery in November 1991. Not only that, but they had never heard of East Timor.

That was the horrific thing, says Tom Hyland: 'We had seen programmes before about Cambodia, Burma, Tibet and El Salvador. But there was something about East Timor. I think it was two things: we had never heard of it; and the extent of the killing that had gone on for so long.'

The scenes also left their mark on Barney McKeon, a neighbour of Tom's, who was playing cards: 'My own feelings were shock, horror, disbelief. The sheer savagery of the Indonesian soldiers left me speechless. I watched this programme amazed that such things, such barbaric murders, could still happen in this day and age, and that those who committed them could get away with it.'

The scenes left everyone stunned into silence. Normally they would play cards late into the night. This time, they just shuffled off home quietly, forgoing the normal pleasantries of a chat and a cup of tea. Tom Hyland went to bed early, but couldn't sleep. 'I got up several times during the night, had a cigarette and several cups of tea,' he says. 'Those images and the cries for help from the East Timorese kept going over and over in my mind.'

Over the next few days, as all the neighbours discussed among themselves what they had seen, they decided to try to find out more about East Timor, a country they knew nothing about. A few inquiries to politicians and journalists yielded nothing: most had never heard of it. Only Amnesty International and TrÛcaire (the Catholic Development Agency) knew something about it, but were not focused on it.

'When we went to look for information we had to scrape around for it,' says Tom Hyland.

That was when the decision was taken to set up the East Timor Ireland Solidarity Campaign (ETISC), recalls Barney McKeon: 'Most of us were unemployed and did not have very much. But those people out there were being killed and slaughtered as if they counted for nothing. We, at least, could speak out; and we do have people to speak on our behalf. We decided that we should at least stand with the East Timorese—it was the least we could do.'

The group also reasoned East Timor needed one group to focus on it, in the same way campaigns had been run for El Salvador, Nicaragua and South Africa. However, unlike these countries, where large numbers of Irish lived and worked, there was no obvious Irish connection to East Timor.

Hyland: 'Our first challenge was obvious: to link an island on the other side of the world and our own, when there was no historical relationship. The connection that we made was that, like East Timor, we had been invaded and occupied by a larger, more powerful neighbour. We had also suffered colonialism. There was the direct link.'

As the problem of linking Ireland and East Timor was overcome, others emerged. Most of the founding group were unemployed and had few resources; none had any experience of campaigning. Acquiring an office was easy: they just took everything out of a bedroom in Tom Hyland's house and that became an office—an empty office. By borrowing money from friends and neighbours, they got a telephone. Friends in a trade union donated an old computer. 'The problem then was none of us were computer literate so we all had to go and learn to use it,' adds Tom.

ETISC was launched in April 1992 outside the British, Australian and American embassies 'because we thought they were the most culpable in East Timor's genocide'.

Initially there was a wave of interest in the media about this group of unemployed people from Ballyfermot—an area normally in the news for crime or drugs—making common cause with an island people half a world away. ETISC members were interviewed on both national radio and television. The 'big break', which gave East Timor a huge national profile, came when all the group's founders were interviewed on the *The Gay Byrne Show*, Ireland's most popular daily radio show, with over one and a half million listeners (out of a population of three and a half million). All the group were interviewed in Tom's kitchen. Although representatives from other NGOs were present, many of whom had long-time experience in human rights, it was those Ballyfermot people who spoke with passion and outrage about what was happening half a world away who caught the public's imagination. The public response was overwhelming. The original five-minute slot was extended to over half an hour, as the station was inundated with calls expressing sympathy and support.

This public support puzzled most politicians, remembers Tom. 'They were caught off balance so to speak. Suddenly East Timor jumped into the public profile. And the question being asked by them was why would a number of unemployed people in one of the most marginalised areas of Dublin become involved in this issue. I have to say they were very receptive to our message. We weren't being confrontational in any way. We just wanted to switch off the violence there; and in some way make a contribution to the East Timorese to get their freedom.'

Tom—who cites Aung San Suu Kyi, Martin Luther King and Heinrich Moller as his heroes—says that the group's aim was to win people over to the cause through reason and argument, by raising public awareness in all sectors of society. Over the years, ETISC has organised talks about East Timor across the length and breadth of Ireland—in schools, colleges, community associations, clubs, trade unions and the local branches of political parties.

ETISC decided to hold its first public rally at the British embassy on 12 November 1992, to commemorate the 270 men and women slaughtered at the Santa Cruz cemetery in Dili (now an annual commemoration). During the remembrance, which consisted of speeches and songs, an event occurred which moves him to this day, recalls Tom: 'Soon after the demonstration, at which a lot of people turned up, a car stopped, an old man got out and gave us an envelope. Afterwards when he drove off, I opened the envelope. There was some money and a small letter. I can still remember the text of the letter to this day. He apologised about not being able to attend because of prior commitments and then said: "I was listening to the Gay Byrne programme and I was very moved to hear of the plight of the people of East Timor. Of all human crime, genocide is the most abhorrent. As a Jew who survived the Nazi Holocaust, I would like to be associated with you." '

In this case, you had someone who had personally suffered sympathising with others. But with politicians and others in power, this is rarely the case. 'There are people like Daniel Moynihan and others in the US of Irish extraction. We would have had the opinion, like most people, that because their ancestors fled oppression, they would be sympathetic to East Timor. However, it doesn't work that way. People work their way up into power positions and, in some ways, they learn to forget their past.

'Think of Kissinger, a Jewish refugee from Germany, and the

role he played in East Timor—and elsewhere. This is how politics operates. But it has been a quantum leap to learn of the role that people of Irish ancestry like Daniel Moynihan have played. In Moynihan's case he blocked the UN from taking effective action, which allowed Indonesian genocide in East Timor to continue apace.'

However, it is the case of former Australian Prime Minister Paul Keating which Tom says should be regarded as a 'classic example' of how power works, 'which should be put in text books and studied by students'.

Tom says he had seen Keating on television and had originally been impressed by him, seeing him as someone who spoke his mind, stood up to the British establishment and championed the underdog. That was his impression up until East Timor. 'Then I saw a different side. I saw that despite the ancestral background, this man was no different from other politicians who were prepared to sell their conscience to the highest bidder. This is the unethical search for profit at any expense where people can actually block out what has happened. I think it is absolutely disgraceful for senior politicians in Australia, like Bob Hawke, who cried tears over Tiananmen Square, who were morally outraged over Iraq's invasion of Kuwait, to act as if Timor never happened.

'We all know the hypocrisy, the double standards. The problem is trying to get others to understand and react. Most people don't want to.'

An example of this hypocrisy is on the question of betrayal. Keating has made a career out of lashing Britain's abandoning of Australia when the Japanese bombed Darwin. Yet this pales in comparison with the betrayal of the East Timorese, 40,000 of whom died helping Australian troops against the Japanese. 'This ranks as one of the greatest betrayals of all time. Not only have they betrayed the East Timorese; not only have they, along with the Indonesians, robbed East Timor's oil, but they have supplied weapons and training. It is the shame of Australia. And they know it.'

The case of Keating is just one side of Australia. The other is represented by a small group of dedicated people, many of whom have struggled selflessly and tirelessly for 22 years to alert the world to what was happening in East Timor.

Notification of Keating's visit to Ireland in September 1993 was released several months before. As a prelude, ETISC members went to visit the Australian Embassy and met the Ambassador, Terence McCarthy. The visit was an eye-opener in the ways and attitudes that underpin international diplomacy. The Ambassador listened to what they had to say, remembers Tom, but then dismissed their concerns: 'We went there to see if we could get them to do something to help. He just ridiculed us. He told us we were being emotional and that we should forget these people. I remember we left that office shaking with anger. Not only was his attitude morally unjustifiable, it was also bad diplomacy because when we left the office so angry, we weren't going to go away.'

The group sat down and discussed what to do. They took the decision to make a stand during Keating's visit. Immediately they realised the dangers: that few in the Irish political establishment or media like it when prominent politicians of Irish origin return and are criticised. It happened with Reagan, it could also have happened with Keating.

Hyland: 'We decided to make a stand on the issue. The media could easily have rounded on us although we had been on good terms with them since the beginning. If you stand in solidarity with the oppressed, you take on the consequences.

'We were very nervous. This would have been our biggest opportunity to date. We knew there would be intense media concentration, not just on him but also on us. I always remember the night before he arrived, I found it difficult to sleep. I had a lot of self-doubt. I lay in bed thinking: "Here you are an ex-bus driver and you are challenging the Prime Minister of a foreign country. I really was so nervous as to what we were taking on".'

However, this self-doubt disappeared with the arrival of Shirley

Shackleton, who came the same day as Keating. ETISC met her at the airport, which was being prepared for Keating's visit. 'We knew that whatever we had taken on was minuscule in comparison to what she had done', says Tom. 'All the self-doubt left. In fact, not only had the self-doubt left, but we decided that since we were in solidarity we would take on the vested interests, or else we would pack it in. For 21 years she has dug for the truth about her husband's murder. But what impressed me was that Shirley was able to put her husband's death behind her and had seen the wider picture—the plight of the East Timorese.'

Shirley's visit engendered a lot of interest. That evening as Paul Keating arrived, RTE (the national broadcasting station) ran with the news of her arrival—proof that East Timor was on the agenda for Keating's visit. Also that evening, ETISC called on the Irish Government to give Keating a qualified welcome—which was also picked up on all stations. The call quickly took effect. A number of politicians—from all parties, both in Government and Opposition— also called for a qualified welcome. Other politicians then said they would boycott his address to the Dail (the Irish Parliament).

'We did not want to confront him or embarrass him,' says Tom. 'We wanted him to look into his heart. There is no-one, in a position like his, who can look into their heart and say, "I didn't know." I can't understand how the man gets up in the morning and looks at himself in the mirror.'

Before visiting Ireland, Keating spent a couple of days in Britain, where much of the mainstream media concentrated on his desire to make Australia a republic and on his breach of protocol with the Queen when he put his arm around her shoulder. East Timor hardly rated a mention.

In Ireland, however, it was a different matter. Before Keating even set foot in Ireland, the trouble that awaited him became clear. Travelling from London to Dublin on Sunday, 19 September, his entourage read Irish Sunday newspapers. When they opened the *Sunday Tribune* they encountered a full-page advertisement, titled:

'Massacre in East Timor'. The advertisement, which had been paid for by sympathisers, showed photos of the Santa Cruz massacre and gave details of Australian military support for the Indonesian military.

At Dublin airport, an assembled group of politicians and dignitaries gathered to welcome Mr Keating. After the initial formalities, Mr Keating was whisked off to the All-Ireland Gaelic football final, the high point in Ireland's sporting calendar, where he was feted as the guest of honour to the 70,000 crowd. However, as Mr Keating settled down to watch the match, several football supporters began shouting: 'What about East Timor, Mr Keating?' —the unexpected question that left him clearly uneasy.

That evening, the Government held a state dinner in honour of Keating, at Dublin Castle, where most official functions are held. Outside the castle gates, over 500 people gathered behind barriers, despite the rain and cold, to show solidarity in answer to a call put in the same advertisement in the *Sunday Tribune* that Keating had read on his journey from London. As the convoy of limousines gathered, everybody in the crowd faced the roadway and held up candles, their flickering in the dark night creating a powerful image. Nobody raised their voices. As Keating's limousine passed he turned his face away, pretending to ignore those protesting.

'However, if he thought that it was over he was wrong,' adds Tom.

Once inside Dublin Castle, as Keating moved among guests from the *crème de la crème* of Irish society, he was confronted by several wearing badges saying: 'Hands off East Timor's oil' and 'Australia: Where is your conscience?' Several guests raised the issue in private conversation.

'I think that by this stage he was left in no doubt as to the extent of Irish solidarity with the people of East Timor,' says Tom.

The next morning the issue confronted him again, as soon as he sat down for breakfast. In that day's edition of the *Irish Times* was another full-page advertisement directed at him personally. It read:

'Welcome Home Mr Keating! Do you remember why your family had to leave Ireland?' The advertisement dealt with Keating's ancestors fleeing oppression in Ireland, and contrasted this with Australia's recognition of Indonesian annexation of East Timor. It also had a photo from the Santa Cruz massacre, and a picture of Greg Shackleton, whose widow, Shirley, had appeared on Irish radio that same morning talking about East Timor. Opposition to Mr Keating's policies on East Timor featured in all press coverage of the visit, including editorials.

That day, Keating was also due to address the assembled members of both houses of the Irish Assembly: the Dail and the Senate. As he was led into the Dail chamber, he could hardly have failed to notice that several of those present—from all parties—wore white carnations, both as a protest against Australian policy towards Timor and as a commemoration of those 200,000 who had died under Indonesian occupation. Several others took their protest a stage further, by boycotting.

The address to the Assembly covered a wide range of topics: the Irish contribution to Australia; economic reform and GATT; the desire to be a republic; and his commitment to justice and fair play. And, as expected, there was no mention of East Timor. However, he wasn't able to escape the issue at the press conference which followed the Dail address, where he was asked about East Timor by several reporters. Newspaper reports describe him as being 'clearly irked by the strong pro-East Timor campaign in Dublin'.

He defended his policy on East Timor, claiming, 'Australia has had a very consistent position on human rights and, in fact, East Timor has been the cause of eruptions on a number of occasions.'

'I suppose after years of mollifying the Indonesian regime in the most craven manner, he seems to think that by slapping Suharto on the wrist with a feather he can absolve himself of his involvement in one of the worst horrors of the late twentieth century,' notes Tom.

By that stage of the visit, Tom believes the point had been made. As Mr Keating prepared to leave for a visit to his ancestral home in

Tynagh, Galway, ETISC decided to cancel a demonstration planned to coincide with his return.

'We hoped that his visit to Galway would give him a chance to reflect on what he has done to the East Timorese and to change his ways,' recalls Trevor Sargent, one of those who boycotted Mr Keating's Dail speech.

Although Keating pretended to be unfazed by the protests, sources indicate that he was privately furious. In the Australian Embassy, he reputedly gave the Ambassador and Embassy staff a dressing-down for leaving him so open and unprepared on the issue that had dogged his career and spoilt what was supposed to have been a trouble-free homecoming party.

Noam Chomsky has been a human rights and peace advocate for four decades. He rose to prominence as a vocal anti-Vietnam War academic and has been involved in the East Timor issue from its beginning. Professor Chomsky has addressed the United Nations General Assembly on East Timor, in 1978 and 1979, and has published numerous works on the issue. He is one of the twentieth century's major linguists and political analysts, a prolific author, and teaches in the Department of Linguistics and Philosophy at the Massachusetts Institute of Technology. At the time of his visit to Australia, one commentator noted that almost more people came to see Professor Chomsky than went to see His Holiness Pope John Paul II. This speech was presented at the Melbourne Town Hall, Australia, to a capacity audience on 24 January 1995.

11

THE CASE OF EAST TIMOR

NOAM CHOMSKY

As you know, the Foreign Affairs Minister of Indonesia, about a couple of years ago, did make a comment how it might be useful to think about getting this piece of gravel out of the shoe, and with some encouragement, that might happen. Well, in the West, the situation is beginning to improve somewhat, at least in parts of the West. So take, say, the US; in the early stage of the invasion, the US support was absolutely decisive. The United States was providing about 90 per cent of the arms. The arms were given to Indonesia under an explicit condition under US law that they be used only for defence. The invasion took place with a green light from Washington, the flow of arms increased and, theoretically, there was an embargo. A public embargo was announced but it was announced rather quietly, so quietly that the Indonesians never heard about it, nor did anyone else. During the six-month embargo, there were new arms shipments, including counter-insurgency equipment. It continued as the atrocities mounted.

Prior to the Indonesian invasion, there had been quite a glut of coverage of East Timor in the American press, reflecting concerns about the break-up of the Portuguese empire and what might follow. After the invasion, coverage began to drop and what was there was disgraceful in character—State Department lies and so on. By 1978, the measures reached their peak, a kind of a near-genocidal peak as new US flows of arms were sent to expedite the atrocities. At that point, the coverage reached absolute zero. There was no word in the American press. The same was true in Canada and other major investors. That was probably the low point. There were people working on it—I testified at the UN by then, as had plenty of other people, but it looked impenetrable, it looked impossible to break through. Well, that's changed. Now things are a good deal better.

We're still a long way from being able to emulate the courage of people like George Aditjondro, the Indonesian scholar who expos-ed the crimes of his Government and has forthrightly condemned them; or the Indonesian Student Associations, whose conditions are a little more difficult than ours, to put it mildly, and who after the Dili Massacre came out with public pronouncements calling on the Government, in their words 'for the sake of humanity and our common wellbeing, to reconsider the fake process of integration in East Timor'. They demanded further that Indonesia withdraw its forces and grant the 'full and free process of self-determination to the people of East Timor'.[1]

I should add at this point, when people here talk about the necessity of good relations with Indonesia and the importance of Australia's ties with Indonesia and so on, there's an obvious question that has to be asked in that and in all other cases, and that is, which Indonesia are you talking about? There certainly are different ones. There's the Indonesia of General Suharto and his cronies and the affiliates of the great corporations. That's one Indonesia. There's another Indonesia that includes people like George Aditjondro and the Indonesian students I've been quoting, like the workers fighting for their rights who were tossed into jail right before the APEC conference to clean things up a little before Westerners showed up, and in fact there's probably the great mass of the population of Indonesia who would join them if they were able to discover what was going on in their name in East Timor, and they're beginning to discover it.

The Government of Indonesia put extremely harsh censorship on what was happening; the only target of that censorship, of course, is their own population—nobody else had to be deceived unless they chose to. The reason for the censorship was the usual reason why governments keep secrets and tell lies, and why the press distorts, and so on and so forth—it's simply hatred of democracy and fear of the population. They're the only ones from whom the facts are kept; it's a lot easier to tell lies—we all know that. If huge efforts go into deceit, distortion and concealment, it's out of fear that the people in whose name you speak simply wouldn't tolerate what's going on if they knew about it. They're beginning to be able to learn the truth, as we all could if we chose, and the reaction is about what you would expect—lots of protest. So there's a different Indonesia, and you have to decide which one you want to be related to.

Well, as I say, in the United States, the censorship initially was so strict that coverage literally dropped to zero in 1978. That has changed through a lot of hard work of actually a very small number of people, mostly young—a couple of young people have worked extremely hard—and it's gotten to the point where, by now, the coverage is way better than it was before. In the United States, editorial condemnation of the Indonesian takeover is almost universal at this point and is indeed very strong. Congress has imposed barriers to the training of Indonesian officers and the selling of arms.

In the increasing coverage, some topics are still unmention-able—for example, the US role—that's one thing you can't talk about. There are many important current issues that aren't yet discussed, for example, what's going on with the oil; stocks of US oil companies every once in a while go up, if you read the business pages, but you have to know something else to know why—somebody found some oil in the Timor Gap. In any event, things are improving, significantly improving, and it's important. It's important because of the role of the United States in world affairs. If the chief Mafia Don makes it clear that he doesn't like some-thing, other people have to take notice, even if someone else will move in and replace the actual job that he was doing. And since, in fact, the world is run pretty much like the Mafia, if we're honest, that change is a significant one, and it shows what can happen when censorship breaks down and a population begins to learn something about what's being done in their name and with their money.

Even the sporadic coverage which you now find in the United States is too much for some prominent figures, for example, a gentleman who is well known here, Gareth Evans, who in his last trip to New York met with *New York Times* editors, according to journalist Brian Toohey, 'to complain about their criticisms of Indonesian human rights violations in East Timor' and to complain about what he called 'their continual harping on the crimes of the Indonesians', that is, the Indonesians he prefers to associate with—remember, you have choices about that. Well, there's no doubt that he's onto something, I mean—maybe that reaction's a bit hysterical, but it's true that the situation has changed.[2]

Even the far-right *Wall Street Journal*, which is essentially the voice of the investor community in the United States—big business, big corporations—has called on Indonesia to get out. The title of the editorial was 'Remove the Pebble from the Shoe'—you know, it's enough, it's not worth it any more, and that's important. There's now a reasonably effective solidarity movement, there's a lot of public awareness and, as I mentioned, there have been moves in Congress across the spectrum which have definitely imposed certain barriers. In fact, they've compelled the Clinton administration to carry out some pretty complicated manoeuvres to evade Congressional legislation. For example, Congress did vote a couple of years ago, in 1992, to bar training of Indonesian military officers because of the aggression and human rights violations in East Timor, and the State Department had to issue a determination that they would interpret that ban as meaning that training of Indonesian officers could continue—they chose delicately the anniversary of the invasion of East Timor to make that announcement—which led to plenty of protests in Congress, though there was very little coverage in the media, which I suppose gratified Senator Evans. But the progress in Congress is significant, and it will be harder to evade next time around.

Unfortunately, as the United States has backed off from its decisive and crucial participation in some of the main crimes of the twentieth century, others have more than eagerly moved in. First among them is Britain, which is now the leading arms seller to Indonesia, and although there are some public protests, they're not yet sufficient to bar these sales, although there are people like John Pilger, who is the most noteworthy and important, who are putting pieces of gravel in the shoes of the 'Douglas Hurds', and you can tell he is getting somewhere from the amount of abuse he gets, both over there and over here, which is a pretty good sign you're doing something right, you know, and he definitely is.

When I landed at Sydney airport, the first headline that greeted me, just to make me feel good, was the announcement that Australia is planning to sell rifles to Indonesia. It's kind of a new niche-market that opened up, thanks to the pressures on the United States to stop selling small arms. Nobody, no sane person at least, has any doubts what those arms are for, and if those sales of rifles go through, that'll be a real scandal. As you may know, there's a six-month campaign opening right now, in fact, focusing on East

Timor, to call—I'm just reading the announcement of it—to call upon the Australian Government to stop arms sales to Indonesia, to withdraw the *de jure* official recognition of the Indonesian sovereignty over East Timor, to withdraw from the Timor Gap Treaty, and to support the right of self-determination of the East Timorese people, which simply means to go along with the demand of the Security Council of the United Nations to all states, and to call on the Indonesian Government to release Xanana and to release all Timorese political prisoners. Well, that's right, and there's not much doubt that the Australian people can easily implement those demands if they want to. This isn't a totalitarian state, and the reaction to popular pressures won't be long in coming. And it'll make a difference, and the same can happen in other countries.

Among the various achievements, and there have been some in the United States, they're not unimportant—I've talked mostly about those because that's what I know—among the achievements in the United States there are others, and some are of some significance—actually, one of them took place in the city where I live, a few months ago, in the city of Boston: there was a Federal Court hearing which awarded $14 million in damages to Helen Todd, a woman whose son was murdered by Indonesian forces in what's sometimes called the Dili Massacre, although to be more precise it's in the extended 'Dili Massacre', because it went on for quite a while and in many horrifying ways. The person who was accused and convicted in the court case was an Indonesian general. The United States has a law which makes it possible for someone to bring civil cases against someone resident in the United States for human rights violations, torture, atrocities and so on, and that's what happened—Major-General Sintong Panjaitan was at that point in the United States—and Helen Todd, the mother of the guy who was killed, who was actually a student in Australia, brought the charge [to court] and she won.

The Dili Massacre was, in the immortal words of your Foreign Minister, 'an aberration'—there was a mistake made: massacres are supposed to be conducted in secret; they're not supposed to be conducted in front of television cameras—I'm sure they teach that somewhere. Well, the Indonesians thought they were carrying it out in secret—it's not that they didn't learn their lessons. The second mistake is: you're not supposed to beat and practically kill two American reporters, even if they're freelance dissidents. I mean, that's not too bad in that case, but that's even a little too much. Now, when you make mistakes like that, there is a routine that you go through. It's like a record—every country knows it, and if they don't, their PR firms explain it to them. The routine works like this: first, the people who are supporting them express their dismay over this 'aberration' carried out by low-ranking soldiers who somehow got out of control, and then the next thing is you call a judicial commission, which produces a whitewash. Meanwhile, the victims who survived, as in this case, get long sentences—in fact, up to life sentences—for such crimes as showing hostility to their Indonesian 'benefactors', and as they say, foreign diplomats are properly impressed and so on. It was also considered expedient as part of this process to send Major-General Panjaitan, who was one of the architects of the massacre, out of the country for a while, away from the glare of publicity. So he was sent off to Boston, to Harvard University, to refine his skills a little bit, to make sure that next time you do it right, you know—don't break the rules.

When local activists in Boston heard about this, I guess from people here actually, they checked at Harvard University, who said they'd never heard of him. They checked further and it turned out, yes, they had heard of him—he was a student at one of their programmes, and the pressures began, and that led to a news story, on the anniversary of the Dili Massacre, which had one of my favourite headlines ever in the Boston paper—'Indonesian General flees Boston', and he did. He was tried *in absentia* and sentenced with a $14 million sentence.[3]

Well, all of these things are of some importance. It's important to make it clear that not everybody puts out a welcome mat for the

State Department's favourite killers and torturers. Furthermore, in this particular case that we're talking about, the training of Indonesian military officers at American universities has had an acknowledged and, indeed, quite admired place in the recent history of Indonesia in ways which relate quite closely—a little indirectly, but quite closely—to the topic that we're discussing. To see why that's the case and to understand what's happening altogether, it's really necessary to look at the background, and I would like to say a few words about that because it's an important one—I think it provides the basis for understanding what's going on now and what's going on in many other places and what we could do about it.

The background in this, as in most questions having to do with contemporary world order, goes back to the end of World War II. At the end of World War II, there was a big change in world affairs: there was a new 'Mafia Don'—in fact one with historically unparalleled power. The United States at that point had about 50 percent of the world's wealth. Its economy had boomed during the war while everyone else was getting smashed—it already had by far the largest economy before the war—and it was now going to be a major player in world affairs. US planners understood very well that they were in a position to organise the world, and they intended to do it. To quote someone else, 'the United States Government out of self-interest, assumed responsibility for the welfare of the world capitalist system'—I'm quoting a noted and respected diplomatic historian, Gerald Haines, who is also the senior historian of the CIA, and that's a very accurate description of what happened.[4]

For the welfare of the world capitalist system, quite extensive and intricate and, in fact, rather sophisticated planning was undertaken, and the primary task was to reconstruct the other major components of the world capitalist system—that is the capitalist system of the rich industrial powers. There were a lot of reasons for reconstructing them: one was that the US needed opportunities for foreign investment. In fact, the multinational corporations just exploded in that period, as part of this reconstruction, and most of them were United States based at that point. Secondly, the US had a huge manufacturing export surplus—it was the only country that had a viable economy during the war with the massive transfer of public wealth to private power that was part of the war effort. There was a huge manufacturing surplus and something had to be done with it, but nobody was able to buy into it because of what was called the 'dollar gap'—nobody else had dollars, since everywhere else was smashed, and concern over the dollar gap was in fact one of the leading elements of US foreign policy at the time.

The idea was to reconstruct the industrial powers around what were called their natural leaders—the great workshops, Germany and Japan. They had just demonstrated their prowess in the recent war, and they were now to be the second-level leaders of the world capitalist system, with the US being the boss—that is, controlling the whole show—with others to be reconstructed around them. They, of course, had to be able to purchase US manufacturing goods for opportunities for US investors to move abroad through growing multinationals and so on, and that meant overcoming the 'dollar gap'. And a lot of methods were tried, like the Marshall Plan, which didn't work but a couple of methods did.

One method that worked was called 'international military Keynesianism'—that is, massive rearmament programmes with offshore procurement and so on. That did revitalise the natural leaders, Europe and Japan, and the countries around them, as it indeed maintained the US economy, and that was of course hailed by the business press for these reasons, quite openly. The other factor that was crucial was the reconstruction of rather traditional triangular trade patterns whereby the traditional imperial powers would sell goods to their former colonies. The US would purchase raw materials from those colonies and the dollars would go back to the imperial power and then they could purchase US surplus manufactures, and in fact that was the core system by which the 'dollar gap' was overcome, along with 'international military Keynesianism'.

It's actually within that whole context that the future of Southeast Asia and, in fact, most of the rest of the world was determined. US planners very carefully allotted to every section of the world a function within this global system. It was done thoughtfully—you look through it, you see it was not stupid by any means. A lot of the planning was done by the State Department policy planning staff, headed at that time by George Kennan, who is one of the architects of the postwar world, and they specifically assigned every area its role, and the roles were different. The western hemisphere was going to be US turf. Finally, the US was able to extend the Monroe Doctrine over the entire western hemisphere and then unceremoniously kick out its traditional enemies, England and France— they were out of there. The Middle East, with its huge energy resources, the US was basically taking over for itself—France was kicked out. England was allowed in because England was regarded as one high planner. They said England was our lieutenant—the fashionable word is 'partner'. The British were supposed to hear the fashionable word, and still have illusions on that score, but as long as the British were just in fact serving as a lieutenant, they were allowed to help out in the Middle East, to take a little share in that.

Africa, as Kennan put it, was to be exploited for the reconstruction of Western Europe. Kennan also added that exploitation of Africa would give Europeans a kind of a psychological lift; they were sort of in a gloomy period at the end of the Second World War, not only because of what had happened but because the United States was taking over a lot of their traditional prizes, and he felt that they would feel better if they had someone to exploit too, so therefore, they were given Africa to exploit. One might have imagined a different relationship—let's say that maybe Africa could have exploited Europe for its reconstruction—but naturally, no such horrendous thought could ever occur to anyone, and I should say that all of this is totally down the memory hall—I mean, it's all in the documentary record but you're really going to have to work to find it.

As for Southeast Asia, it too had a function. Southeast Asia was, as Kennan's policy planning staff put it, to fulfil its main function, as a source of raw materials and other resources for the reconstruction of Western Europe and Japan, and of course for the United States as well. As Kennan then went on to explain, the United States was going to reconstruct Japan's 'Empire toward the South'. In other words, Japan had tried to create a 'new order' including Southeast Asia, and the United States basically had no objection to that as long as the US was allowed in. And there was some conflict about how well they were allowed in, which is what brought on the Second World War. But now the US was 'in', I mean there was no question about that—they ran the world, and therefore, they had to reconstruct Japan's 'Empire toward the South' and Southeast Asia had to fulfil its main function in this fashion.

That was the basic story, and it went down to small details. For example, Timor was mentioned, believe it or not. As far as I know, Timor only got about one sentence in all of this extensive planning, but it did get a sentence. One of Franklin Delano Roosevelt's top-level advisers, Sumner Welles, mentioned that Timor did deserve independence, but he thought that they shouldn't be too pushy about it, that they should wait their turn. He suggested that it might take about 'a thousand years'. That policy has a technical name—it's called 'Wilsonian Idealism': self-determination of peoples.

Well, that's the rough structure of the new world order of the day. Southeast Asia fits in it and Indonesia was crucial. Indonesia was the richest prize in Southeast Asia. It had most of the resources, most of the wealth, and they were aware of it. So in 1948, as you'll remember, there were a lot of complicated things going on in the world, a lot of threats and threats of nuclear war and so forth, but in 1948, Indonesia was considered, and I'm quoting from the declassified record, 'the most crucial issue of the moment in our struggle with the Kremlin'—that was Kennan again. 'Struggle with the Kremlin' is another one of those technical phrases—there wasn't any Kremlin around—but it means conflict with independent nationalism. That means some forces within the country pressuring that country to move on a path of independent development—that's known as struggle with the Kremlin and you know it doesn't matter whether the Russians are there or not. As Kennan went on to explain, there was a danger that if things went the wrong way in Indonesia, the 'infection', as he described it, might spread all through Southeast Asia and South Asia, causing all kinds of unravelling of the system that was being constructed —Japan's 'Empire toward the South'. The infection was the disease of independent development—that's always been the problem.

In 1948, Indonesia was the main problem, and the big problem was that there was a major independent political party—the PKI, the Communist Party—and they were very much concerned that it would win a political victory. If winning a political victory has a name, it's called concealed aggression, or internal aggression, and in fact that's the actual term that's used, even in public, and so it looked like there might be a chance for a concealed aggression there.

Well, as I say, Kennan said that a political victory would be an infection that could sweep over South Asia. Specialists on Indonesia think that the expectation of a political victory was not unlikely. One of Australia's leading specialists, Harold Crouch, in his history *The Army and Politics in Indonesia*, writes that 'the PKI had won widespread support, not as a revolutionary party, but as an organisation 'defending the interests of the poor' within the existing system,'[5] and the idea that a party that's defending the interests of the poor might win political power is totally inconsistent with the conception of democracy, so therefore, that has to be stopped by all means, and that's why there was such a serious problem at that time.

The West does like democracy—in fact it loves it; it loves it as much as it loves human rights—but democracy is understood in terms of outcome, not process. So it's a democracy, the right people win, and if the wrong people are going to win it's not democracy and you have to do something to prevent it. In fact, the future history of Indonesia—and incidentally, East Timor—sort of follows from all of this with the simplicity of elementary proof and logic, almost.

Concerns continued through the 1950s. In 1948, the Secretary of State, John Foster Dulles, informed the National Security Council (that's the highest planning body) that there were three major crises in the world: one of Indonesia, the other Algeria, the third the Middle East, the oil-producing regions. And he also pointed out, in now declassified secrets, that in these three major crisis areas, there were no Soviet plots. And when there were some questions about that in the internal meeting, the note-taker pointed out that President Eisenhower vociferously agreed that there were no Soviet plots—for the public, it's all fighting the communists, but they were talking to each other internally.

They have just recently declassified the 1958 volume of records of official State Department history, and if you read through it, there is a lot of censorship but there is one theme that goes all the way through. For example, at one point the US Embassy in Jakarta in mid-1958 sends a cable to Washington, reporting the attitude of the Sukarno Government, and says the Sukarno Government was 'beginning to reach the conclusion that the communists could not be beaten by ordinary democratic means and elections. Program of gradual elimination of communists by police and military to be followed by the outlawing of the Communist Party [is] not unlikely in the comparatively near future'[6]—that's quoting the Indonesian Foreign Minister.

Naturally, the US agreed with that—the physical elimination and the outlawing of the party defending the interests of the poor. The Joint Chiefs of Staff the very same day urged (in their words) that 'action must be taken, including overt measures as required' (meaning terrorism and aggression) 'to ensure either the success of the dissidents or the suppression of the pro-Communist elements of the Sukarno Government'.[7] The dissidents that they were referring to were the so-called revolutionary government that had been established in the outer islands with very substantial US military support, though within a certain degree of ambivalence in Washington, because they weren't exactly clear what the outcome would be and the military support for the rebellion was alienating the pro-American Indonesian generals in Jakarta and they didn't want to do that either, so it's kind of a tricky balancing act. That was what was going on at the time.

Direct military support for the rebellion was in fact revealed when an American pilot was shot down, and caught with papers in his pocket and so forth—another bad mistake, and intelligence isn't supposed to do that—and that blew the cover. By then, the Indonesians knew that there was US support coming from Taiwan and Singapore and, possibly Australia, though it isn't certain and the whole thing ended. The US had to switch to another tactic and US intelligence concluded in 1958 that these events had 'greatly strengthened the position of the Indonesian communists (the PKI)', and if there were elections, they said, they would 'probably emerge the strongest party in Indonesia and be in a strong position to demand cabinet representation',[8] which is, of course, completely impossible and unacceptable for a party that defends the interests of the poor, according to prevailing democratic theory.

At that point, the US just had to turn to its standard operating procedures in such circumstances. You want to overthrow a civilian government, which is what it had to do because it's getting out of hand. Can't allow an election, because the wrong people are going to win—what you do is cut off aid to the government but send aid to the military. It makes perfect sense—you send aid to the military and you keep with exactly the kind of people who are able to overthrow the government, and very often they do it. That went on through the early 60s, and it's going on in exactly the same way at the very same time in Brazil, with the same results: the Brazilian generals took over and destroyed Brazilian democracy in what was called a great victory for democracy at the time. In Indonesia, as you know, the same thing happened very shortly after in 1965, and that just goes on constantly and is 'standard operating procedure'.

Right after the overthrow of the Shah in 1979, the United States first tried to sponsor a military coup, and that didn't work out. It then immediately started sending arms to the Iranian military via Israel, with Saudi Arabian funding which later became known as the Iran scandal. That was then called an arms-for-hostage deal, but it had nothing to do with that because there were no hostages at the time: it was just straight standard technique for overthrowing a civilian government.

The technique is routine and it's perfectly understandable and it's completely rational, and it's the only way to deal with the fundamental problem that arises over and over. And the fundamental problem is also discussed in the internal record, quite frankly in fact. For example, back to 1958, there was a private discussion, later declassified, with President Eisenhower, John Foster Dulles (who was Secretary of State), and his brother, Allen Dulles (who was the head of the CIA), when they were discussing this big problem—remember, Indonesia is one of the main crisis areas—they were deploring what they called the communist ability to get control of mass movements, something we have no capacity to duplicate.

'Unlike us,' President Eisenhower complained, 'they can appeal directly to the masses'—and we don't seem to be able to do that. John Foster Dulles, who's the smart guy, explained the reasons for this unfair advantage that they have: 'the poor people are the ones they appeal to and they have always wanted to plunder the rich'. That's the real problem of world history, if you look, and somehow we have a problem with this. We find it really difficult to convince people of our values—that the rich are supposed to plunder the poor—and it's probably that they have better PR people than we do, so we have to work on it. But anyway, there's this constant problem that they appeal to the poor, who want to plunder the rich, and we are trying to tell them 'no, the rich have to plunder the poor'. And that somehow gives them the advantage to appeal to the population, and that leads to all sorts of threats of democracy and chances that they may take over the political system, and there's just nothing that we can do except turn to our own comparative advantage in violence and terror.

By the early 1960s, US experts were urging their contacts in the Indonesian military 'to strike and sweep their house clean'. At the very same time, the very same concerns were being expressed with regard to South Vietnam, but they had the same worries. Right then, Kennedy's Ambassador, Henry Cabot Lodge, distinguished American diplomat, wrote an 'eyes-only' cable—that is, a cable just for the President—in which he said there is a problem here too: 'Vietnam is not a thoroughly strong police state ... because, unlike Hitler's Germany, it is not efficient' and it is thus unable to suppress the 'large and well-organised underground opponent, strongly and ever-freshly motivated by vigorous hatred', and furthermore, he said, 'the Vietnamese appear to be more and more ever anxious to be left alone'.[9]

The coup did take place in Vietnam shortly after, and Diem was killed, but the generals never did meet US standards there, as exemplified by Hitler's Germany. However, the Indonesian allies and students turned out to have a better appreciation of Western values and they did act like the Nazis, and took over and carried out a huge massacre, killing nobody knows how many people, maybe half a million or so in 1965–66, and they wiped out the party that was representing the interests of the poor, the PKI.

The country was very quickly turned into what was called a paradise for investors. Investment boomed and everybody was delighted, and the threat of a political party that represented the poor was put off for a long, long time, so the right people were going to do the plundering. The reaction in the West was highly revealing. It was absolute euphoria, despite the biggest slaughter since the Holocaust and nobody had any doubt about the dimensions. The major study of the killings is actually published here by Monash University. Robert Cribb, in the introduction, points out that 'in most cases the killings did not begin until elite military units had arrived in a locality and had sanctioned violence by instruction or example',[10] moving swiftly to destroy the PKI, having gained the right orientation in American universities. So, incidentally, going back to what I said before, you can see the importance of sending people like Major-General Panjaitan to Harvard to make sure they understand civilised values.

The media were uniform, and again, you have to really read it to get the feel, so *Time* magazine had an eleven-page cover story which began with what they called 'The West's Best News for Years in Asia'. The cover of *Time* magazine read 'Vengeance With A Smile'. It described what they called 'the boiling bloodbath' that had taken at that time 4000 lives, and then there were wonderful pictures of people slaughtered and 'what great news' and so on.

The leading liberal, crusading columnist of the *New York Times*, James Reston, had a column with the headline 'A Gleam of Light in Asia'. Reston was a hotshot. He had a lot of contacts with high-level people in Washington, and using those, he said that the US role was much greater than was claimed in this hopeful development—in other words, Washington was being too modest by saying they didn't have much to do with it. He said 'it's doubtful that the Suharto coup would ever have been attempted without the American show of strength in Vietnam' or 'would have been sustained without the clandestine aid it received from Washington'. The *New York Times* agreed: they praised what they called the Indonesian moderates who had carried out what they called a 'staggering mass slaughter'. They did note that the 'staggering mass slaughter' carried out by the moderates raised 'critical questions for Washington' but 'fortunately, the questions had been answered correctly', the editors concluded—namely, Washington didn't embrace the killers too effusively and too openly, which might have harmed them, although it did give them generous aid, so the critical questions were properly answered.

There was no condemnation of the slaughter, not a word in the halls of Congress. No major relief organisation offered any aid. The World Bank, however, did react by restoring Indonesia to favour, making it very quickly its third-largest borrower. Western incorporations' and governments' followed suit, and in fact, everybody was very happy. The *Christian Science Monitor*, which in the United States is one of the few elite national newspapers, reported recently (and correctly), that after his 1965 achievement 'many in the West were keen to cultivate Jakarta's new moderate leader, General Suharto', who is 'at heart benign', the London *Economist* assured its readers in 1987, perhaps thinking of his attitude to corporations.[11]

Now we are up to the East Timor period and the *Economist* and our leading journal (the *Christian Science Monitor*) dismissed what it called the 'propagandists for the guerrillas' in East Timor who 'talk of the army's savagery and use of torture'.[12] The 'propagandists' include the bishops and other Church sources, Amnesty International, thousands of refugees, Western diplomats and plenty of journalists by then—but they're all lying: the *Economist* knew that by 'doctrinal necessity', so we have this guy who is a 'moderate' and who is 'at heart benign'.

It also provides a good part of the context for the East Timor invasion and the Western reaction to it. The Indonesian generals had performed a major service—remember, this was at the core of a large piece of the world system: they had eliminated the threat of democracy by a 'staggering mass slaughter' that had destroyed the political party that had gained popularity by 'defending the interests of the poor'. By then, they had also compiled one of the world's worst human rights records, offering enormous riches to Western investors.

These are services to Western values that are not easily forgotten. There were no other reasons necessary for the West to support the invasion of East Timor. Another staggering mass slaughter could hardly be expected to disrupt the friendly relations that had been established in this fashion by such successful emulation of the Nazis. There were, of course, specific reasons for the West to lend its support to the new atrocities.

I mentioned earlier that there had been a good bit of coverage of East Timor in the United States right before the invasion. That was in the context of the break-up of the Portuguese empire, and we often make a mistake when we look at these things by focusing narrowly on one or another region of the world. The place to focus is where the planning goes on, in Washington, and then you find that the same kinds of things are happening everywhere at the same time, and that's true here too. So what was going on in East Timor was also going on in Angola and Mozambique at exactly the same time and in the same context: concern over the collapse of the Portuguese empire and the various infections and viruses and so on that might spread as the Portuguese imperial system collapsed and people got independence with maybe the wrong ideas about who ought to plunder whom.

Harold Crouch again, pretty plausibly I think, writes that one of the factors that motivated the Indonesian generals and their Western supporters was 'the fear that an independent Timor would become a source of subversion in Indonesia itself'.[13] How are a couple of hundred thousand people going to subvert Indonesia? In the usual way: by providing an example that others might want to follow, and that leads to the threat of democracy, and the threat of political groupings to represent the poor, and the wrong people doing the plundering, and therefore, naturally, you've got to put an end to it. The dread demonstration effect has always caused great terror.

Western backing for the Indonesian invasion probably has roots in similar concerns—there were also strategic interests and others, but my strong suspicion is that when, or if, the records ever come out, we'll discover that the debt of gratitude to the Indonesians, and the concern over the spreading infection, whether it was Africa or Southeast Asia or elsewhere, plays a large part. There's also another factor, the one that was emphasised by the Australian Ambassador to Jakarta, Richard Woolcott, in August 1975. You remember, that's right before the invasion and when everyone was pretending they didn't know it was happening, although we now know, of course, that they did know it was happening.

Woolcott wrote a secret cable, which was later leaked—an important one, I'm sure that you've seen it. He advised in secret that Australia go along with the impending invasion because, he said, Australia could make a better deal on the oil resources in the Timor Gap with Indonesia 'than with Portugal or with an independent East Timor'.[14] What's good for the energy companies is always in the 'national interest'—that's virtually by definition. Australia's *de jure* recognition of the annexation was in that context, it seems: the context of trying to make a better deal to steal the oil. The treaty was actually signed in 1989, ratified by the Australian Parliament a year later, and went into effect immediately after the Dili Massacre when the Indonesian and Australian joint authority began signing exploratory contracts with major oil companies to rob the country of what the treaty calls 'the Indonesian province of East Timor', which does not deserve the inalienable right of self-determination guaranteed by international law and explicitly by the United Nations, we are told, because it is not viable economically—that's what we are told by the people who are robbing its resources.

You've got to admire the gall, I have to say, but people listen to it. Your Foreign Minister has a scholarly treatise on Australian foreign policy in which he offers the Timor Gap Treaty as an example—stellar example, of what he calls 'a non-military solution to a problem',[15] a model to follow in a peaceful world. That's pretty impressive—not a lot of people would do that. Well, you know the rest of the story, I'm sure, and I'm not going to recount it—it's mostly the story of terror and atrocities, and Western complicity in extraordinary crimes.

World attention again focused on East Timor after the Dili Massacre, that unpardonable 'aberration', the technical error that I mentioned, and in fact it has stayed at a fairly high level since then, and that gives us some real opportunities. We can just conclude with what is the most important thing: this horror story can be brought to an end if Westerners can exhibit even a fraction of the integrity and the courage that's been shown right now by Indonesians who are protesting what their Government is doing under conditions vastly more onerous than any of us face, and I don't even speak of the incredible courage of the Timorese which shames all of us, perhaps Australians in particular because of the 'debt of blood' remaining from World War II, which I'm sure you know about.

I think there is good reason to believe that we may be at a kind of turning point, that with enough energy and commitment to change Western policy, there's reason to believe that the Government of Indonesia can be encouraged to do what it's thinking about anyway, and that is to remove the piece of gravel from the shoe. If so, there is a good possibility that one of the world's major atrocities can be brought to an end, that the people of East Timor can enjoy the inalienable right of self-determination, and perhaps even in less than a thousand years.

Endnotes

1 Statements made by the Indonesian Student Council one week after the Santa Cruz massacre of 12 November 1991.

2 See Brian Toohey, *Australian Financial Review*, 24 November 1994, and the editorial 'Indonesia's Pebble', in the *Wall Street Journal*, 17 November 1994.

3 See Randolph Ryan, *Boston Globe*, 25 and 28 October 1994.

4 See Noam Chomsky, *Year 501,* Verso, London, 1993.

5 Harold Crouch, *Army and Politics in Indonesia*, Cornell University, 1978, p. 351.

6 *Foreign Relations of the United States, 1958–60*, Washington, 8 April 1958, Vol. XVII.

7 Ibid.

8 Ibid., 12 August 1958.

9 See Noam Chomsky, *Rethinking Camelot*, South End, 1993, for background details of the recently declassified record.

10 Robert Cribb, *The Indonesian Killings of 1965–1966*, *Monash Papers on Southeast Asia*, Monash University, Melbourne, 1991.

11 John Murray Brown, *Christian Science Monitor*, 6 February 1987, *Economist*, 15 August 1987.

12 Ibid.

13 Op. cit., p. 341.

14 J. R. Walsh and G. J. Munster, *Documents on Australian Defence and Foreign Policy 1968–1975,* Hong Kong, 1980, p. 200.

15 Gareth Evans and Bruce Grant, *Australia's Foreign Relations*, Melbourne University Press, 1991, p. 109.

In October 1995 there were claims made in the media by several East Timorese living in Australia that they had new evidence about the circumstances surrounding the deaths in October 1975 at Balibo, East Timor, of five Australian and Australian-based journalists, and the death in December of the same year of Roger East in Dili, the capital of East Timor. The then Labor Government initiated a new inquiry under the retiring Chairman of the National Crime Authority, Tom Sherman, to evaluate any new evidence and to establish the existence of prima facie *weight to such evidence. The findings of the Sherman Inquiry were released in June 1996 by the new conservative Government and although it was established that Roger East had been summarily executed by an 'unidentified Indonesian soldier', the finding that the Balibo Five were 'killed in the heat of battle while fighting was continuing to occur' was condemned by the activist community. The following is an evaluation of the Sherman Report which was first published in the Melbourne University journal, 'Protocol', 1996.*

12

OUR COMMON ALLEGIANCE

JIM AUBREY

On 6 May 1976, in the Federal House of Representatives, Labor MP Tom Uren, an ex-prisoner of war in West Timor during World War II, spoke with 'no doubt in my mind' about a conspiracy in the Department of Foreign Affairs to mislead both the Government and the people. Almost one month later, on 2 June, the statement he made in the House that day would become extremely prophetic—'the way in which the five young people were ill-treated and the attitude of the Indonesian authorities will have an enormous

211

influence on our relationship with the Indonesian Government in the future'.[1]

The conclusions of all previous independent investigations into the deaths of Greg Shackleton and his colleagues as well as statements made within Federal Parliament suggest sections of the Federal Government not only knew about the fate of the journalists almost immediately after their deaths, purportedly from intercepted communications intelligence traffic. It has also been stated on many occasions that the Prime Minister of that period was aware as early as September 1974 of the wishes of President Suharto for the incorporation of East Timor into the Indonesian Republic. (Prime Minister Whitlam and President Suharto held a meeting in Central Java in September 1974 and again met the following year in Townsville, Australia.

The secret cable of the Government's Ambassador in Jakarta, Mr Richard Woolcott, which was sent to the Department of Foreign Affairs on 17 August 1975 and which was later leaked to the media, in January 1976, certainly alludes to a prior knowledge of Suharto's intentions—'Indonesia still wants to know whether privately we still sympathise with their objectives (incorporation of Timor), even if we cannot condone the means they have adopted in pursuing it'.[2]

Labor MP for New South Wales Senator Arthur Gietzelt stated in the Senate on 7 April 1976 that Mr Woolcott is 'one of the guilty men', and that 'there are people who have blood on their hands in this issue'.[3] In the same speech, he stated that the order to shoot the Australian newsmen was actually heard on naval radio (said by Senator Gietzelt on 3 June to be at Shoal Bay, near Darwin), which was being used to monitor the Indonesian troop movements taking place near East Timor. In the first week of May, the *National Times* newspaper claimed that the Joint Intelligence Organisation had informed the Department of Foreign Affairs about the fate of the newsmen two days after the Indonesians executed them.

Bruce Juddery, of the *Canberra Times*, reported on 31 May allegations that Mr Woolcott had altered a Ministerial statement in

October of 1975 from the Foreign Affairs Minister, Senator Willesee, 'to conceal the fact that Australia knew Indonesian troops were active in East Timor more than three months before the all-out invasion of the territory on December 7th'.[4] From another leaked cable sent by Mr Woolcott to the Department of Foreign Affairs dated 29 October, he stated that: 'if the Minister said or implied in public that the Indonesian Government was lying, we would invite a hurt and angry reaction'.[5]

Gough Whitlam was a seasoned parliamentarian, of considerable skills in the arts of exhortation and admonishment. However, he was remarkably recumbent to the fate of the Balibo Five, and when the story from Jakarta finally surfaced that they had been caught in 'cross-fire' between anti-Fretilin and Fretilin forces, we can easily assume that the often-mentioned pro-Indonesia lobby inside the Department of Foreign Affairs who were responsible for advising the Prime Minister met this news with a collective genuflection and three Hail Marys.

During the weeks that followed the newsmen's fate the policy of the Government went no further than to regard the two television crews as missing in East Timor, perhaps due to misadventure. Mr Whitlam, in a reply in the Federal House of Representatives on 21 October 1975, one full week after the event, stated that: 'the Government is gravely concerned about the fate of the missing journalists.'[6]

On 25 March 1976, the Federal Labor MP for Fraser, Mr Kenneth Fry, stated in the House of Representatives that members from both sides of the House had visited East Timor because 'the people of Australia were being denied the real truth. Five Australian journalists were murdered by the Indonesian forces because the Indonesians did not want the truth to come out. There is no doubt about it'.[7]

On the same day, Don Chipp, the soon-to-be leader of a new political party, the Australian Democrats, and the then Liberal MP for Hotham, made the only explicit reference in the 1975/76 parliamentary debates concerning the depth of Mr Whitlam's involvement in Indonesia's territorial ambitions for East Timor. 'The truth is yet to come out about the infamous conversation he [Mr Whitlam] had with President Suharto and Mr Malik [the Indonesian Foreign Affairs Minister] in Bali and north Queensland last year. The secrets discussed in these conversations have yet to come out.'[8]

It is now time for these 'secrets' to 'come out', because there are serious questions regarding the alleged absence of communications between Canberra and Jakarta to confirm the non-combatant status of the journalists or even to warn them of the danger of an impending invasion. Then there is the other area of serious conjecture concerning the acceptance of the debatable 'cross-fire' theory suggesting 'misadventure' for the journalists' deaths.

Newspaper reports in Australia as late as 6 November 1975 had still not officially confirmed the deaths, and it is rather illuminating to see on 7 November in the *Age* newspaper an article announcing the second year of a three-year military-aid programme to Indonesia, with the expected aid for that year amounting to 25 million dollars, including naval boats and twelve military aircraft that were almost certainly used in the armed aggression against thousands of innocent men, women and children in East Timor.

Roger East, who was later executed in a massacre on the wharf in Dili, was as good as dead when he first thought of going to East Timor to find out what had happened at Balibo. He was as good as dead because of the unbelievable tolerance emanating from Canberra: you could murder defenceless Australian citizens and get away with it.

The conclusions of the Sherman Report perpetuate the myth of engaged combat in Balibo, whereas every independent investigation, including the extensive investigations made inside East Timor and Indonesia by James Dunn, a former Australian Consul to Portuguese East Timor, dispute this key point about the fate of the newsmen.

I have been able to corroborate from my own sources the same conclusion as that reached by Mr Dunn that there was no engaged combat at Balibo; that Fretilin had abandoned Balibo as a strategic liability; and that an Indonesian force with only a few anti-Fretilin Timorese had more or less strolled into the village. Indeed, the single most critical flaw of the Sherman Report is that the urgency of the 'cross-fire' theory is given unequivocal credibility by the adoption of the phrase: 'that the Balibo Five were killed in the heat of battle while fighting was continuing to occur.'[9]

The same theme reoccurs later in the Sherman Report with the newsmen concluded to have been [killed] ... 'in circumstances of continuous fighting between the Fretilin and the anti-Fretilin forces'.[10]

I do not possess the legal expertise to conduct an inquiry of this nature. However, I am bewildered as to why Mr Sherman would choose the evidence of the single witness known as witness 'L1', whose account supports a battle in Balibo whereas, from the list of 33 witness statements, nine of these, including accounts made some time after 13 October by Greg Shackleton himself (in his diary and on the Channel Seven news footage), refer to Fretilin's decision not to contest Balibo, refer to the decision by the Fretilin soldiers safeguarding the newsmen to retreat without them, or state that there was no fighting at Balibo when the Indonesians entered the village.

Even the anti-Fretilin Timorese whom one witness stated had unwittingly told him that he had 'killed the two journalists by knife'[11] told another witness: 'How can I be a hero? There were no fights; there was no firing, nothing.'[12]

From all the witnesses interviewed by Mr Sherman, no fewer than four different houses were said to be the place where the bodies were burned, with two witnesses stating that the bodies were burned in the open—at different places. It is necessary to point out that not one of these people was an immediate eyewitness to the murder of the newsmen.

Further discrepancies, just as alarming, again involve witness 'L1', who told Mr Sherman that three of the bodies were inside the house and 'two were in the doorway with their feet sticking out, on the verandah'.[13] This apparently occurred while 'L1' was in the middle of a rather serious military engagement which, according to him, involved grenades and rocket fire. He even had a scar to prove it! The claims of 'L1' not only about being engaged in combat but also very relevantly about the position of the bodies are in stark contradiction with the accounts of sixteen other witnesses.

If the accounts of these sixteen witnesses lead us to be able to make any conclusion, it can only be that there is no possible way the bodies of the newsmen could be together in the one house, as the information of these witnesses is that two of the Balibo Five were 'despatched' well outside the house.

Very pertinent conclusions of Mr Sherman's inquiry were made upon a dubious evaluation of the testimony of a single 'witness' whose account is at glaring variance with so many other accounts. To discredit the version of the 'many' for the 'one' without any corroboration does not make any sense to me. Perhaps Mr Sherman would like to explain?

Recently, I held a press conference in Parliament House, Canberra (4 December 1996), where I disclosed the fact that I am in possession of a hand-written eyewitness testimony to the brutal murder of the Balibo Five. I am under an oath of confidentiality whereby I am unable to release very pertinent details of the act of murder which took place, because to do so would be to jeopardise the eyewitness and other innocent lives.

What I can say did happen at Balibo was the cold-blooded summary execution of Greg Shackleton, Tony Stewart, Gary Cunningham, Brian Peters and Malcolm Rennie in the most brutal manner, in circumstances of no engaged combat or any fighting whatsoever.

Since I released this information, the 1996 Nobel Peace Prize co-laureate, José Ramos Horta, has also released information in an

SBS radio interview with Andrew Kruger on 3 December, about another eyewitness, an East Timorese who had actually been forced to burn the journalists.

Mr Ramos Horta went on to release details, and I am now able to state, without breaking my oath of confidentiality, that, apart from one discrepancy—the Horta witness states that one of the journalists was at first killed, whereas my witness states that two of the journalists were at first killed—everything after this is word for word, verbatim. Here is a part of the transcript of the Horta/Kruger interview recorded 3 December 1996 (courtesy of SBS).

José Ramos Horta is speaking: 'According to this source ... of the five journalists, only one was dead when he arrived on the scene ... The four that were alive were ordered to be tied up. So the East Timorese was himself the one who tied up the four. Then the one that was dead was thrown on top of the four ... Then the East Timorese was ordered to pour petrol on the five. Then he was ordered to light a match. And all five were burned beyond recognition. The other four—it's significant, very disturbing—apparently, allegedly, were alive'.[14]

Roger East was also executed in cold blood, in a massacre of several hundred East Timorese on Dili wharf on the morning of 8 December. Jill Jolliffe, an Australian journalist who was evacuated from Dili on 2 December 1975, describes Roger East as 'a rugged individualist'.[15] Pilot Paul Spottiswood states that when he offered to fly him out of East Timor, East replied, 'I can't leave these people, everyone else has but I can't leave them. We've been sending messages all around the world requesting observers to come and see what is happening here, and we've had no response. I just can't leave these people.'[16]

The scandalous reaction of the print media to the Sherman Report was a united call to now put this matter to rest. Not one journalist has stepped forward to investigate the veracity of the conclusions reached by Mr Sherman. Jill Jolliffe reported a witness stating that while Roger East was being dragged along Dili wharf, with his hands bound with wire while being kicked and prodded by the bayonets of the Indonesian soldiers, he 'hurled a constant stream of abuse at his captors'.[17]

If Roger East was alive today, he would no doubt be hurling similar abuse at all and sundry—media and politicians—for the whitewash of these crimes. We must remember that East and the Balibo Five were among 60,000 victims in just the first three months of East Timor's invasion at the hands of the brutal Indonesian army. In twenty-two years there have been more than 200,000 victims. Are these the 'different values' that Mr Howard and his predecessors argue we should accept when defining our relationship with Indonesia?

It is pertinent at this point to quote from an account by one of the East Timorese taken from Michele Turner's book *Telling East Timor, Personal Testimonies, 1942–1992*, which Mr Sherman quotes in his report. After describing being part of a work party to throw condemned men and women, including friends and neighbours, into the sea, Mr Siong (a pseudonym) described Roger East's death and the further atrocities:

'They push him, tell him to face the sea. He [East] refuses to do this. The Indonesians just fire at him. He falls straight into the sea. Next they bring the ten that had been working with us, digging the graves. The Indonesians tell them to stand in line and face the sea and then they are shot with a machine-gun. Four people in that first sixteen of us digging graves were father and son, but the Indonesians didn't know this. There on the wharf they kill the father, and the son must tie and throw his father into the sea. Then they kill the other son and his father is one of the six of us who must tie and throw his body'.[18]

In 1975, Richard Woolcott advised the Whitlam Government to let 'events take their course' and to 'act in a way which would be designed to minimise the public impact in Australia'.[19] However, I believe that every Australian feels a very deep shame over our role in the course events have actually taken in East Timor.

Furthermore, I believe it is a shame that Australians would like to see reversed today.

The fate of the Balibo Five and that of Roger East will be far more crucial than we can ever imagine, in determining who we are as a people, as a nation, even more so twenty years after the tragedy, and whether, willingly or not, the conclusions in the Sherman Report have continued the ugly policy of deception. It really appears that only a full judicial inquiry into Balibo can achieve justice, silencing once and for all the conspiracy of denial instigated twenty years ago by those among us who had forgotten our common allegiance.

I should end this article with some of the inspirational words of Xanana Gusmao, the jailed leader of the East Timorese, but I am certain he would forgive me for choosing another 'legend', Gough Whitlam. In the Federal House of Representatives, on 1 June 1976, the former Prime Minister stated that 'a peaceful Southeast Asia can only be achieved by the nations of the region solving their problems in cooperative endeavour, free of external interference from whatever source'.[20] If only Mr Whitlam had espoused those noble sentiments just one year earlier and made a principled stand against Suharto and his brutal thugs!

Endnotes

1 T. Uren, Hansard, Australian House of Representatives, 6 May 1976 and 2 June 1976.

2 Several sources, G. J. Munster and R. Walsh, *Documents on Australian Defence and Foreign Policy 1968–1975,* Sydney, 1980; Munster and Walsh, *Secrets of State: A Detailed Assessment of the Book they Banned*, Angus and Robertson, Sydney, 1982; Geoffrey C. Gunn with Jefferson Lee, *A Critical View of Western Journalism and Scholarship on East Timor*, Journal of Contemporary Asia Publishers, Manila, 1994; Dale Van Atta and Brian Toohey, 'The Timor Papers' (Part One and Part Two), *National Times*, 30 May–5 June, 6–13 June 1982.

3 Senator Gietzelt, Hansard, Australian Senate, 7 April 1976.

4 *Canberra Times*, 31 May 1976.

5 Ibid.

6 G. Whitlam, Hansard, Australian House of Representatives,
21 October 1975.

7 K. Fry, Hansard, Australian House of Representatives,
25 March 1976.

8 D. Chipp, Hansard, Australian House of Representatives,
25 March 1976.

9 Sherman Report, Australian Government, Canberra, 1996,
p. 110.

10 Ibid., p. 137.

11 Ibid., p. 58.

12 Ibid., p. 63.

13 Ibid., p. 75.

14 José Ramos Horta/Andrew Kruger, SBS Radio, PM
3 December 1996.

15 Sherman Report, op. cit., p. 120.

16 Ibid., p. 130.

17 Jill Jolliffe, *Canberra Times*, 28 October 1980.

18 Michele Turner, *Telling East Timor: Personal Testimonies
1942–1992*, University of New South Wales Press, Sydney, 1992,
p. 104.

19 G. J. Munster and R. Walsh, op. cit., et al.

20 G. Whitlam, Hansard, Australian House of Representatives,
1 June 1976.

*Bishop Hilton Deakin is an Assistant Bishop in the Catholic Archdiocese
of Melbourne, Australia. His human rights activities stem from his work
among the Aboriginal people and East Timor's refugees and orphans.
Bishop Deakin is currently a trustee and patron of several children's
relief foundations as well as the Chair of the East Timor Human Rights
Centre. He remains actively involved in the Catholic Aboriginal Ministry
in Melbourne as well as the struggle for freedom in East Timor.
This chapter outlines the history of the Catholic Church in East Timor
as well as its role in the struggle.*

13

EAST TIMOR AND THE CATHOLIC CHURCH

BISHOP HILTON DEAKIN

The Portuguese were the first known European visitors to land on
Timor, some time between 1512–22 AD. For Europe, it was a
time of discovery urged on by a collective inquiring mind, but also
by an acquisitive urge to gain economic advantage for expanding
trade and industry. Timor had little to offer. The coastline offered
some haven and protection for ships on the move across the scatter
of islands that made up the East Indies. And there were fine stands
of the much sought-after sandalwood tree that gave some return for
efforts at settlement. Most often, each Portuguese ship had its chap-
lain on board. And a ship on discovery trips would most likely have
had instructions to lay the groundwork for Christian evangelisation.

The first recorded visit of missionaries to the island occurred in 1561, when a Dominican friar, Father Antonio Taviera, sailed from Flores to Lifau, situated in the former enclave of Oecusse in present-day West Timor. Records of the early days of missionary contact are few and scarce. As a result, little is known about events of the time. Nor is anything of certainty known about the efforts and success rate of the early missionaries. It seems that one consistent policy of the friars was to convert the local chieftains, or *liurai*, to the new ways, rather than follow a policy of attempting wholesale conversions. The common view seemed to be that local people would follow their *liurai* along the Christian path.

SLOW RESULTS

Within a century, all but one of the five *liurai* in what is today West Timor became Catholics. But just one *liurai* in today's East Timor took up the new ways. For reasons whose explanation seems now to be lost in the mists of time, there were no mass movements of conversion. People seemed to be slow, even loath, to give up the ways of their forebears. The missionaries attended to the religious needs of the few settlers, the small but growing number of people of mixed descent, and the trickle of converts from the efforts of the missionaries.

In 1621, a band of twenty missionaries came to the island. They heightened the pressure for conversion. For their efforts they gained a foothold on the island, but not much more. Besides doing the work of the Church, the Dominicans developed areas of self-interest in the political and economic spheres of activity on the island. Such would not have been well developed, but the close relationship the missionaries had with the secular colonising power gave them the opportunities for defining their own areas of interest.

However, it appears that the Church personnel encouraged rapport with the local people. This relationship became apparent when the missionaries sided with the local people during some of the skirmishes and rebellions that proved to be a constantly reoccurring feature of life on the island. Every now and again, a record or document shows up to provide a glimpse at the state of affairs of the Church. A document from 1750 records that East Timor had 50 churches. If such was the case, there was little enough to show for 150 years of missionary work.

EAST AND WEST

The island suffered disturbances and ravages from time to time over the disputes between the Portuguese and the Dutch, who cast their own trade-sensitive eyes over the hapless island. The end result was the division of the island into two parts, West and East, with Portugal retaining only the eastern section of the island. The division brought about differences between the two sections that last to this day.

Back in Portugal, political events from time to time affected the state of affairs in East Timor. One such was the emergence of anticlericalism in the nineteenth century. The Dominicans were expelled from Portugal and its overseas territories in 1834. This left only four or five priests to service the entire East Timorese Church for half a century. There was little support for missionary staff such as religious orders or trained lay leaders. Consequently, any drive to evangelise the people was severely blunted for many decades.

NEW GROWTH

However, in 1874, as the result of a policy to rationalise lines of communication and authority, the Vatican arranged for East Timor to become ecclesiastically dependent on the Portuguese Diocese of Macau, in China. Shortly afterwards, eleven diocesan clergy arrived in East Timor. They were to lay the foundation of a local body of diocesan and, eventually, native-born clergy, who would become a significant group in East Timor's historic struggle for independence. In 1898, four Jesuits arrived to open a secondary college and a meteorological observatory at Soibada in the mountains, to the middle south of the colony.

The positive and encouraging moves made on behalf of the East Timor Church came about through the interest and influence of a remarkable man, Bishop Antonio Joaquim de Medeiros, who worked in Goa and Macau. He visited East Timor several times. His correspondence indicates a sensitive and decision-oriented pastoral care for the area. He died in the colony, and was buried in the old Cathedral in Dili. After the building was destroyed, as a result of a Japanese bombing raid during the Second World War, his remains were re-interred in the bayside church of Motael, where they have a place of honour to this day.

By 1910, for instance, the Church was conducting sixteen schools for boys, and four for girls. This was nothing like a universal education system, nor one for boys and girls equally, but it was laying the foundation stone for an emerging educated group who could provide ideas and also services as the needs of the local society grew. Also, the system broadened and defined the Portuguese cultural base of the emerging educated class. This had its effect on the civil order and on the Church.

Back in Portugal, one result of a recent revolution was the forcing of all religious orders out of Portuguese territory. The Central Government restricted the activities of local diocesan clergy as well. It was all part of a prevailing anticlericalism that motivated politicians to restrict wherever possible the influence of the Church. This policy had its intended effect on the Church in East Timor. The number of diocesan clergy declined from twenty-two to ten between 1910 and 1922, one period for which there are accurate figures. Religious orders, male and female, still provided personnel for missionary work. Nearly all such male personnel were expatriates. Some of the women's congregations attracted local women into their ranks. It was all slow work, and the results were generally on the low side.

CENSUS PICTURE

Another clue to the results of Church efforts was a Church census of 1930, which claimed 18,984 Catholics as members of the Church and another 1100 preparing for membership. By any standards this does not represent a remarkable entry into the East Timorese population, colony-wide. The three likely major results were:

a)   the growth of a large Portuguese-oriented group of people, for whom Portugal was the second homeland across the seas and the continuing source of culture and ideas;

b)   the conversion of the larger part of the body of *liurai*, their education and that of their families and clans; and

c)   the small but steady growth in the number of diocesan native-born clergy. The increase in numbers of all Church personnel was significant nonetheless.

SECOND WORLD WAR

The Second World War almost passed by East Timor. Almost, but not quite. The damage done to person and property was enormous. Dili was created a diocese in 1940, but nothing could be done about the new diocese, including appointing a bishop. The clergy was scattered. Three were killed, one died during hostilities from his sufferings, and six took to the mountains, partly to escape the Japanese soldiers and partly to be with those of their people who had also fled. Ten others fled to Australia, and remained there for the duration of the war.

FIRST BISHOP

In 1945, the first Bishop of Dili was consecrated in Sydney. He was Dom Jaime Goulart, a Portuguese priest, nephew of the Cardinal patriarch of Goa, India, of which Archdiocese Dili became a dependent See. Goulart was a well-educated and urbane man, much travelled and deeply committed to East Timor. He began working there in 1933, and remained, except for the time spent in Australia, for thirty years. On his return with his fellow refugees in 1945, he went about the task of raising the Church and the people generally from the ashes. He sought help from abroad: from Portugal; from the Vatican and its offices, which gave aid and other support to mission countries; from Goa, which eventually provided volunteer diocesan clergy; and from Australia, where he had made friends and useful contacts.

One important move was the setting up of the first stages of a seminary at Dare, in the hills behind Dili. The Jesuit Fathers were given charge of the new institution. It proved to be the only post-secondary educational centre in the colony for many years. It gave its students an educated and long look at the world of ideas, culture and science. Few of its students became priests. But the college provided a layer of articulate and educated men who became leaders in 1975, when leadership was most needed by the population.

Constant work and the climate took their toll on the health of the bishop, and he handed in his resignation in 1966. He had given his required five-yearly report on the state and shape of his diocese in 1964. No doubt he pulled the diocese back from the ruins of war and laid a foundation for growth.

STATE OF AFFAIRS

The accuracy of the figures of the Goulart report cannot be guaranteed, but the trends are detectable. The report claims there were some 560,000 non-baptised people in the colony. There were 113,500 Catholics and a staggering 14,000 being prepared for baptism. The previous year saw nearly 9000 baptisms. The figures are an almost certain sign of a shift to the Church taking place well before the eventual invasion of 1975, questioning the usual explanation that the growth in Church membership took place following that event.

It appears that the invasion and occupation and East Timor's absorption into the Indonesian Republic may have been a partial cause of the shift. But there was already large movement going on.

Interestingly, the report noted there was a handful of other Christians, but no further information is included. There are claimed to be c.5300 Timorese of Chinese origin, of whom about 490 are noted as Catholics. Altogether there were forty-four priests, of whom just seven were locally born. Of these, five were Jesuits and nine were Salesians. Also there were twelve religious brothers and thirty-seven religious sisters. Six of these were Timorese. The figures showed not only an increase in all numbers, but also a small group of locally born Timorese males and females developing a presence in the professional personnel of the local Church.

The report indicates that the colony had less than adequate schooling facilities, of which about half were Church-run. They consisted of three secondary and forty-one primary schools, holding 4667 boys and 1957 girls, respectively.

SECOND BISHOP

Goulart handed over his diocese to his successor, Bishop José Joaquim Ribeiro. A Portuguese priest with experience in parish and seminary staff life behind him, Ribeiro proved to be a man of vastly different temperament and capacity. He was an avowed conservative, at a time when the world-wide Church was in a state of theological ferment and about to absorb the impact of the second

Vatican Council. He belonged to the school of strongly anti-communist clerics, who were products of the Cold War period. Within a short time of his taking over his diocese, Ribeiro developed an intensely integrationist approach to East Timor. He saw its future as being at one with the future of its huge neighbour.

The Bishop carried on Goulart's expansionist policies, at the same time consolidating what his predecessor had accomplished. But affairs in other parts of the world were catching up with East Timor, and would take them along a road of suffering and death, even to a struggle for survival.

The ferment in the Church was one thing. Political changes in Europe and the Portuguese colonies were another. Forces working and fighting for freedom and independence broke out in the old colonies and took to arms against colonial power and administration from Europe. Some of the Portuguese troops took recreational leave in East Timor from the privations of battle in various other countries. They, and the few political prisoners who found themselves banished there, fed ideas into the inquiring minds of the Timorese locals and prepared them for the days ahead.

NEW ERA

Portugal itself found its national life at a crossroads with the passing of the fascist dictator Salazar. The Government forced the pace of change and the decolonisation of the old empire. The political pulse in the far-away colony quickened as people took up the challenges that the European scene presented. Political parties emerged. One came to be known eventually as Fretilin, and it slowly built itself into a strong populist force that could claim majority support in town and country. It also produced from its midst the core of the Resistance fighters who carried on the struggle for freedom after the invasion and occupation of the colony and its forced incorporation into the neighbouring Republic of Indonesia.

The second most significant party, UDT, was rather town-based and sought to have stronger ties with Portugal. They also held a strong line for independence. The third party, Apodeti, was small but not significant, and sought integration with Indonesia.

The ravages of the civil unrest fed Ribeiro's fears of a communist takeover. He even passed on a piece of political gossip, as it turned out, of a band of Vietnamese Reds entering the island to train Fretilin in guerrilla warfare. The terrible damage done to people and their land following the invasion of the island on 6 December 1975 almost brought the Bishop down. He proved himself to be a brave man through it all, as he strode out to minister to his people and to bring them aid and comfort. However, he never really understood what was happening, and eventually found himself mentally isolated from all around him. He suffered from the sight of all the atrocities he had to witness. No doubt he must have been particularly humiliated by the sight of all the cruelties and destruction borne by his people at the hands of the very people in whose company he had believed the East Timorese people would find their national identity. His health gave way, and he handed in his resignation in 1976. No doubt he would have had a hand in suggesting a successor.

THIRD CHURCH LEADER

For the first time the Vatican named a Timorese to head the diocese. Martinho da Costa Lopes was a diocesan priest, who had to his credit a long list of appointments in the diocese, in parish, mission station and chancery and even a stint as a parliamentarian in Lisbon. The Vatican did not appoint him to the rank of bishop, but nominated him as Apostolic Administrator, with the title of 'Monsignor'. He had the common touch. He was much loved by his clergy and admired by his fellow citizens. He took charge of a Church that was fighting for its very life, along with the rest of the nation.

Six of the local clergy had gone to the hills and joined the guerrilla movement. He found it difficult to seek priests and religious staff from outside the colony, since conditions of war prevailed. He had to head a people, most of whom suffered terribly and from among whom many thousands fled to other countries, among people who had differing views about what was going on and where the island must go. Through it all, Lopes pleaded for help from the outside world. His cries for help went unanswered for the most part. The world powers were fast accommodating their views of the matter to the practical necessities associated with keeping Indonesia contented. Constantly he pleaded with military commanders and with police officers to release prisoners and to give information of the whereabouts of citizens under arrest.

Lopes was quickly isolated from the wider world. The Timorese people were seldom more left alone. The experience of isolation and seeming rejection forced the people to turn inwards for survival. Priests, usually as poor as their people, suffered with them. Somehow the identity in suffering forged a new oneness. Statements, speeches, letters and suchlike gave testimony to the silence and the suffering and marked an emerging sense of a unity of purpose and destiny. In the early days of the struggle, the Indonesian bishops spoke out in defence of their co-religionists. But it did not last for long. However, they did organise fellow citizens in their nation to send in relief and much-needed medicine.

The persistent lack of international support forced the Timorese people to rely on their own inner resources. Inexplicably, a major drift towards membership of the Catholic Church began to occur. Why it happened has never been convincingly explained. But it helped to shape a strong unity of opposition to the enforced absorption into the Indonesian Republic and the adoption of its laws and customs.

SURVIVAL WORK

Lopes worked tirelessly for sheer survival. His lonely role began to become apparent as other people in the common tragedy began to show their hands. As Apostolic Administrator, Lopes was not structurally part of the Indonesian Church, nor did he have the right or duty to participate in the Indonesian Bishops' Conference. This was the ecclesiastical state of affairs, in spite of the fact that East Timor had been absorbed politically into the structures of the Republic as the 27th province. Lopes' immediate superior, the one to whom he reported, was the Pope's representative in Jakarta. He held the office of Papal Pro-nuncio, or Papal Ambassador to the Jakarta Government.

Many Timorese saw the Nuncio as no friend of their nation or of their cause. In public speeches in East Timor, he admonished the priests for his perception of their interference in politics. It was widely believed also that he gave little comfort or support to the Apostolic Administrator.

THE END FOR A HERO

In the early days of his administration, Lopes confessed an abhorrence for communism, and for its alleged connection with Fretilin. Much has been made of the communist influence in the Fretilin movement. One suspects the point is made for political advantage, rather than in pursuit of the fact of the matter. The Fretilin leadership of the time had about 50 to 60 Catholics and some seven communists. This would indicate a containment of influence. But it did not prevent Lopes from being deeply concerned about Marxist influences. His pastoral work brought him close almost daily to his fellow Timorese, who were suffering terribly at the hands of the occupying army. He made formal contact with the guerrilla forces to influence them towards moving away from their Marxist orientations. Fretilin did make a separation, and many credit Lopes with effecting the change. But he became a marked man.

Under pressure from the Papal Nuncio, Lopes was forced to resign. Those who were in a position to know what happened simply say he was sacked. He left East Timor when he resigned, in 1983. The people gave him one of the largest send-offs ever seen in Dili. He never returned. He settled eventually in Lisbon, living in near-poverty. He travelled the world speaking publicly of his beloved Timor, pleading its cause, begging for help and relief, attempting to turn the world's critical eye to what was happening in East Timor. He saw little of his work succeed. But he kept the cause of East Timor's suffering in the public eye. He died in Lisbon in 1991. As the years pass, his reputation as a brave and resolute leader grows. He is becoming revered as a hero of his people.

A NEW CHURCH LEADER

Lopes was succeeded by another East Timorese priest, Salesian Father Carlos Ximines Belo. A young man, he had spent a large part of his training for the priesthood in Portugal and Rome. When he returned to East Timor, the country was caught in the grip of fierce guerrilla warfare. The Vatican appointed him to replace Lopes, and gave him the rank of Monsignor and the task of Apostolic Administrator. He was a relatively unknown quantity among the clergy. The fact that he was a Salesian did not endear him to the diocesan clergy either. His own views of his country's affairs were not well formed at the time. But he had been a quick learner and a close observer of the Lopes style. Particularly did he learn of Lopes' dedicated concern for people and their problems.

As did his predecessor, Belo acted as advocate with the military and police authorities. He constantly visited the prisoners, and the sick and wounded in the hospitals. He also travelled about the country, calling in at every village and hamlet of his wide diocese.

At a grinding pace, and persistently, he came to know and be known by the population generally. Occasionally he would make a loud call for justice and cry out over the sufferings his people were enduring. He wrote to the Secretary-General of the UN, to various political leaders, to bishops and to friends. He found that such pleadings were not what some people wanted to hear. An occasional lecture from the Papal Nuncio, or a dressing-down from a military commander or a political authority in Jakarta taught him to be careful. He also learned to backtrack his comments, and to select times and places where he could tell the truth in a measured manner while at other times appearing to say either the opposite or something rather different.

It was said that he was chosen for the top position because he appeared to be a pliable personality who would follow orders when given. He did, in fact, and still does, but not in quite the way that others may have hoped. But he has also seen the deep suffering and continuing oppression across the land. Slowly but with a sure step, he began to win the respect and admiration of his clergy and people.

Gradually Belo organised the personnel of the diocese to cope with the huge influx of new members. The work placed great strains on a thin line of priests and religious workers, and on the even thinner economic resources available to the diocese. Belo met with many refusals to his pleas for help. But he also slowly won over people of goodwill who had deep sympathy for the troubles his people endured and the struggle for justice they continued to fight.

He invited a number of eager religious congregations to come to East Timor to work. As far as the immigration laws and regulations of the Republic would allow, some dozens of new recruits entered the country to staff parishes, take on educational work at all levels, provide medical and paramedical services, assist in developmental programmes and take on general pastoral work.

In 1987, the Pope nominated him as a bishop, but still kept him on as Apostolic Administrator of the Dili Diocese. He was often called the Bishop of Dili, when in fact he was the Bishop in Dili only. The year after his ordination he was host to Pope John Paul II, who visited the suffering colony for some hours, providing the occasion for a massive gathering of the Timorese people and some fierce clashes with the military and police.

He kept up the ever-increasing pace of pastoral care. World opinion kept alive the cause of East Timor. Hardly a week passed by without a report of some incident or statement or political move that involved the country.

Eventually his long years of work for peace and justice gained world recognition. To universal acclaim, he was awarded the Nobel Peace Prize in 1996. This time he was seen as a world leader. His people could hardly contain their delight and pride. When he returned from Oslo, Norway, following the presentation of the award, East Timorese gathered in Dili in the tens of thousands to welcome home their national hero. It was a high point of a proud life of service.

In December of the same year, the Vatican announced that there would be another Bishop in East Timor, to head the new Diocese of Baucau. He was Father Basilio Nascimento, a diocesan priest, widely acclaimed and popular. He was also appointed an Apostolic Administrator. It meant that the East Timorese Church was still not incorporated into the structures of the Indonesian Catholic Church.

UNFINISHED BUSINESS

The military occupation has not allowed a let-up, nor a cessation of oppressive measures and abuses of human rights. The youth are inheriting a legacy of suffering, death, deprivation of rights, and an intense hatred for those who have caused such conditions to persist. Probably one of the most significant experiences in recent years has been the growth in the migration programmes, by which thousands of people come into East Timor from other parts of the Republic. It presents an immense challenge to the cultural integrity of the Timorese people, to historical continuity, and to the reasonably homogeneous religious character of the people, and points to a continuation of the oppression of Timorese ways and aspirations. So the struggle continues.

The Australian Government has undertaken a legal challenge to determine the status of 1360 East Timorese who are seeking asylum in Australia. Whether or not Australia is legally obliged to grant them refuge will determine not only their future, but could as well, in the scenario of a High Court decision favouring the Government, unleash a civil disobedience challenge unique in our history. The Sanctuary Network was started in late 1995 by a Christian group, and the Josephite nun Sister Kath O'Connor has been involved from its inception.

14

THE SANCTUARY NETWORK

KATH O'CONNOR

The Sanctuary movement was begun in November 1995 by a group of concerned people in response to the Australian Government's declaration that it was going to deport East Timorese refugees because they were considered to be Portuguese citizens. It was called the Christian Sanctuary Network and has since grown to well over 10,000 people including unions, political parties, pensioners, lawyers, doctors, families, parishes, individuals and other groups. At this stage it is a national movement that is ready to be fully activated in the event that deportation is threatened. All have pledged to hide the East Timorese refugees here in Australia despite the risk of being jailed.

We believe that all laws are not necessarily good or moral, for example, slavery was once legal as was the extermination of the Jews under the law of Germany at the time. There is a greater law of morality and compassion that seems to be lacking in the Australian Government's policy-making. It is every Australian's responsibility to stand up for just and fair resolutions to issues.

The Government's position on the East Timorese refugees in general is that they will not be allowed under any circumstances to stay in Australia. The case of Kim Koe Jong found that he had dual citizenship but that Portugal would/could not guarantee safety and protection. The Portuguese Government has refused to take any refugee who does not want to go there.

The hypocrisy of both the Labor and Liberal Governments is clearly set out in the events beginning in 1995. Prior to this, East Timorese asylum-seekers had access to the same process as every other refugee seeking asylum.

Portugal, on behalf of East Timor, had taken Australia to the International High Court protesting the legality of the Timor Gap Treaty which gave Indonesia and Australia exclusive rights to the massive oil deposits. Because Indonesia was not part of the proceedings, the court could not adjudicate and in early 1995 the case was dismissed. Australia, in its defence, vehemently denied Portugal's right to speak for the people or the land of East Timor.

In mid-1995, General Mantiri, whose record of atrocities and brutality in East Timor was well documented, was nominated as the new Indonesian Ambassador to Australia. The Australian people's reaction to this nomination forced the Australian Government to reject him and diplomatic relations between the two countries became very tenuous. About the same time eighteen boat people arrived from East Timor and Australia was warned by Indonesia of the repercussions if they were given refugee status.

A statement by the Department of Immigration soon followed, directing the independent Refugee Review Tribunal (RRT) to declare East Timorese applicants to be Portuguese citizens and therefore ineligible for refugee status.

The Australian Government is one of the very few that

recognises Indonesian sovereignty over East Timor. That recognition, however, only applies when it is a matter of economics and trade. When it comes to the people and their needs they suddenly recognise Portugal.

Most cases are at Immigration level and have been for up to five years. A number are at RRT level. At present all are on Asylum Seekers Assistance (ASA) except for about a dozen who have been rejected by the RRT. The Government hopes to reject them at both levels, therefore making them ineligible for the funding. This would effectively put them on the streets as they have no other source of income while awaiting their appeals. The Government is saying—you can starve here in Australia while you wait for your cases to be heard or go back from whence you came.

International support of East Timor's fight for self-determination has taken centre stage, especially in the last twelve months, and Australia is finding itself more and more out of step with this opinion. It would follow that Labor would use this platform to push this new policy. Successive Governments have bowed to Suharto's Indonesia and it is difficult to believe there will be any basic policy shift that will put them off side with the Indonesian dictatorship. Martin Ferguson, Shadow Immigration Minister, has already stated that Labor agrees with the Government's refugee policy and this just reflects their stance on Indonesian matters when they were in Government.

There was a time when people fleeing persecution from their home country could find a welcome here in Australia or at least access to due process. Where the plight of the East Timorese is known in parishes the support is almost unanimous. Once the full story is known by any group, whether it is a Church group, university group, a club group, the response is offers of support in whatever way they are best able.

Maria and Josip exemplify the deep need for sensitivity and a change of policy on behalf of Canberra. As young teenagers, they fled to Australia after the 1991 Dili Massacre to escape the Indonesian Government's persecution and oppression which is the distressing plight of the people of occupied East Timor. Their grandparents protected our Australian soldiers following our invasion of their neutral territory during World War II. We said we would never forget them. Australia's response to their pleas for refugee status was to recommend that they be deported to Portugal, the former colonial power in East Timor. Neither of the two was born when Portugal withdrew in 1975, they do not speak Portuguese, they have no friends or relatives there and will, if sent there, in all likelihood never see their families again.

It is difficult to explain to Maria and Josip why our Government is traumatising them by dragging out their appeals for years, why it is repaying a moral debt with cold-hearted economic policy. It's hard to explain why we trade in arms, train the anti-insurgent squads and intelligence officers in interrogation methods that are used against them and their people.

It's hard to explain Australia's 'softly softly' approach that for twenty-two years has ignored the slow genocide of the East Timorese. An approach that flies in the face of international condemnation of Australia's stance. Numerous censures from the United Nations Commission on Human Rights, Amnesty International and the International Jurists have been ignored while the United States, the European Parliament, South Africa and other Asian countries have openly condemned the human rights abuses perpetrated by Indonesia in East Timor.

It is even harder to explain that in a democratic country, where dissent and debate are becoming less tolerated, a Government can obstruct independent bodies such as the Refugee Review Tribunal by directing them in their cases and removing those members who protest at the interference and its threat to impartial judgements. A Government which has withdrawn funding from the Refugee Advisory Council and is in the process of cutting off applicants' right to court appeals.

It is almost impossible to explain that for justice and a fair go to prevail, ordinary Australians have to threaten to break the law and declare Sanctuary and 'safe houses' if the 1360 East Timorese are to be deported. The Christian Sanctuary Network has over 10,000 people around Australia committed to this cause. The law of compassion and morality takes precedence over a law that denies a fair go under the International Refugee Convention to which Australia is bound.

Successive Government actions have affirmed their determination to give priority to economic policy over a moral-social policy. It is within their power to grant a Special Humanitarian visa to the 1360 that would save the East Timorese and at the same time not offend the Indonesian Government. It is not a matter of throwing out economic policy, that would be detrimental to Australia's future; it is a matter of reclaiming our reputation as a fair, responsible, compassionate people, who value human rights and morality as equally as we do economics.

Until that reputation is reclaimed, it is we, the people, who must take responsibility and stand up and say 'Enough'. By our silence we are colluding with the Government in its unjust and dishonourable deeds.

Dr George Aditjondro is a leading Indonesian academic living in self-imposed exile in Australia since 1995. His outspoken views have called for democratic reform in Indonesia and an end to the Indonesian occupation of East Timor. Dr Aditjondro first visited East Timor in 1974 and returned ten days after the Santa Cruz massacre to Dili in 1991. He has maintained his contact with all the political factions in East Timor since 1974 while working as a journalist with Tempo *magazine as well as when studying at Cornell University in the USA. In 1993 and 1994 he went to East Timor to assess the post-Xanana period. Dr Aditjondro has published a number of research papers and books outlining the human rights violations, the economic dispossession and the cultural marginalisation of the Maubere people of East Timor. This research paper is his latest work and was presented in 1997 to the UN Special Rapporteur on Women under the title 'Violence by the State Against Women in East Timor' as a report by the East Timor Human Rights Centre and is reproduced with their kind permission.*

15

THE SILENT SUFFERING OF OUR TIMORESE SISTERS

DR GEORGE ADITJONDRO

*This report is dedicated to Odilia Victor,
who died in childbirth in August 1997.*

INTRODUCTION

This report has been prepared for the UN Special Rapporteur on Violence Against Women who, in 1998, will report to the UN Commission on Human Rights on the issue of violence perpetrated by the state against women throughout the world. In the East Timor context, very little material is available about violence by the Indonesian authorities against East Timorese women. Further documentation of these violations is still required in order to more accurately report to the international community the true situation of women in East Timor.

In keeping with the mandate of the Special Rapporteur, this report does not attempt to cover all violations perpetrated against East Timorese women, but focuses on gender-specific violations. The report documents recent cases of gender-specific violations by the Indonesian authorities against women, and also surveys gender-specific violations against women throughout the twenty-two-year history of the Indonesian occupation of East Timor, thereby providing a useful historical perspective on the issue.

The meaning of 'violence' in the context of violations by the state against women could be interpreted widely to encompass a whole range of violations. However, the full range of violations is not covered here, principally because of the dearth of information available. Few organisations have been able to gather information about violence by the Indonesian authorities against East Timorese women, as human rights groups are denied official access to East Timor. Partially because of these difficulties, these kinds of violations have largely avoided international scrutiny.

This report therefore focuses on some of the main gender-specific violations being perpetrated by the Indonesian authorities against East Timorese women: rape and other forms of sexual abuse, sexual harassment, forced 'marriage', the use of women as 'sex slaves' or 'comfort women', and prostitution. These are some of the most pressing issues of concern to East Timorese women and, indeed, to the international community.

The ETHRC has already published a detailed report on the issue of violence against East Timorese women in the form of coercive sterilisation and coercive family planning under the Indonesian national family planning programme (*Keluarga Berencana Nasional*).[1] That report contains additional information about rape and sexual abuse, forced marriages and prostitution, some of which is also included here.

CONTEXT

Women subjected to gender-specific violations in East Timor generally live in poor, isolated communities and as such have limited access to independent lawyers or human rights organisations. This not only makes them more vulnerable to human rights violations, but also means that when their rights are violated, they are less likely to report the violations or seek justice. Furthermore, gender-specific violations, especially rape and sexual abuse and harassment, often go unreported because of human rights monitors' lack of access to East Timor and because of the high level of military surveillance.

East Timorese women who are the victims of rape and other forms of sexual abuse are less likely to report the violations, because they feel a deep sense of shame for themselves and their families. They are reluctant to pass on information about rape and sexual abuse to non-government organisations (NGOs), let alone report them to military or police authorities. Women are more willing to talk to priests or nuns about their experiences, but Amnesty International reported that an Australian lawyer assisting East Timorese asylum-seekers found that:

'Most asylum-seekers who have histories of sexual assault have indicated that they have not spoken to anybody about these instances'.[2]

Of the human rights violations that are reported, some have been investigated by the Indonesian Human Rights Commission

(KomnasHAM) and the military. But according to Amnesty International, there is no evidence that violations are systematically and independently investigated or that the members of the security forces responsible are brought to justice. Cases which are investigated are usually those taken up by the local or international community. Even then, the security officers are tried in military courts and, if sentenced, receive sentences which do not generally take into account the seriousness of the crime. Meanwhile, military and police authorities consistently deny that human rights violations such as rape take place.[3]

Despite official denials, there have been persistent accounts of gender-specific violations which are detailed enough to conclude that there are substantial patterns of rape, sexual abuse and other types of gender-specific violations being perpetrated against women in East Timor.

Indonesia has ratified the Convention on the Elimination of All Forms of Discrimination Against Women (CEDAW), creating a responsibility for Indonesia to promote and protect the rights of East Timorese women. In 1994, Indonesia played a prominent role in preparations for the 1995 Beijing Conference on Women by hosting the Second Asian and Pacific Ministerial Conference on Women. At this conference the Government restated its commitment to women's rights, in Ministerial speeches, and also signed the Jakarta Declaration, affirming that women's human rights are 'inalienable, integral, and indivisible parts of universal human rights', and that it regarded the implementation of CEDAW as 'crucial'.

This commitment has not yet been borne out in practice, and gestures towards international legitimacy will remain meaningless until the Indonesian Government takes concrete steps towards ending violations of women's rights in East Timor.

RAPE, SEXUAL ABUSE AND HARASSMENT

Rape is the most common form of gender-specific torture perpetrated against East Timorese women, and constitutes a violation of both sexual and reproductive rights. This type of violation is not simply a matter of sexual imbalance between the influx of male soldiers and the local women. It is a weapon of the occupying troops, used to subdue the local population. It is also a weapon used to destroy the opponent's culture, by biologically 'de-purifying' their ethnic constituency.[4]

Unfortunately, this inhuman behaviour has already been followed by some of the East Timorese members of the Indonesian military. In June 1994, 'DDS', an East Timorese member of the Indonesian security forces, was detained in Baucau for allegedly raping and then killing an eighteen-year-old East Timorese woman in a village in Quelicai, Baucau. He was handed over to the Indonesian police commander in Dili to be prosecuted.

In 1975, when the Indonesian troops landed in East Timor, they 'asked for girls or simply chased any women they found attractive'. Stories could be heard throughout East Timor about Indonesian soldiers abusing and raping girls of twelve to thirteen years of age and women, including pregnant women. They seemed to prefer the 'mestiza' girls, those of mixed Timorese and Portuguese descent, but they were also interested in other East Timorese.[5]

An East Timorese of Chinese descent, who spoke Bahasa Indonesia for trading with West Timor, was forced to interpret for the soldiers. After coming back, he told his niece, 'Olinda' (not her real name), how the Indonesian soldiers were raping East Timorese women. She became so frightened that she cut her long hair and cried and cried. Many young East Timorese girls also cut their hair and wore T-shirts and shorts, to disguise themselves as boys. Sometimes, although they dressed like boys but did not really look like boys, soldiers touched their breasts, to check whether they were boys or girls. So, to avoid being touched, the girls had to look dirty so the soldiers would not be interested in touching them. They wore dirty clothes, didn't comb their hair, went barefoot and, if their breasts had started to develop, they wrapped their breasts in order to flatten them.[6]

From 1975, the residence of the then Bishop of Dili, Dom Martinho da Costa Lopes, was full of girls seeking refuge from the soldiers. Typically, soldiers came in the evening to the parents' house, saying that the commander wanted to interview them, or wanted to ask the girls to go on Indonesia's national television (TVRI). Even after the Bishop went to complain to the highest-ranking officer, there were still soldiers who tried to sneak around the Bishop's fences to get the girls, but they were thrown out of the house by the Bishop himself.

As Dom Martinho tells his story, before he was replaced by the Vatican for his outspoken criticisms of the Indonesian occupation forces:

'People came all the time to tell me in secret, to clear their conscience of the things they were forced to do or see. Even out of the confessional, all the time people were coming, knocking softly on my door to talk to me because they felt so guilty when they were forced by the soldiers to do things they knew were wrong ... They come to tell it, women too, even young girls ... One young girl was put in a tank of water together with a Timorese man and the soldiers tell them to have sex. They're in front of the soldiers in a tank of water! The Timorese do not even know each other. They cannot do this thing of course, they turn away, they are shy. Some of these sorts of things make me think they are quite mad, these soldiers. They seemed to have no moral sense, no humanity. One of their favourite customs was to rape the wife in front of the husband, right there, sometimes the children there too. For Timorese people worse than physical suffering was the moral suffering of these things, the humiliation, taking away the dignity of people. I said to Indonesian officers, "Don't you have mothers, sisters, do you know what it means to be human?" '[7]

In the smaller places, far away from Dili, the soldiers could carry out their sexual attacks without having to worry about the Bishop's protests. On one occasion in Manatuto, the soldiers came to a house when they knew that the husband had gone to Dili for business, and raped the wife, in front of her three small children. The soldiers took turns raping the poor woman, while the others stole things from the house. When the husband returned and complained to the soldiers' commander, none of the soldiers was punished. His wife survived, but she was very sad after the experience.[8]

In 1978, young Timorese women, detained by the local military command (Kodim) in Viqueque for being members of the women's movement of the Resistance, the OPMT (Popular Organisation of Timorese Women), were subjected to rape for their involvement in the OPMT. Domingos Sarmento Alves, a young East Timorese leader studying in Portugal, testified:

'Every night one [OPMT member] would be taken by the troops and raped, sometimes as many as three rapes a night. We children had to watch this. This was when I began to hate the Indonesian soldiers who I thought were "communists".'[9]

'Security-linked' rapes

The wives, sisters and other female relatives of freedom fighters have been subjected to rape by Indonesian soldiers as a form of revenge against the freedom fighters, or to force the freedom fighters to surrender to the Indonesian troops. This is illustrated by the testimony of Donaciano Gomes. Gomes had been detained in four different military headquarters in Dili for fifteen days from January to February 1990, for his involvement in the demonstrations during the earlier visit of Pope John Paul II to Dili. After his release, he was eventually able to flee East Timor, and gave the following testimony to Amnesty International:

'Among the other prisoners there were women, who we were told were raped. There was one woman who was from Iliomar [south Lautem], whose husband had been a guerrilla commander and had been shot dead at the same time that she was captured. She was kept in a separate room, where she was raped, and had become pregnant, supposedly by a captain. Her name was Justina Moniz'.[10]

In 1995, one woman and her family were tortured for several days by Indonesian soldiers in Baucau who were looking for her twenty-two-year-old son, a freedom fighter. When she denied knowing his whereabouts, she was stripped naked, beaten, and kicked and subjected to torture by electric shock. Three days after her arrest, one of her nephews and her unmarried sister-in-law were called in for questioning. They too were interrogated under torture; her sister-in-law was also sexually abused.[11]

On 25 November 1992 at 4.30 am, Armandina dos Santos, a former Indonesian civil servant and youngest sister of the imprisoned East Timorese Resistance leader José Alexandre ('Xanana') Gusmao, was detained by the Indonesian army's Special Forces, Kopassus, in their main interrogation centre in Colmera, Dili. She was arrested with her husband, Gilman Exposto dos Santos, two of their teenage children, another of Xanana's sisters and her husband, six of their children, and both of Xanana's parents.[12]

Armandina and Gilman, however, were the longest-term detainees among Xanana's relatives. While in detention, Armandina was interrogated and had to sleep in a separate room from her husband. During the interrogation sessions, she was sexually harassed and raped by the Kopassus soldiers. Apart from 'getting back' at Xanana, the soldiers also seemed to be furious that a sister of Xanana had been appointed as the personal secretary of Mrs Carrascalao, the Governor's wife. They suspected Armandina of being a political link between Xanana and Carrascalao.[13]

Other rapes

According to an undated Clandestine Front report, received from a confidential source, Lourenca, aged 18, from Dare, a village to the south of Dili, was raped on 20 August 1990, by soldiers from

Battalion 164. The rape saved her brother from being extra-judicially executed by the soldier.

Another six rape cases, committed by Indonesian soldiers between 1990 and 1992 in the district of Ainaro, were reported in the same undated Clandestine Front report:

Alianza (14), who was born in Mulo, Hatu Bui Liku, and lived in Mau Siga, was raped by the 613th Battalion commander in Mau Siga on 15 February 1991, and was forced to continue having extra-marital sex with the commander, to save her life.

Rosa (13), born in Mau Siga, Hatu Bui Liku and lived in Mau Siga, was raped by a soldier from the 613th Battalion in Mau Siga on 30 May 1991, to force her to uncover her contacts with the guerrilla fighters.

Lorena (15), born in Tatiri Mulo, Hatu Bui Liku and lived in Tatiri, was raped by a soldier from the 164th Battalion in Tatiri on 19 September 1990, and was threatened to be killed.

Mariana dos Santos (16), born in Mulo, Hato Bui Liku and lived in Dare, was raped by a soldier from the 164th Battalion on 10 March 1990, and was threatened to be killed.

Rosa Kurvan (17), born in Mulo, Hatu Bui Liku and lived in Dare, was raped by a soldier from the 726th Battalion on 1 May 1992, and was threatened to be killed.

Aida (19), born in a place between Hatu Kero, Mau Siga and Hatu Bui Liku and lived in Hatu Kero. She was raped by the commander of the 164th Battalion on 13 May 1990, to save the life of her brother.

New soldiers are stationed in East Timor every three months, and schoolgirls are particularly vulnerable to sexual abuse because of their visibility as they walk to school each day: 'The soldiers go to schools looking for girls, [and] follow them home. Then the soldiers call the boys on watch duty, and the unit will go to the girls' houses while the boys are away. They take the girls, go and rape them, and do all kinds of rape. Girls know they have to be quiet and can't tell anyone.'[14]

In East Timor, as in other societies, pregnant women are respected and well protected by the rest of the society. It is not surprising that 'Edhina' (not her real name), in an interview with Michele Turner, said she was shocked when her nephew's wife was raped by an Indonesian soldier. As she told her story:

'My nephew's wife was a pretty girl pregnant with their first child, soon to give birth. The husband went to work and the wife was home alone and a Javanese soldier came and raped her. The baby died. All of us were so shocked. In all our lives before nothing like this could ever happen. Pregnant women everyone respected, even a husband didn't make love with his pregnant wife in case of harm. They told us the war was over in Dili but still they act like that. These foreigners are not human, they are devils. Of course it doesn't just happen to this girl, it happens to many other girls. Sometimes they rape the wife in front of the husband. If he does anything he will be killed.'[15]

On 3 September 1995, Reuters published the story of Maria (not her real name), 25, who hid the bulk of her unborn baby under a dirty T-shirt. She was six months pregnant by an Indonesian soldier who allegedly forced his way into her house in a village near Lospalos, past her mother and father, and raped her. 'He had a gun and I was afraid,' she said, crying. She added, 'I have not heard from him since. Not a letter or anything.'

'Isabella' (not her real name), 29, lived in the same village as 'Maria', a primitive hamlet of leaf and mud huts on East Timor's northern coast. She had two daughters, one seven years old and one two years old, from two fathers, both of them Indonesian soldiers whom she said raped her. The girls were given Indonesian names in bitter memory of their fathers. 'I have no protection because I live alone with my younger sister, as my parents are already dead, and one of my brothers was killed by the Indonesians,' she said in her interview with Reuters.[16]

A recent case, which received extensive media publicity and was reported to the National Human Rights Commission

(KomnasHAM) in Jakarta by fourteen human rights organisations, was the case of Alianza Henrique dos Santos, aged 23.[17] Alianza was arrested on 5 December 1995, together with seven members of her family, by more than ten soldiers in Atabae, Bobonaro district, where she was in hiding after being accused of harbouring members of the armed East Timorese Resistance at her home in Lizapat. All eight detainees were beaten, and Alianza was reported to have been tied up and threatened with a knife before being taken to KORAMIL (Sub-District Military Command) in Ermera. In the fourteen days Alianza was detained there, she was subjected to torture and was also raped by an unidentified Indonesian soldier. The soldier threatened to kill her if she reported the rape.

Alianza and the other detainees were transferred to a Rajawali military post at Luli Rema, where she was raped twice by a soldier ranked sergeant (*Sersan Kepala*). At night the soldiers slept all around her. While detained at the post, Alianza was forced to obey orders from the soldiers and accede to all the needs of the post such as boiling water and other duties. It was only after the group of detainees were discovered by a parishioner, who reported the case to the parish priest, that Alianza and her relatives were released on 16 December.[18] One media report about Alianza's case said that Colonel Soekotjo, an official at the Dili Military Command, denied the report of rape.[19] It is believed an investigation into the allegations is being undertaken by KomnasHAM[20] and the ETHRC welcomes this investigation.

In January 1996, Juliana Pereira and Martinha Pereira were arrested, together with Domingos de Jesus Xavier, and accused of harbouring Falintil guerrillas. They were reported to have been severely tortured by a policeman named Afonso and the local military head there, and the women were also reported to have been raped.[21]

In July 1996, the Free East Timor Japan Coalition presented three rape cases in their petition to the UN Special Committee of 24:

Sometimes the rape takes place in the presence of the husband, as in the case of the wife of Lucas Bayasa. In this case the husband became mentally unstable after witnessing his wife's rape, and the woman herself gave birth to the child of the rapist.

Ms A, who lives in a village in the Lospalos area, was six months pregnant at the time of the interview as the result of rape by a Private Second Class 'W' of the 612th Battalion. According to Ms A, the soldier burst into her house armed with an M16 rifle and attacked her. He threatened to shoot her parents if she resisted, and told them that they would be shot if they interfered. He returned a number of times after that. She became pregnant as a result, but the soldier went back to Indonesia when his twelve months of duty were up, taking no responsibility for the child.

Ms H (30), another woman interviewed, has two children, two and seven years old, conceived as a result of rape by two different soldiers belonging to Battalion 511. Neither of the soldiers took any responsibility for the children.

Mr X, a man interviewed in one village, said that as many as fifty women in the village had been sexually abused by Indonesian soldiers. His younger sister, Ms B (25), gave birth to a baby (ten months old at the time of the interview) conceived when she was raped by an Indonesian soldier.[22]

On 23 March 1997, thirty-three East Timorese youths, including two women, were detained at Becora prison for their alleged involvement in a demonstration which took place that day at the Mahkota Hotel in Dili. They have since been charged and are awaiting trial. It has been alleged that the two female detainees, Celina da Costa, 20, and Olga Quintao Amaral, 19, had their clothes torn and were severely beaten and raped by members of the Indonesian military.[23]

On 25 March 1997, Rajawali troops arrested Celestina of Ataubu-Lasaun village in the Atsabe sub-district. It has been alleged that prior to Celestina's arrest, her house was sprayed with bullets and she was taken to the bush, where she was tortured and raped several times. Also arrested were Armando Magalhaes, who was taken into the bush, where he was strung up from a tree and punched and kicked, and Cosme. The three young people were accused of co-operating with Falintil by providing logistical support.[24]

Other forms of sexual abuse and harassment

In addition to rape, East Timorese women allege that they have been sexually abused and harassed by members of the military during periods of mass arbitrary arrests when house-to-house searches are conducted. Often this occurs when the husband is already detained or in hiding, and sometimes the intention is to obtain information about family members.

Madalena Pinto was intimidated and interrogated on 16 August 1996 and accused of contacting members of the Resistance. It is believed the interrogation lasted all night and at approximately 10 o'clock the next morning she was coerced into declaring that she had had sexual relations with a member of the Resistance forces.[25] Two days later, Luciana Alves was interrogated and accused of giving refuge to a Resistance guerrilla. During the interrogation she was slapped and punched four times in the back. At a subsequent interrogation she was coerced into saying that she had had sexual relations with a Resistance guerrilla. On 1 September, soldiers from the Rajawali battalion again visited her in her home, beat her again, claiming that she had been visited by three Resistance fighters.[26]

Some women are harassed simply because of their family relationship with alleged members of the Clandestine Resistance or Falintil. Teresa de Fatima and her four children, Elda Pinto, Rita, Bicau and Bi-Soi, were arrested on 2 August 1996 in Nunuhou, after fleeing to the mountains for safety following the military crack-down in the area. After Teresa de Fatima and her children fled, her house was burnt down by the Indonesian military. Teresa de Fatima was the wife of Julio 'Maureha', a Falintil commander who was alleged to have been involved in the killing of an Indonesian army captain.[27]

Beatriz Ximenes was picked up by police on 3 June at 11.30 am, following the arrest of her husband, David Dias Ximenes, on 31 May 1997. David Dias Ximenes was arrested under suspicion of being the mastermind behind the 28 May assault on BRIMOB (Mobile Police Brigade) headquarters. Police told Beatriz she was being taken to see her husband's lawyer but she was in fact taken to POLDA (the local police station) in Comoro, where it is believed she was interrogated. She was released at around midnight that day but it is believed she continues to be subjected to intimidation.[28]

FORCED 'MARRIAGES' AND 'COMFORT WOMEN'

Becoming mistresses, or 'local wives' of Indonesian soldiers, offers some 'protection' for certain East Timorese women from continuous rape by other soldiers. The soldier keeps the young woman with him while he stays in East Timor, and when he goes, abandons her. According to an East Timorese woman who fled to Australia and later submitted a testimony to the 1982 Australian Senate Inquiry into the situation of the people of East Timor, the country is full of children born out of those compulsory relationships.[29]

Miranda Sissons reported that accounts of forced 'marriages' to Indonesian soldiers, in which soldiers forced women into sexual relationships or to commit sexual acts under threat of violence or retribution, were common:

'This is a way of surviving there, for them to survive. It's a very common thing in Timor, if the father has passed away and they have a family. It's not that they want to become prostitutes, but they are forced to do it because if they don't, the others are going to get killed. So they're forced to do certain things with them. If the mother doesn't do it, they go to the daughters, or to their younger daughters'.[30]

Women forced into marriages with Indonesian soldiers are usually abandoned when soldiers leave the province at the end of their duties:

'Many young women become prostitutes because of the army. They force them, to save their parents or because they've lost their virginity. At night in the country, they used to force the men to go on guard duty, and then come and abuse the women. In the country-side this is still happening. They make a girl choose between her parents and a soldier'.[31]

Adriana dos Reis, a young woman living in the village of Abafala in the sub-district of Quelicai, Baucau, had been kept as the mistress of the local army commander (Dandim). Eventually she got pregnant and gave birth to a son. Later the Dandim's wife came to join her husband in Baucau and Adriana dos Reis and her baby had to return to the village. However, Adriana continued to be harassed and was threatened by the officer's men not to show her face and not to tell the officer's wife that she had been the officer's forced mistress. In early 1994, to prevent the young woman from reporting the officer's misbehaviour to his superiors in Dili, Adriana was forced to sign a letter addressed to Indonesian-appointed Governor José Abilio Osorio Soares, in which she stated that she apologised for besmirching the officer's good name, and admitted that she had tempted the officer into having sex with her. Fortunately, the letter was intercepted by Bishop Belo before it was sent, and the Bishop went to the Governor to explain the back-ground of the letter.[32]

Emilia Baptista Gusmao, wife of the most well-known Resistance leader, Xanana Gusmao, was often picked up in the middle of the night to be interrogated. The soldiers told her to write a letter to Xanana and his comrades, urging them to surrender. Sometimes they threatened her by pointing a gun at her head. At other times they tried a softer tactic, suggesting she move to Jakarta, for the sake of the children's education. Eventually, on 20 May 1990, she managed to migrate to Australia with her two children, through the assistance of the ICRC (International Committee of the Red Cross).[33] On 25 May 1993, three years after settling in Melbourne, she wept when speaking publicly of the child she bore by an Indonesian army officer after the Indonesian military took over her home in Dili. She said the child had died. In an interview with Australian Radio National, she described the experience with the Indonesian officer as the worst of her life. Yet, she grieved when the child died and said she would carry the grief of the dead child all her life, 'because that child was my child'.

In 1990, six women from one village[34] were abducted by Indonesian troops. They were ordered to pass themselves off as supporters of the Resistance guerrillas, with whom they were to make contact for the purpose of gathering information for the Indonesian troops and leading them to the guerrillas' hideout. The women were also used as sex slaves by the troops. Ms 'C', the woman who related these events, said she had been forced to do these things since 1990 and was still forced to provide sex to the soldiers who came to her house. The soldiers told her that if she refused, they would take it that she was cooperating with Fretilin.[35]

In March 1994, a widow called Joana Maria, from a village near Same, the capital of Manufahi, was used as a sex slave by soldiers from Battalion 312, who were supposedly stationed in the village as part of the army's 'Territorial Operation', an operation which is supposed to provide civic support.[36]

In July 1996, during a speaking tour of Japan, Odilia Victor, one of the two East Timorese women who sought asylum in the Australian Embassy in Jakarta in January 1996 and later went to Portugal as a refugee, spoke on the issue of sexual abuse of East Timorese women. She told of the tragic experience of her sister as a 'local wife' and 'sex slave', and of other women also used as sex slaves by the soldiers. At the time of the Indonesian invasion, Odilia's sister was married and expecting a child. Her husband fled to the bush, while she stayed behind in Dili. The Indonesian military took her to a house, where she was confined as a sex slave for about one year. There were seven other women there, also forced to serve the Indonesian soldiers. The house was located on Kakau Lidun Street in Dili and right in front of it was the headquarters of the Mobile Police Brigade (BRIMOB) police.

In 1978, this same sister was forced to become the 'local wife' of an Indonesian air force officer, Agus Korek, and she later bore a child by him. The Indonesian officer had a wife in his own country, and after his six months' duty ended in East Timor he went home, leaving behind Odilia's sister who was expecting his child. The house her sister lived in as the local wife of the officer was next door to her family home, but she was never able to set foot in her own home, nor did any of her family dare try to get her back. One might think that a woman in such a situation could simply run away. Odilia pointed out, however, that the women who are singled out to work as 'comfort women' usually have a low level of education, making them particularly vulnerable to intimidation. But, she said, it is also very difficult to run away because of the extensive presence of plain-clothes intelligence agents living in the community, who constantly monitor people's movements.

Her sister's tragedy did not end there. Although she was eventually able to get out of her situation as a 'local wife', when her own husband came back from the bush his family spoke ill of his wife to him, accusing her of having sold herself to the Indonesians. Although her husband understood the true situation, the couple never lived together after that.

Odilia testified that women are forced to act as sex slaves for Indonesian soldiers in other areas outside Dili. In the village of Aileu, Odilia saw several women who were targeted as sex slaves. They were visited almost every night by different Indonesian soldiers in turn. The soldiers gave the women canned foods from their military rations, not money. The women could not get out of their situation even when the soldiers they served were transferred back to Indonesia, because the soldiers would tell their replacements that these women were there to serve them.[37]

This system of segregating certain women in a village for sexual exploitation has another unfortunate result, that of creating divisions among women themselves. The 'sex slaves' are cut off from the sympathy and support of other women because they are seen as 'women who take goods and money for sex'.[38]

Apart from the old 'divide and rule' tactic, this Indonesian military practice of keeping sex slaves has another function, namely surveillance. The wives of guerrilla leaders, left behind in the towns and villages, are frequently forced to live with Indonesians or East Timorese in the pay of the Indonesian authorities. This is particularly the case if their husbands are in important positions in the Resistance. This is both in order to monitor any communication with their husbands in the bush and in order to compromise the women in the eyes of the Timorese community as 'unfaithful' wives, thereby isolating them. This practice is, in other words, part of Indonesian military strategy to weaken the unity and morale of the East Timorese Resistance.[39]

PROSTITUTION

One of the consequences of ongoing violations against East Timorese women is the increase in the number of women becoming prostitutes. In interviews of East Timorese women conducted by Miranda Sissons in Australia, many women unilaterally raised the issue of prostitution as a significant problem. According to one twenty-two-year old woman, 'Even if you are a good girl you have to do it.'[40]

There are three main reasons why large numbers of East Timorese girls and young women have been forced into prostitution. First, some women become prostitutes as a 'post-rape consequence'. This point was emphasised by Maria Transfiguracao Sarmento and Odilia Victor, the two female freedom fighters who sought asylum in the Australian Embassy in Jakarta in January

1996. They linked this prostitution 'drive' with the fact that many young East Timorese women had lost their virginity due to rape by the occupation troops.[41]

Second, as pointed out by Shirley Shackleton,[42] other women resort to prostitution because of the high levels of unemployment for East Timorese people in the territory.[43] Third, and this point is linked to the previous two, many women need to support themselves and their children during the absence of their men fighting in the mountains, or after the men have been killed by the Indonesian troops.

An official survey, carried out on the 500 prostitutes officially registered by the Dili municipality police unit (MAPOLRES), shows that 60 percent of them became prostitutes because of economic difficulties, 20 percent because they were divorced by their husbands, and 20 percent because of frustration. These statistics, however, applied to the entire population of 500 officially registered prostitutes, who came from East Java, South Sulawesi, West Timor, as well as from East Timor.[44] It does not tell us the proportion in each category for the East Timorese prostitutes. Nor does it tell us anything about the East Timorese women who are not officially registered but are having to work as prostitutes.

An increasing number of East Timorese women have joined the influx of prostitutes from Java, Sulawesi and West Timor, who since 1984 have entered the territory and contributed to the population of 3000 prostitutes.[45] In Dili, prostitutes operate from a brothel near the Comoro airport, in the Areia Branca (white sand beach) tourist resort to the east of the town, and even in Dili's two luxury hotels, Hotel Mahkota and the New Resende Inn. The brothels are not confined to Dili, though, since the prostitutes also operate in all district capitals, mostly under the cover of restaurants, where customers can ask for 'raw meat' (*daging mentah*), borrowing from the local Indonesian language. These brothels have been frequented by Indonesian bureaucrats and officers, whose cars with red registration plates have often been seen parked in front of the shops.[46]

RECOMMENDATIONS

In order to ensure greater promotion and protection of the human rights of women in East Timor, the East Timor Human Rights Centre urges the Indonesian Government to:

1. End its tolerance of violations of women's human rights in East Timor and conform to its international obligations under the Convention on the Elimination of All Forms of Discrimination Against Women (CEDAW).

2. Ratify and implement the Convention against Torture and Other Cruel, Inhuman or Degrading Treatment or Punishment (which the Indonesian Government signed in 1985), the International Covenant on Civil and Political Rights, and the International Covenant on Economic, Social and Cultural Rights.

3. Invite the Special Rapporteur on Torture to visit East Timor in 1997 so that he can report to the UN Commission on Human Rights by March 1998. The invitation would be in keeping with the undertaking made by the Indonesian Government in 1996 to invite a Special Rapporteur to the territory and could include consideration of gender-specific forms of torture perpetrated against women.

4. Also invite the UN Special Rapporteur on Violence Against Women to visit East Timor to examine violations of women's human rights and thereby assist the Indonesian Government to fulfil its international obligations.

5. Request the Indonesian National Human Rights Commission (KomnasHAM) to conduct a full and impartial investigation of human rights violations, including rape, perpetrated against East Timorese women, in particular in the last two years. Perpetrators should be promptly brought to justice, removed from Government service and given sentences appropriate to the severity of the crimes.

6.   Establish a section within KomnasHAM to deal specifically with allegations of violations against women, especially allegations of rape. Sufficient resources and logistical support should be given to KomnasHAM to enable it to fulfil this function.

7.   Act on all KomnasHAM findings of human rights violations against women, especially rape.

8.   Ensure that female guards are present during interrogation of female detainees, in order to reduce the risk of rape and sexual abuse. Also ensure that female detainees are held separately from male detainees.

9.   Provide fair and adequate compensation and appropriate medical care to women who are victims of rape and sexual abuse perpetrated by Indonesian authorities.

10.   Allow full and unrestricted access to all areas of East Timor for journalists and independent human rights organisations, including the East Timor Human Rights Centre, to enable monitoring and reporting of violations against women.

Endnotes

1 Sissons, Miranda E., *From One Day to Another: Violations of Women's Reproductive and Sexual Rights in East Timor*, East Timor Human Rights Centre, SR 2/97, Melbourne, 1997.

2 Amnesty International, *Women in Indonesia and East Timor: Standing Against Repression*, AI Index: ASA 21/51/95, London, 13 December 1995, p. 14.

3 Ibid., p. 15.

4 Seifert, R., 'War and rape: a preliminary analysis', in Stigmayer, A. (ed.), *Mass Rape: the war against women in Bosnia-Herzegovina*, University of Nebraska Press, Lincoln, 1994, pp. 62–64.

5 Turner, M. (ed.), *Telling East Timor: Personal Testimonies 1942–1992*, New South Wales University Press, Sydney, 1991, pp. 110–111, 121.

6 Ibid., pp. 146–147.

7 Ibid., pp. 147, 164–166.

8 Ibid., p. 121.

9 *Tapol*, June 1995, pp. 21–22.

10 Amnesty International, *East Timor—Amnesty International Statement to the United Nations Special Committee on Decolonization*, Amnesty International, London, 7 August 1991, p. 11.

11 Amnesty International, *Women in Indonesia and East Timor: Standing Against Repression*, ibid., p. 21.

12 The *Age* and the *Australian*, 25 November 1992; *Sydney Morning Herald*, 25–26 November 1992.

13 Interviews with Armandina and Gilman in 1993, 1994 and 1997.

14 Sissons, op. cit., p. 32.

15 Turner, op. cit., p. 111

16 Friends of East Timor (WA), 1996 Report, p. 4.

17 Asosiasi Perempuan Indonesia untuk Keadilan (APIK) et al, *Kasus Perkosaan atas diri Alianca Henrique dos Santos: Laporan pada Komisi Nasional Hak Asasi Manusia (KomnasHAM)*, Jakarta, 22 January 1997.

18 ETHRC, *Continuing Human Rights Violations in East Timor: Annual Report of Human Rights Violations*, Melbourne, January 1996, p. 13.

19 *Kyodo*, 7 February 1997; and ETHRC, op. cit., p. 13.

20 *South China Morning Post*, 23 January 1997.

21 ETCHRIET Urgent Action Appeal no. 4, 26 January 1996.

22 Free East Timor Japan Coalition, Violence Against Women in East Timor Under the Indonesian Occupation, and Suggested Measures to be Taken: Petition to the United Nations Special Committee of 24, Free East Timor Japan Coalition (FETJC), 23 July 1996, p. 3.

23 ETHRC, *Human Rights Deteriorate in East Timor, Bi-Annual Report of Human Rights Violations in East Timor*, SR 1/97, Melbourne, 30 August 1997, p. 2.

24 Ibid., p. 5.

25 ETHRC, *Continuing Violations in East Timor*, op. cit., p. 18.

26 Ibid., p. 18.

27 ETHRC Urgent Action UA 7/96, 23 August 1996.

28 ETHRC Urgent Actions 12/97, 4 June 1997 and 12/97PR, 6 June 1997.

29 Turner, op. cit., p. 111.

30 Sissons, ibid., p. 31.

31 Ibid., p. 32.

32 Aditjondro, G.J., *In the Shadow of Mount Ramelau: the impact of the occupation of East Timor,* INDOC, Leiden, 1994, p. 47.

33 Barreto, P., *Feto Rai Timor—Mulheres de Timor, Fundacao de Relacoes Internacionais, CDPM and APPTL,* Lisbon, 1991, pp. 5–7.

34 Referred to as Ms C, 20, Ms D, 35, Ms E, 35, Ms F, 37, Ms G, 2, and Ms H, 30.

35 FETJC, op. cit., p. 4.

36 Santo, Aitara de Spirito, report of clandestine student activist, 16 May 1994.

37 FETJC, op. cit., pp. 4–5.

38 Ibid., p. 5.

39 Ibid., p. 6.

40 Sissons, op. cit., p. 31.

41 The *Australian,* 13–14 January 1996.

42 Shackleton, S., 'Planting a tree in Balibo: a journey to East Timor', in Carey, P. and Bentley, G. C. (eds), *East Timor at the Crossroads: the forging of a nation,* Social Science Research Council, New York, 1995, pp. 109–119. Shirley Shackleton is the widow of one of the four Australian-based journalists killed by Indonesian troops in East Timor on 16 October 1975.

43 Ibid., p. 116.

44 *Fakta,* 1 April 1994, p. 74.

45 Figure as at November 1991.

46 *Jakarta-Jakarta,* 4–10 January 1992, p. 100; *Fakta,* 15 February 1993 p. 3 and 1 April 1994, pp. 45 & 74; *Surya,* 18 November 1993 and 10 December 1993; *Media Indonesia,* 8 December 1993; *Suara Timor Timur,* 9 July 1993, 10 February 1994 and 26 May 1994.

Justice Marcus Einfeld (Federal Court of Australia and the Supreme Court of the Australian Capital Territory) has been many times a member of the Australian delegation to the UN Commission on Human Rights and has participated in several international missions of inquiry and investigation of human rights and refugee issues. As Ambassador and Patron of a wide-ranging variety of organisations, for example, UNICEF Ambassador for Children, Patron of the Children of Chernobyl, AUSTCARE's Ambassador for Refugees, Australia Day Ambassador, Ambassador of Hope (Jewish Community Services), and with involvement in equally wide-ranging groups and issues, such as the struggles for freedom and democracy in Tibet, Burma and East Timor, Aboriginal medical services, AIDS, victims of torture, and War Crimes investigations, Justice Einfeld has been recognised as one of Australia's foremost activists for human rights, both at home and abroad. He has been very outspoken on the persecution and the ongoing human rights violations in East Timor. The speech reproduced here was presented at the Melbourne Town Hall on 15 December 1997, where, as Patron, Justice Einfeld launched the photographic exhibition Stop Operation Annihilation, an expose of the Nazi Holocaust and the genocide in East Timor.

16

UNTIL JUSTICE IS THEIRS

THE HONOURABLE JUSTICE MARCUS EINFELD

I welcome the opportunity to speak out again in the cause of the East Timorese people. The exhibition which I am launching today is a graphic reminder that East Timor is the site of one of the most enduring human rights tragedies in our lifetimes. This photographic study is also a powerful reminder that the world has failed to learn the lessons of the Nazi Holocaust, called in Hebrew 'the Shoah'. But whereas that unique example of human barbarism took place on the other side of the world, timidity and political motives on the part of Australians have allowed human tragedy and suffering to continue unabated for the last twenty-two years in a country close to Australia's borders.

Fifty-two years ago, the world was forced to confront the atrocities of the Shoah. The international community could no longer deny that the Nazis had conducted a systematic campaign of genocide against European Jewry. As the atrocities of the concentration camps were revealed, people were horrified beyond belief at the wickedness and inhumanity that human beings could inflict on their own kind.

Through the creation of the United Nations, and international law declaring the fundamental entitlements of human beings everywhere, the world community united in a vow never again to allow such evil to darken the lives of humankind. However, despite the lessons the world then said it had learned, the evils of genocide are still occurring—starkly in countries like Cambodia, Bosnia and Rwanda, insidiously in Tibet and too many other places, and both starkly and insidiously in East Timor.

There are so many lessons that the Nazi Holocaust could and should have taught us. One is that it could not have occurred without the racist and anti-Semitic mania of the German population as a whole and the prevalence of virulent anti-Semitism in many of the countries occupied by the Nazis. In other words, the attempt to annihilate European Jewry—almost entirely successful—was made possible only because the idea did not greatly offend the bulk of the German population or the Nazi collaborators throughout Europe. What the Shoah proved is that, ultimately, the people can be led only where they want, or are prepared, to go.

It also showed us the evils of racism taken to its horrifying conclusion—a lesson that, given the current climate in our country, everyone in Australia should heed. Finally, the genocide committed against the Jews should have taught us that ambivalence and indifference towards large-scale persecution in other countries only encourages governments to continue and intensify their attacks on fundamental human rights.

When General Suharto ordered the invasion of East Timor just days after it declared independence, and announced its annexation a few months later, he and the Indonesian leadership ignored the deep racial and historical differences between the Melanesian Timorese and the Indonesians of Malay origin, and their totally separate cultures and histories. After a brief flurry of activity in the United Nations, during which the invasion was condemned by the Security Council, the world seemed to lose interest. After all, Indonesia was a large and populous nation which at the height of the Cold War had impressed the West by obliterating its Communist Party. One day it would certainly be the regional superpower, whereas by comparison, East Timor was tiny and insignificant.

In 1975 the population of East Timor was around 660,000. Of them, up to 40 per cent are believed to have died as a result of the invasion, either directly through the fighting, or from the effects of the fighting, such as starvation, malnutrition, lack of medical care, and other indirect events. Not satisfied with a death toll that, in terms of percentage of population killed, ranks alongside the Nazi Holocaust and the killing fields of Cambodia, the Indonesians thereafter deliberately set out to destroy the indigenous culture of East Timor.

Having annexed the territory, they have tried to make it ethnically and culturally part of Indonesia. The teaching of Portuguese has been forbidden and Bahasa Indonesian, widely spoken in Indonesia, has been promoted over Tetun, the East Timorese language. Like the Chinese in Tibet, Indonesian immigration from the more populated centres has been encouraged, pursuant to their policy of *transmigrasi*, so that many believe that within a decade, even Dili will no longer be predominantly East Timorese.

In the first half of this year, nearly 800 families from outside East Timor had arrived, 521 of them through an assisted transmigrant programme. And there are no signs that this policy of marginalising the East Timorese in their own country is to ease. These transmigrants generally move onto land that, for the most part, was previously worked by East Timorese people until they were forced to vacate it through relocation and resettlement programmes in the aftermath of the 1975 invasion. Christianity, the religion of most East Timorese and a focus for opposition to the invasion, is being suppressed in an effort to 'Islamicise' the island.

It is now just over six years since the Armed Forces of Indonesia, under orders, fired on a group of unarmed civilians attending a funeral at Santa Cruz cemetery in Dili. The Dili Massacre has been described by a Special Rapporteur of the United Nations Commission on Human Rights, in a masterly understatement, as a 'planned military operation designed to deal with a public expression of political dissent in a way not in accordance with international human rights standards'.

An inquiry into the massacre held by the Indonesians was able to find only about 40 people who had been killed, and concluded that these murders were the result of a few young officers who feared for their own lives at the hands of unarmed civilians. The inquiry's assessment was that the whole thing was all one most unfortunate incident. Even a general of the Indonesian army interviewed by the *Sydney Morning Herald* after the massacre admitted that over 200 people were shot dead. The general was reported as having said that he was sorry it was not more. There is in fact more than ample evidence that the true casualty figures were 271 killed, 280 wounded and 250 missing, every one of them an unarmed, peaceful and defenceless civilian, the victims of the very armed forces who were supposed to protect them.

A few mostly young officers were tried and sentenced to, at most, short periods of detention. However, dozens of civilians were also tried and convicted, of inciting a riot and similar offences. Unlike the soldiers who shot people dead in cold blood, the unarmed civilians were sentenced to long terms of hard labour, some to life imprisonment. This response to a brutal, unprovoked massacre was described by our Government at the time as 'credible'. As the International Commission of Jurists reported, our response, let alone what the Indonesians did, was incredible.

A view is sometimes put in Australia, by people who should and do know better, that we should not speak out on our neighbours' or other countries' human rights failings for fear of offending them. Such an attitude would finally make credible the old rhetoric of Cold War days, still espoused by China and a few other totalitarian countries, that human rights breaches and abuses are what they call the 'internal affairs' of the oppressors and are not subject or susceptible to international analysis and exposure.

In my opinion, this is a recipe for entrenching and conniving in the violations. The Nazi Holocaust and many other acts of genocide in this century, such as those in Armenia, Ukraine, Eritrea and Cambodia, as well as what has happened in East Timor, have been the results of this supremacy of so-called 'diplomacy' over humanity. They should have, but apparently have not, made it unnecessary to remind ourselves that human rights are not the prerogative or in the discretion of any nation state or leader to grant or withhold as a matter of personal or national whim. They are, as the most famous human rights declaration says, universal.

And those who suffer abuses of their rights are entitled, indeed have no option but, to appeal to others to rescue them from their hell. Those who do not listen, and respond, are nothing less than the accomplices of the perpetrators. To hold back, because it may be difficult or embarrassing, from criticism of human rights violations and gross affronts to the rule of law by countries affecting to be upholders of internationally accepted standards and seeking a voice in the councils of free peoples is, to me, a wholly unsustainable attitude. I have always found odd the apparent belief of Australian

Government Ministers and officials over recent decades that we will be respected by others for being completely untrue to the human dignity which our nation professes to hold so dear.

Much has undoubtedly been done by successive Indonesian administrations which has been of benefit to their people. It is certainly true that their consciousness of the importance of human rights has shown improvement, such as, for example, in their ratification of the Convention on the Elimination of All Forms of Discrimination Against Women and the incorporation in domestic legislation of Indonesia's responsibilities under that Convention and of international standards on reproductive issues. Indonesia has also signed the UN Declaration on the Elimination of All Forms of Violence Against Women as well as the Convention on the Rights of the Child.

Recently, an office of the Indonesian National Commission on Human Rights (KomnasHAM) was opened in East Timor. However, the ability of the office to conduct independent investigations of human rights violations is severely constrained, and it has not been able to gain the trust of the East Timorese people themselves, a problem compounded by its location directly opposite the District Military Headquarters in Dili.

Since its initial invasion in 1975, East Timor has refused to be absorbed. To the East Timorese, the issue of their future is far from decided. Undeterred by the deaths of over 200,000 of their fellow citizens, they have fought on desperately, despite an almost total lack of international support and completely inadequate weapons and ammunition. There is still some distance to go to obtain their political emancipation, but courageously, they have kept their pride and integrity, and are slowly but surely involving the world in their struggle. The voices of Australians must be heard in this quest. We must send a message to the East Timorese people in East Timor in loud and unequivocal terms—stand straight, be strong, we are with you. Together, we can do it!

In October 1996, the Nobel Peace Prize was awarded to Bishop

Carlos Belo and José Ramos Horta for 'their work towards a just and peaceful solution to the conflict in East Timor'. The announcement led to renewed international interest and concern for the plight of the East Timorese, but it also foresaw an intensification of human rights violations by the Indonesian military in East Timor. It must not be forgotten that the Indonesian administration remains a military government with an unenviable record of bullying oppression of its own people by a large and well-equipped army with no aggressive external enemies.

The human rights situation in East Timor has continued to deteriorate throughout this year. In response to a number of guerrilla attacks during the May elections, the Indonesian military launched *Operasi Gerakan Tuntas*—Operation Annihilation—on the civilian population. Hundreds of East Timorese men and women have been rounded up by the military, arbitrarily detained for days or weeks, and intimidated and tortured. In just the first half of 1997, it is believed that at least 707 East Timorese people were arrested and 49 killed—double the number of arrests and killings recorded by the East Timor Human Rights Centre for the whole of 1996.

Unrest has escalated. Last month, demonstrations and riots by East Timorese students were met with a quite excessive use of force by the military. Following a confrontation at the University of East Timor on 14 November, the local Human Rights Commission office confirmed that students had suffered near-fatal injuries, including gunshot wounds, and that they were beaten and had their teeth broken, faces swollen, and legs injured and bruised. The university's blackboards were riddled with bullets. Of the 16 students arrested immediately after the confrontation, some with serious injuries, three have since disappeared and five remain in detention.

The victims of the Indonesian military are not only those who protest against Indonesian rule. On 12 November, three young East Timorese women were killed when police and soldiers opened fire on a group of people laying wreaths and lighting candles to commemorate the sixth anniversary of the Dili Massacre.

Torture, inflicted by electric shocks, lighted cigarettes, and instruments such as rattan, metal pipes and electric cable, is a standard form of interrogation used by both police and army personnel. Currently there are fears for the safety of a man named Sabino Barbose Ximenes. Arrested back in September, Sabino has already been subjected to electric shock, burnt with cigarettes, and cut with razor blades. He also had his fingernails pulled out. Without access to his family, independent legal counsel and humanitarian assistance, he is at severe risk of further torture.

Reports of extra-judicial executions are frequent. The death, in June this year, of David Alex, a guerrilla commander, drew international attention. He died from gunshot wounds received during his capture by a military team. The official version of the event asserted that the refusal of the guerrillas to surrender forced the military to open fire, and that David Alex died from blood loss whilst undergoing hospital treatment. The capture apparently took place at 11.00 am but David was not transported to hospital until 6.00 pm. What happened in those intervening hours to a bleeding human being?

The Resistance leader Xanana Gusmao, a truly popular figure, continues to be incarcerated, despite the efforts of South African President Nelson Mandela to obtain his release. The Indonesians apparently refuse to heed the experiences of the governments who kept the likes of Mandela, Mahatma Gandhi, Andrei Sakharov, Robert Mugabe and hundreds of other heroes of resistance to tyranny in prison or exile for years while their governments vainly tried to obliterate the legitimate political and national aspirations of their people.

Indonesia's refusal to allow international human rights groups official access to East Timor, the severe restrictions or bans placed on overseas journalists in the region, and the high level of military surveillance make it extremely difficult—as is the intention—to compile detailed studies of human rights violations. This is particularly true with regard to violations committed against women, because the feelings of shame brought on by rape and other forms of sexual violence add to their reluctance to talk of their experiences.

An overall picture of the human rights situation in East Timor has, however, been pieced together from the many personal stories that are told by asylum-seekers or smuggled out in clandestine reports and interviews. One man told that as many as 50 women in his village had been sexually abused by Indonesian soldiers. His younger sister gave birth to a baby conceived when she was raped by an Indonesian soldier. A woman has told of having been attacked in her home by a soldier armed with an M16 rifle. He threatened to shoot her parents if she resisted and told them that they would be shot if they interfered. He returned a number of times, and she became pregnant as a result. The soldier returned to Indonesia after twelve months, taking no responsibility for the child. There are any number of similar stories of barbarity and cruelty.

Indeed, since the Indonesian invasion, in 1975, hundreds of East Timorese women and young girls have been the target for rape and other forms of sexual violence, sexual harassment, forced 'marriages', and prostitution. The systematic abuse and violation of East Timorese women by the Indonesian military not only traumatises and often isolates the immediate victims, it also creates fear among all East Timorese. Sexual violence thus becomes a deliberate weapon to subdue the people. Insidiously, through the many pregnancies that result from rapes, it is also a way of diminishing the racial and cultural purity of the East Timorese. The wives, mothers and female relatives of Resistance members are particularly targeted for arbitrary arrest, sexual assault and intimidation, with the aim of obtaining information on Resistance members or forcing them to surrender. When the soldiers leave at the end of their tours of duty, the women and resulting children are abandoned.

Until the Indonesian Government ceases to tolerate the rape and persecution of women in East Timor, its internationally proclaimed commitment to the human rights of women will ring hollow.

No less disturbing are the allegations of persistent human rights abuses perpetrated through the implementation in East Timor of Indonesia's widely acclaimed national population control programme, *Program Keluarga Berencana* (the 'KB' programme). A 1997 report by Miranda Sissons, *From One Day to Another: Violations of Women's Reproductive and Sexual Rights in East Timor*, published by the Melbourne-based East Timor Human Rights Centre, documents numerous examples of covert sterilisation in the early 1980s, and finds strong evidence of widespread covert forcible injection of young women with hormonal contraceptives and denial of treatment in life-threatening circumstances during pregnancy. In addition, continuing military involvement in both recruitment and service provision of birth-control programmes contributes to a strong element of structural coercion, and the lack of basic follow-up care for users of injected or IUD contraceptives.

Sissons concluded:

(T)hese and other abuses have contributed to a strong belief on behalf of the local population that the KB programme is used by the Indonesian Government as a politically-motivated instrument to deliberately undermine the survival of the East Timorese as a national group, an activity expressly forbidden by Article II (d) of the Genocide Convention.

Such abuses, combined with poor communication and insensitive administration, and set against a background of extreme political oppression, have created an intense distrust of Government health services, such that women frequently do not seek medical assistance at all, despite its need. Many choose not to let their daughters go to school, because young East Timorese girls have consistently been targeted for unexplained injections. This has, in turn, contributed to high levels of infant and maternal mortality. In 1996, the United Nations World Population Report recorded the infant mortality rate in East Timor as 149 per 1000, almost three times that of the rest of Indonesia and one of the five worst in the world. Reports also indicate relatively high levels of malnutrition, sexually transmitted diseases, tuberculosis, malaria, respiratory illness and poor hygiene.

For some reason, successive Australian Governments have felt unable to protest these developments. They surely cannot be unaware of the feelings of the Australian people in these regards. They surely cannot believe that the Indonesians will respect us and our culture for our silence on such basic affronts to human dignity and decency. Whatever our political stance, it is time—indeed it is way past time—for our immoral and inadequate approach to the lives and wellbeing of the East Timorese to be corrected and reversed.

Until the maturing of our political relationship with Indonesia can permit a serious addressing by our officials of the plight of East Timor, Australians as individuals must look to protect and save the East Timorese from brutality and oppression. We should be enraged at the attempted destruction of yet another culture, at the repression of yet another peaceful people, and at the passive disregard—yet again—of the watching world. We must act to change the status quo. And exhibitions like this help to do just that.

I refuse to accept that, in the protection of humanity, it is wrong to be right. This is not lecturing or hectoring; it is upholding the sanctity of the human condition. Nor can it be wrong to be right. If abuse, injustice and human wrongs are practised, it is not merely our right to speak out, it is our obligation.

I congratulate Australians for a Free East Timor, especially Jim Aubrey and Amandio da Costa Gomes, on putting this poignant and evocative exhibition together. I compliment the photographer Emmanuel Santos on his sensitive capturing of scenes of true agony. I thank those whose generosity has made it all possible, including Jewish groups and individuals in Melbourne who have so honourably linked themselves—and those whose memories they daily honour—with the current plight of the East Timorese people. I am privileged to have been invited to be patron of the exhibition and honoured by the invitation to launch it.

When, despite its important symbolism, an apology for the Aboriginal Stolen Children on behalf of the Australian people is beyond the capacity of an Australian Government, it is appropriate to remind ourselves that the train of racial and other forms of discrimination never stops at the first station. Already, the people of East Timor have suffered genocide in many of its ugliest forms. It is time to act—before their culture is completely destroyed. They are crying out for our help. Let us all stand strong with them until justice and right are theirs.

This lecture was given on a 1997/1998 tour of several major international cities as part of a photographic exposition of the genocide of the Nazi Holocaust and East Timor. The photo exhibition titled Stop Operation Annihilation was organised by Australians for a Free East Timor in conjunction with encouragement and support from the Jewish community of Melbourne, Australia, as well as the other communities in Australia and from solidarity groups in many parts of the world. Encouragement and inspiration also came from His Holiness the Dalai Lama, Bishop Desmond Tutu, Holocaust survivor Elie Wiesel and Jesuit peace activist Daniel Berrigan.

17

COMPLICITY IN GENOCIDE

JIM AUBREY

The case against Australia in East Timor's genocide

On 12 November 1991 in Dili, the capital of East Timor, several thousand East Timorese had gathered to march to the Santa Cruz cemetery in remembrance and mourning for a young man who had been murdered two weeks earlier by Indonesian soldiers. His name was Sebastiao Gomes, and Sebastiao, like all young people in East Timor, had lived a life of unremitting persecution. As one of Sebastiao's spiritual elders had once written, 'the luck of the Timorese was to be born in tears, to live in tears, and to die in tears'.[1] However, no-one could have guessed how many tears would be shed on this fateful day in East Timor's painful history under

Indonesian occupation. The young people at the march were encouraged by the simple fact of being together, and so an outpouring of pro-independence sentiment followed. These several thousand unarmed civilians expressed the same hope for self-determination that Sebastiao had been murdered for doing. What began as a day of mourning to highlight East Timor's long years of suffering came to symbolise the sadism and brutality of the Indonesian Armed Forces, the defencelessness of the victims, and the estrangement and abandonment from the moral conscience of the international community of the ethical responsibility to protect and to defend these victims of genocide.

The reaction of Indonesia's 'finest' soldiers was swift. Once positioned, they began to shoot with rapid fire from their American-made M16 rifles into the crowd gathered around the cemetery entrance. A handful of foreigners were amongst the crowd, namely filmmaker Max Stahl and photographer Steve Cox. And so the horror of the bloody massacre of 271 people was captured on film, and subsequently shown on television around the world once the films had been smuggled out of East Timor. Along with the East Timorese victims, one New Zealand student had been shot dead, an Australian aid worker had been wounded, and two American journalists had been badly beaten. What had not been captured on film was the murder of the wounded who had been taken to hospital and the later summary execution of other East Timorese who were guilty of participating in the plea for freedom at Santa Cruz. The death toll from these savage acts was over 500 people. That this massacre was unique lay in the fact that it is the only one of East Timor's massacres to be witnessed and documented by foreign journalists. This provoked both international condemnation and the activities of people like my colleagues and me to support East Timor's right to self-determination, their freedom from human rights abuses, and to inevitably confront my Government's record of complicity in one of the longest ongoing acts of genocide since the Nazi Holocaust.

Equally, other campaigners confront the complicity of their respective Governments, namely Belgium, Britain, Canada, Finland, France, Germany, Italy, the Netherlands, Sweden, Switzerland and the USA, through their accommodation of a brutal regime and their collective willingness to fulfil economic and defence sales contracts rather than moral and humanitarian obligations regarding the sanctity of life, the sovereignty of human rights as the foundation for policy-making, and the common concern for the welfare of all people regardless of the shallow expedients of the geopolitical bias in international relations.

The crimes against humanity and the acts of barbarity that these governments have unequivocally condemned in other parts of the world have, in the case of East Timor, been characterised not only by indifference and accommodation, but also by a policy of apologetics whereby various world leaders and their respective State Departments have consistently expressed the necessity for a deeper or more sophisticated understanding of Indonesia's special needs, as if genocide in a Third World developing state is somehow acceptable or tolerated when seen as conditional to that state's prevailing human rights standards. Indeed, a feature of the apologetics of consecutive leaders and their foreign affairs bodies has been their constant attempt to minimise the severity of the brutality that is the daily reality in East Timor. I am reminded here of attempts by a handful of people to deny the existence of the Nazi Holocaust and also of mischievous and misleading interpretations of the Allied response to the Holocaust. The world turned away from the pre-war crisis confronting European Jews, and in fact, the first reports of the Holocaust were disbelieved. Equally, the world has reacted with indifference towards the genocide in East Timor. What is more, those democratic countries who fought the evil and the tyranny of Nazi Germany have, in turn, subsidised the genocide in East Timor with their accommodation of the criminal regime in Jakarta—a regime which bears the vicious hallmarks of the Nazis.

A classic example of the obfuscation of East Timor's tragedy is the response of the Australian Foreign Affairs Minister, Senator Gareth Evans, to the 1991 Santa Cruz massacre. Senator Evans attempted to defuse the domestic condemnation of Indonesia by describing the massacre as 'not a matter of deliberate or calculated government policy but rather represented some aberrant behaviour by a section of the military.'[2] The one commonality in the two decades of Indonesian occupation has been a plethora of such 'aberrations', accounting for the genocide of more than one-third of the population. A United Nations investigator called the massacre 'a planned military operation designed to deal with a public expression of political dissent'.[3] Nine months prior to this, Senator Evans had stated that 'the truth of the matter is that the human rights situation in East Timor has in our judgment conspicuously improved particularly under the present military arrangements' and that the guerrillas should 'accept the reality of the situation' and surrender.[4] The Australian Government's indifference to East Timor's plight must first be qualified by a piece of history, that being the support given during the Second World War by East Timorese to Australian commandos sent to the then Portuguese colony of East Timor before the arrival of the Imperial Japanese Army.

With the landing of the Japanese forces, the East Timorese sided with Australia, and they fed, hid, sheltered and helped the Australian commandos in their campaign of guerrilla warfare against superior numbers. The reaction of the Japanese to this partisan support for Australia left up to 60,000 East Timorese dead, twice the number of Australia's war dead in all theatres of fighting in that war. Indeed, towards the war's end, the Royal Australian Air Force dropped hundreds of thousands of leaflets over Portuguese East Timor in recognition of East Timor's sacrifice for Australia's war effort. This leaflet began with the declaration: 'Friends, we will not forget you!' It is the greatest irony that a Royal Australian Air Force navigator and future Australian Prime Minister, Gough Whitlam, who had been stationed in the Northern Territory at this time, may have been involved in this operation. During the past year, I have questioned Mr Whitlam on this matter but, as yet, I have not been honoured with his reply.

It is to Mr Whitlam that I now turn, and the year 1974. In April of that year, the old fascist regime in Portugal was swept from power in the Carnation Revolution. The new, left-wing Government began to decolonise its empire, and within one month of the revolution in Lisbon, three political parties had formed for the first time in East Timor. After 550 years of Portuguese colonial status, the dream of independence looked set to become a reality. In the era of the Cold War, the American defeat in Vietnam, and international relations characterised by the totally unscrupulous and even sinister machinations of 'realpolitik', Indonesia viewed an independent East Timor as a threat to its identity as a republic, a 'Cuba' in its own backyard, and a possible base for rebellious groups within Indonesian borders.

In a total contradiction of his progressive views on decolonisation, the Australian Prime Minister, Mr Whitlam, supported East Timor's incorporation into the Republic of Indonesia. Mr Whitlam had played a major role in the Australian decolonisation of Papua New Guinea, yet, at a meeting with Indonesia's President Suharto on the island of Java, Mr Whitlam let it be known that Australian-Indonesian relations were the priority and that 'an independent East Timor would be an unviable state and a potential threat to the area'.[5] As East Timor was economically no more or no less viable than Papua New Guinea, it is difficult and puzzling to know exactly what Mr Whitlam is referring to in his statement. Equally, the petroleum wealth of East Timor in the ocean bed lying south towards Australia had been well known since the 1930s with concessions to Australian companies dating back to that period.

Perhaps the Australian Ambassador to Indonesia was more forthcoming when he stated in a telegram sent to Canberra in August 1975 (which was later leaked to the media) that: 'we leave events to take their course, and act in a way which would be designed to minimise the public impact in Australia and show private understanding to Indonesia of their problems. I am recommending a pragmatic rather than a principled stand but that is what national interest and foreign policy is all about.'[6] What was an essential and an inalienable right to self-determination in Papua New Guinea became, under the unholy designs of realpolitik, an expendable human right for the people of East Timor, and so President Suharto received the green light from the Australian Government and even the alleged understanding from the conservative Opposition, as was later on divulged by the principal Indonesian figures involved in a purpotedly clandestine discussion of the conservative party's position on Indonesia's intentions regarding East Timor. The conservative Coalition was to replace the Labor Government a few weeks before the invasion of 7 December 1975, and the disclosure by the Indonesians of the meeting between them and the new Foreign Affairs Minister, Andrew Peacock, while he was on 'holiday' in Bali in September 1975, was strongly denied by Peacock when questioned about this in Australia's Parliament.[7]

The 'unofficial' invasion began with a policy of subterfuge and political destabilisation during the course of 1975. This period involved a number of clandestine incursions by the Indonesian military over the border that divides Indonesian West Timor from Portuguese East Timor. The depth of the Australian Government's acquiescence to and appeasement of Jakarta's intentions, and Canberra's accommodation of the Indonesian regime's crimes against humanity, begin in full earnest with the murder, on 16 October 1975, of five Australian and Australian-based television journalists. Having gone to East Timor to find out the truth behind the accusations concerning Indonesian plans to invade East Timor, they were brutally murdered by Indonesian soldiers, whom it appears had crossed the border with the singular purpose of eliminating the newsmen. Canberra's reaction was not only silence but, as well, an unquestioning and subservient acceptance of Jakarta's explanation that the newsmen had died in cross-fire during a battle with East Timorese soldiers. Canberra displayed a greater common allegiance with the criminal murderers than with its own murdered citizens, and Indonesia readily saw that it could act in East Timor with impunity. On the fate of the journalists, eyewitness testimonies now in existence totally contradict the Canberra-Jakarta 'crossfire theory', rejecting the suggestion that any fighting took place on the morning of the murders.

The 'official' invasion took place after a two-day visit to Jakarta by the American President, Gerald Ford, and his Secretary of State, Henry Kissinger. Leaked documents from this period, and finely detailed research by American academic Noam Chomsky and Australians George Munster and Richard Walsh (whose original book was banned by Canberra for compromising intelligence-monitoring concerns), revealed that Western Governments knew well in advance Jakarta's plan for invasion. A CIA operations officer at the time of the invasion, Mr C. Philip Liechty, stated in an article for the *Washington Post* newspaper published on 6 January 1992, that: 'there is not one shred of truth in the Indonesian version of events. East Timor was an undefended sitting duck for the expansionist Indonesian generals. A slaughter of tens of thousands followed.'[8] In a subsequent interview with well-known journalist John Pilger, Mr Liechty stated that President Suharto was given the green light by the United States to do what he did and that the American military equipment provided 'everything that you need to fight a major war against somebody that doesn't have any guns'.[9]

On 7 December Indonesia invaded East Timor and two months after the invasion, 60,000 East Timorese had perished—the same number of East Timorese that are believed to have died in Australia's war against Japan in the 1940s. On the opening days of the invasion, several hundred civilian men, women and children, including another Australian journalist, were shot, one by one, on the wharf in Dili harbour. One eyewitness reported that 'the Indonesians tore the crying children from their mothers and passed them back to the crowd. The women were shot one by one, with the onlookers being ordered by the Indonesians to count'. Another eyewitness described how a father had to tie the hands and feet of his murdered son and throw him into the sea, while a boy was forced to repeat the same grisly act on his murdered father.[10]

Australian Governments have not been alone in supporting the illegal occupation of East Timor which has never been recognised by the United Nations. The policies of the Australian, American, Belgian, British, Canadian, Dutch, Finnish, French, German, Italian, Swedish and Swiss Governments have all subsidised the military strength and subsequent brutality of the Indonesian regime, through weapons sales, defence aid and defence training. Their appalling positions can be best characterised by the 1975 British Ambassador to Indonesia, Sir John Archibald Ford, who stated: 'if it comes to the crunch and there is a row in the United Nations, we should keep our heads down and avoid siding against the Indonesian Government'.[11] For his part, the American Secretary of State, Henry Kissinger, was furious that he had been sent cables through official channels telling him that the Indonesians were breaking US law by using American weapons for the invasion. Being aware of the illegality in using American weapons, Mr Kissinger was more concerned that this aspect may be used against him, and as pointed out in a study of this period, 'as the killings increased American arms shipments doubled'.[12]

Strategic and security interests featured prominently in Australian and American compliance with the Suharto regime, in particular, the concern that American nuclear submarines retain the right of passage through the Ombai-Wetar deep water channel that runs parallel to East Timor. So, the goodwill of the Indonesian dictatorship was to remain essential if these submarines were to operate undetected while crossing between the Indian and Pacific oceans. The petroleum wealth in the seabed between East Timor and Australia was an equally important consideration for Canberra's security interests, as it was estimated to be one of the richest oil and natural gas reserves in the world. Referring back to former Prime Minister Gough Whitlam's comment about East Timor's viability as an independent state, the oil and gas deposits in the area known as the Timor Gap render such an analysis to appear utterly ridiculous.

Australia signed an exploration agreement with Indonesia in 1989 to exploit this billion-dollar oil and gas field. By this time, well over one-third of the East Timorese population had perished under the Indonesian occupation. That amounts to more than 250,000 people. For his part, Mr Whitlam went uninvited in 1983 to the United Nations, in an attempt to persuade the General Assembly to drop East Timor from its agenda—he was not successful, and to this day, he remains recalcitrant, to the extreme of being unable to condemn the indiscriminate violence against the civilian population of East Timor.

The position of each of the successive Australian Governments is more than criminal negligence. It is direct complicity in genocide. Consecutive Australian Governments have perpetuated their compliant mimicry to the physical, cultural and ethnic genocide in East Timor. The successor to Gough Whitlam, conservative Prime Minister Malcolm Fraser, made Australia the first Western country to grant recognition to the annexation of East Timor, which was further supported and clarified by Fraser's successor, Labor leader Bob Hawke. The next Prime Minister, new Labor leader Paul Keating, expressly went to Washington in September 1993, at a time when American human rights endeavours were being fine-tuned, with the result that a number of restrictions were placed upon defence sales and defence training to Jakarta. Mr Keating urged President Clinton to withdraw human rights considerations from underpinning economic and defence contracts. In 1995, the Keating Government awarded the Order of Australia to the Indonesian Foreign Affairs Minister, Ali Alatas, at a time when many countries in the world were giving peace awards to Bishop Belo and José Ramos Horta. Then, in December 1995, without one debate in Australia's Parliament, the Keating Government signed a defence pact with Indonesia, to the disdain of Opposition parties and the general public alike. The current Prime Minister, Liberal leader John Howard, as Minister for Business and Consumer Affairs in the Fraser Government, was involved in the confiscation of a boatload of medical supplies that well-meaning Australians had tried to send to the civilian population of East Timor in 1976.

I thank you for your patience. It is impossible to encapsulate and to condense the 23-year history of a struggle for freedom into a one-hour lecture. I will now move forward to the present situation. There is still a small guerrilla force fighting the Indonesian occupation, and although the scale of the armed conflict has subsided in recent years, the human rights violations have continued unabated. The systematic campaigns of rape, torture, arbitrary arrest, disappearance and summary execution have terrorised the people of East Timor, with the result that they live in perpetual fear. In 1996, Amnesty International stated that it continued to receive reports of disappearances, extra-judicial executions, arbitrary detention, torture and ill-treatment. In the same year, the United Nations Special Rapporteur on Extra-judicial and Summary or Arbitrary Executions remained deeply concerned about the level of violence and ongoing abuse in East Timor.

During the first half of 1997, in spite of increased attention to the suffering in East Timor following the award of the 1996 Nobel Peace Prize to East Timorese Catholic Bishop Carlos Filipe Ximines Belo and East Timorese political activist José Ramos Horta, at least 707 arbitrary arrests and 49 deaths have been documented at the East Timor Human Rights Centre in Melbourne, Australia. Bishop Belo, having himself survived a recent assassination attempt, described 'a wave of detention and torture raining down on the young in the territory', and says that the human rights situation is at its worst point since the 1991 Santa Cruz massacre at Dili. The group Human Rights Watch/Asia also described in a recent report widespread arbitrary arrest and detention, often accompanied by torture, after a build-up of Indonesian paramilitary counter-insurgency forces. This report further states that 'torture, particularly with electric shocks but also with a variety of instruments such as rattan, metal pipes and electric cable, is a standard method of interrogation used by police and army personnel alike'.[13] In early October, a source inside East Timor who managed to make phone contact with Australia said that the situation in the country was very grim and that '53 people had been killed' in the previous few weeks. Much to the advantage of the Indonesian military, there is still no United Nations or international human rights group presence in East Timor to check such reports, and so the human rights violations continue to avoid international scrutiny.

This brings me to the photographic evidence that has been smuggled out of East Timor during the 23 years since the invasion. All the types of human rights violations described in the reports of Amnesty International, Human Rights Watch/Asia and the East Timor Human Rights Centre are exposed in full grisly detail in the photos of this exhibition. These photos have either been sold to a member of East Timor's Resistance by a corrupt Indonesian soldier or have been passed on by another Indonesian soldier disillusioned with the job he has been sent to perform in East Timor.

The most recent photos depict the torture and murder of young East Timorese women, some of whom we believe to be schoolgirls, due to their attire. It is believed that they were arrested at, or just after, the return of Bishop Belo from receiving the Nobel Peace Prize in Oslo in December 1996. In one particular photo, there is a sign saying 'Long Live the Nobel Peace Prize'. Another sign written by the torturers mocks a poster portraying a transfigured Jesus Christ asking 'if you really are a God come down and bring her back to life'. These photos are a shocking and confronting testimony of genocide, and women in particular are subject to gender-specific human rights violations. The women in these photos were tortured, beaten and raped until dead.

When these photos were first displayed some two weeks ago by Australians for a Free East Timor, in Darwin, they were confiscated by the Australian police over the concern that the photos were obscene. Two days later, at the launch of Stop Operation Annihilation, in Melbourne, well-known Jewish-Australian Federal Court judge Justice Marcus Einfeld stated to the media: 'what is obscene is the conduct that put them in this terrible, humiliating state.'[14] I believe the police action in Darwin to have been politically motivated, and this richly exemplifies the depth of the Australian Government's subservience to the Indonesian regime.

Systematic patterns of rape and sexual abuse are the brutal daily reality for East Timorese women, and this type of abuse begins for them from juvenile age. This has been an effective weapon used by the occupying forces to terrorise the population. Other gender-specific violations include the widespread use of the injectable hormonal contraceptive Depo-Provera to deliberately impair and limit the reproductive ability of the East Timorese women. The population is already subject to dislocation from Jakarta's transmigration policy of repopulating East Timor with migrants from the overpopulated islands of Indonesia. One testimony on prostitution states: 'Many young women become prostitutes because of the army. They force them to save their parents.'[15]

Particularly vulnerable are schoolgirls, who are followed after school and raped. The net result of these human rights violations is the absence of East Timorese women from family planning programmes and from the school system. According to a recent study by researcher Miranda Sissons, nearly two-thirds of the adult women in East Timor have never attended any type of school, the figure being one-half for adult men. The illiteracy level is 52.7 per cent and East Timor remains the poorest of Indonesia's provinces, with a conservative 1993 Indonesian statistic showing 36.84 per cent living below the poverty line. At the time of the invasion, in 1975, the population was approximately 688,000—as I have already mentioned, at least one-third of this number has perished under the genocide of the occupation.

The idea for this exhibition came about when I found myself

replying to those who would suggest that East Timor is a lost cause. What about the Holocaust? What about the survivors of the Holocaust? Were they supposed to give up? To have no hope? In 1941 before Operation Barbarossa, Hitler and his storm-troopers looked unstoppable. Were we to have no hope? Hope was the one thing that kept many survivors of the Holocaust alive, and in looking back on those dark, evil days, I wonder how many times these survivors were told that their hope was a lost cause?

So this exhibition crystallised with the support and encouragement of the Jewish Holocaust Museum (Melbourne), Descendants of the Shoah (Melbourne), and, indeed, the survivors themselves. A number of distinguished human rights campaigners, namely His Holiness the Dalai Lama, Bishop Desmond Tutu, Professor Elie Wiesel, Justice Marcus Einfeld and the inspirational Jesuit peace activist Daniel Berrigan, have endorsed this project, and expressed their solidarity with the East Timorese people.

There can be no comparison with the Holocaust. It is unique, and just as unique is the heroic struggle for freedom in East Timor. Australia's record, in particular with East Timorese refugees seeking asylum in Australia, is reminiscent of Canberra's refugee policy in the 1930s pre-war period. That policy offered only a token hope of sanctuary for German and Austrian Jewish refugees. For example, during the crisis years of 1937 and 1938, only 3173 German/Austrian refugees were able to meet Australia's strict and racist immigration criteria—a drop in the ocean when contrasted with the 1937 and 1938 immigration statistics which reveal a total of 147,730 immigrants entering the 'lucky country'.

At the opening of the 6 July 1938 Roosevelt-inspired refugee conference at Evian, France, the Cabinet Minister representing Australia stated that 'we do not have a race problem in Australia and we are not desirous of importing one'.[16] Not so far away on the very same day, the then Australian Federal Attorney-General and future Prime Minister, Robert Menzies, was at the opening of a Commonwealth conference in London to discuss the declining *l*

white population growth rates of Commonwealth countries. The resolution of this conference was to promote immigration of 'assimilable types', but a unique opportunity to galvanise assistance for the German/Austrian refugees was never on the agenda.

There are 1360 East Timorese asylum-seekers in Australia, and Canberra is at present conducting Federal Court action to have them deported to Portugal. At the same time, a Sanctuary Network established by Josephite nuns in Sydney has spread across the broad length of Australia, and now includes 10,000 Australians who are willing to break Australian law if the Government is successful with its court action, by hiding the East Timorese refugees, as East Timorese had done for Australian soldiers during the Second World War.

In the middle of 1996, the American Council of Rabbis released a two-page statement in support of the people of East Timor, saying that: 'No people on earth has seen a greater proportion of its population perish under tyranny since the nightmare of the European Holocaust'.[17] Every week in East Timor, civilians are tortured, raped and disappear. Tens of thousands of innocent, beautiful children have been, and continue to be, victims of crimes against humanity that could have been easily prevented if those Governments who have supported this 'death of a nation' had taken a responsible and principled stand rather than a cowardly and pragmatic one.

In the United Nations Convention for the Prevention and Punishment of the Crime of Genocide, it is written not only that genocide is a crime under international law which the 'Contracting Parties' undertake to prevent and to punish, but also that complicity in genocide shall be punishable. The Australian Government, with its unique 'blood debt' to the East Timorese, leads the many Western Governments guilty of complicity in this genocide. In full knowledge of the annihilation of the East Timorese people, they have blatantly pursued policies of accommodation with the persecutors and exploitation of the victims.

The spark of my humanitarian ideals was ignited by a visit to the

Yad Vashem Holocaust Museum some ten to eleven years ago. I vowed then that if I ever saw a people in my lifetime who were abandoned like the European Jews had been and in dire need of help I would not be a bystander—I would not stand by and do nothing. With great shame I must condemn my Government, the Government of Australia, of complicity in genocide.

Since the Nobel Peace Prize, the current military campaign of the Indonesian Armed Forces in East Timor has been code-named 'Operation Annihilation'. The aim of this campaign is to eliminate the Resistance by torturing and murdering civilians and by gaining access to the location of the armed Resistance through this practice. As an Australian, I must ask at what point in the balancing of international relations is our national integrity and honour dispensable? Before or after the people of East Timor completely disappear? As a testimony of our civilisation, it cannot be said that we have advanced the humanity of our nation, and with just cause our children and our children's children will condemn us for our indifference, our apathy, and our Government's appalling record of complicity in the genocide in East Timor.

We are at the dawn of a new millennium, with the fading century one of injustice, pogroms, holocaust, genocide, massacres and killing fields. The approaching century must be one that we can call the era of justice, where the long-suffering peoples of Tibet, Burma, Rwanda, Cambodia, Bosnia, Algeria, and Mexico, indigenous Australians and indigenous people from many parts of our world, together with the people of East Timor, will, with all our help, see an end to their persecution. For now, however, the suffering continues, but just as there is never darkness without the distant light of a flaming star, so, too, there is never evil without hope. Just as it was hope that kept many survivors of the Holocaust alive, so too it is hope for an end to their suffering that sustains the struggle for freedom in East Timor. Ladies and gentlemen, help us stop Operation Annihilation.

Endnotes

1 James Dunn, *Timor: A People Betrayed*, The Jacaranda Press, Milton, 1983, p. 313.

2 Commonwealth of Australia Parliamentary Debates, Senate, Tuesday, 26 November 1991, p. 3298.

3 Bacre Waly Ndiaye, Special Rapporteur to the UN Secretary-General, *Special Report Mission to East Timor, 3–13 July 1994 (E/CN.4/1995/61)*, United Nations publications, New York, 1994, paragraph 48d.

4 Statement made by Gareth Evans at a press conference in Bali 9 February 1991. His meeting with Indonesian Foreign Affairs Minister Ali Alatas was for the purpose of a new agreement in security and anti-terrorism arrangements covering the 'zone of cooperation' Area A ocean area within the Timor Gap.

5 Peter Hastings, *Sydney Morning Herald*, 16 September 1974.

6 *Canberra Times*, 16 January 1976.

7 See *Commonwealth of Australia Parliamentary Debates*, House of Representatives, 3 May 1977, Ken Fry and Andrew Peacock, p. 1439. Ken Fry's questions concerning the allegations were first raised in Parliament on 31 March 1977, pp. 806 and 807.

8 *Washington Post*, 6 January 1992.

9 John Pilger and David Munro, *Death of a Nation: the Timor Conspiracy*, Central Television, London, February, 1994.

10 Michele Turner, *Telling East Timor: Personal Testimonies 1942–1992*, University of New South Wales Press, Sydney, 1992, pp. 104–105.

11 Dale van Atta and Brian Toohey, 'The Timor Papers', *National Times*, 30 May–5 June, 6–13 June 1982.

12 John Pilger, *Distant Voices*, revised edition, Vintage/Random House, London, 1994, p. 300.

13 Human Rights Watch/Asia, *Deteriorating Human Rights in East Timor*, New York, 29 September 1997.

14 The *Australian*, 16 December 1997.

15 Miranda E. Sissons, *From One Day to Another: Violations of Women's Reproductive and Sexual Rights in East Timor*, East Timor Human Rights Centre, Melbourne, 1997, p. 32.

16 *New York Times*, 8 July 1938.

17 American Council of Rabbis, *East Timor Statement of Support*, New York, June 1996.

18

EPILOGUE

THE LAST WORD FROM BALIBO
and
VICTOR'S LETTER

*This is part of the last on-camera report of Greg Shackleton and his
Channel 7 Melbourne crew — Gary Cunningham and Tony Stewart.
It was filed on 15 October 1975.*

… Something happened here that moved us very deeply. It was so
far outside our experience as Australians that we'll find it very
difficult to convey to you, but we'll try.

Sitting on woven mats, under a thatched roof, in a hut with no
walls, we were the target of a barrage of questioning from men who
know they may die tomorrow and cannot understand why the rest of
the world does not care. That's all they want: for the United Nations
to care about what is happening here. The emotion here last night
was so strong that we, all three of us, felt we should be able to reach
out into the warm night air and touch it.

Greg Shackleton at an unnamed village which we will remember
forever, in Portuguese Timor.

Brian Peters and Malcolm Rennie (Channel 9, Sydney) were also with the Channel 7 crew at Balibo. Brian Peters wrote a letter dated 15 October 1975, the day before an Indonesian invasion force crossed into East Timor murdering in cold blood all of the newsmen. This letter remained unknown for 21 years until an incomplete copy surfaced during the 1996 Australian Government Sherman Inquiry. The copy was presented by Mr Sherman to Brian's sister, Maureen Tolfree, on 26 April 1996. It is reproduced here with her kind permission. The original remains missing.

Balibo. East Timor.
Wed 15th Oct.

Hi,

Intended to send you the second half of the story about my trip to Timor this week, but I'm back up here again. Left Sydney a week ago for Dili, now I'm on the border between East Timor and Indonesian Timor. Nine asked me to come up here because fighting has broken out on the border, UDT forces who retreated into Indonesian Timor have been staging counter attacks with the aid of Indonesian forces.

If the Indonesians stage an all out attack the Fretilin troops here would not stand a chance. Balibo is an old Portuguese fort about 5 miles from Batugade, which is a town on the border held by UDT and Indonesian forces. We've suffered a few heavy bombardments here, mainly mortars which quite honestly frighten the shit out of me, there does not seem to be any way to predict where they are going to land, and it is a real bitch trying to film them going off as there's so much schrapnel flying around.

The main worry for the Fretilin here at the moment (and me) is the fact that the Indonesians have 6 ships just on their side of the border, a couple of destroyers, a few patrol boats and what looks like supply boats. We can see them quite clearly, signalling to Batugade, but if the Indonesians decide to get really involved and start shelling from the ship there will be no chance for this place. Our main worry if that happened (apart from being blasted apart) is how to get out of Balibo (there are 5 Aussie pressmen here) because of the shortage of transport if the Indonesians start shelling. I'm sure that these Fretilin troops would panic and head right back to Dili, which is along one of the worst roads I've ever been on, only four wheel drive vehicles can get along it, in fact it took 8 hours to go 60 miles.

I've not eaten for about four days, most of the soldiers seem to eat goat's stomachs and rice, but this morning we had our first feast, coconuts and bananas, we stuffed ourselves so much that we've all had stomach cramps.

We're all hoping that we'll get a bit more action; the mortar attack was difficult to film because I was too scared to stick my head up, but I think I'll be able to handle it again.

Yesterday we went on patrol in the jungle, just about the hardest work I've ever done, I can see how 300 Aussie commandos ... [*letter ends here—Editor*]

Rob Wesley Smith from Australians for a Free East Timor (Darwin) sent me this letter he had in his records. Victor passed away some time ago but I thought his letter adequately illustrates the depth of feeling that exists in our community for the East Timorese.
For anyone who wishes to contact Australians for a Free East Timor, just send us an e-mail on Free_East_Timor@bigfoot.com or write to Australians for a Free East Timor, PO Box 4389, University of Melbourne, Victoria, Australia 3052.
Viva Timor Leste

Dear Friends   1 February 1976

I own a (very) small Caravan ... quite nice, air-conditioned, with a quite large annex: unfortunately—for you—I live in it!

If this is no objection, well, you can use it as much as you like, provided you allow me to do my own cooking and allow me to sleep in it overnight!

Actually, I know pretty well what you're fighting for: just like me, you feel that East Timor is oppressed as Europe was during the second W.W.: I've been in a Concentration Camp and my wife has been killed by the Gestapo ... I realise that this is happening, now, in East Timor so those people got all my understanding and love.

The Sunday before he left Darwin, I briefed Mr Roger East: he was a skilled journalist and needed only some technical details, mainly about photography from me ... I know that Mr East went over there simply to find things out ... the Indonesians didn't, probably, like it!

I wish—I really wish—that I could help you in your struggle ... can I?

yours sincerely
Victor Vanderveken